Theory and Interpretation of Narrative
James Phelan and Peter J. Rabinowitz, Series Editors

Social Minds in the Novel

ALAN PALMER

THE OHIO STATE UNIVERSITY PRESS • COLUMBUS

Copyright © 2010 by The Ohio State University.
All rights reserved.

Library of Congress Cataloging-in-Publication Data

Palmer, Alan, 1950–
   Social minds in the novel / Alan Palmer.
     p. cm.–(Theory and interpretation of narrative)
   Includes bibliographical references and index.
   ISBN 978-0-8142-1141-0 (cloth : alk. paper)—ISBN 978-0-8142-9240-2 (cd)
   1. Narration (Rhetoric) 2. Fiction—Technique. 3. Fiction—History and criticism. 4. Social interaction in literature. 5. Social perception in literature. 6. Cognition in literature. I. Title. II. Series: Theory and interpretation of narrative series.
   PN3383.N35P35 2010
   809.3'9355—dc22
           2010029339

This book is available in the following editions:
Cloth (ISBN 978-0-8142-1141-0)
CD-ROM (ISBN 978-0-8142-9240-2)

Cover design by Janna Thompson-Chordas
Text design by Jennifer Shoffey Forsythe
Type set in Adobe Minion Pro
Printed by Thomson-Shore, Inc.

∞ The paper used in this publication meets the minimum requirements of the American National Standard for Information Sciences—Permanence of Paper for Printed Library Materials. ANSI Z39.48-1992.

9 8 7 6 5 4 3 2 1

CONTENTS

ACKNOWLEDGMENTS / *vii*

CHAPTER 1 *Cognitive Approaches* / *1*
CHAPTER 2 *Introduction to Social Minds* / *39*
CHAPTER 3 *Middlemarch* / *65*
CHAPTER 4 *Little Dorrit* / *105*
CHAPTER 5 *Persuasion and Other Novels* / *145*
CHAPTER 6 *Conclusion (Including* Enduring Love*)* / *179*

WORKS CITED / *203*
INDEX / *211*

ACKNOWLEDGMENTS

I WOULD LIKE TO offer heartfelt thanks to the following (with apologies to anyone whose name is missing) for making a significant contribution to this book, usually by commenting on earlier versions of parts of it: Porter Abbott, Jan Alber, Maria Bachman, Michael Bamberg, Lars Bernaerts, Renate Brosch, Robert Caserio, Monika Fludernik, David Herman, Emma Kafalenos, John V. Knapp, Uri Margolin, Brian McHale, Jan Christoph Meister, Jarmila Mildorf, Kate Nash, Greta Olson, Ruth Page, Laurence Porter, Linda Raphael, Brian Richardson, Marie-Laure Ryan, Elena Semino, Ellen Spolsky, Peter Stockwell, Bronwen Thomas, and Lisa Zunshine.

The following, however, deserve another mention in a paragraph all to themselves for their much-valued support in a variety of other ways: David Herman, Monika Fludernik, Elena Semino, and Lisa Zunshine.

In addition, I am extremely grateful to the four people who read through the whole manuscript and made many substantial and important suggestions that greatly improved it: Porter Abbott (who did it simply as a kindness), the series editors James Phelan and Peter J. Rabinowitz, and the anonymous reviewer for the Press. Remaining shortcomings are all my own. I would also like to thank Sandy Crooms, Senior Editor at The Ohio State University Press, as well as her colleagues at the Press, for their notable help and support.

Most of all, though, I would like, again, to thank Sue: sine qua non, still.

•

Earlier versions of much of the material in this book have previously appeared in print, and, although I have substantially revised much of it, I am grateful for permission from the publishers to draw on it here:

"Attributions of Madness in Ian McEwan's *Enduring Love*." *Style* 43.3 (2009).
"Attribution Theory: Action and Emotion in Dickens and Pynchon." In *Contemporary Stylistics*, edited by Marina Lambrou and Peter Stockwell. London: Continuum, 2007.
"Intermental Thought in the Novel: The Middlemarch Mind." *Style* 39.4 (2005).
"Large Intermental Units in *Middlemarch*." In *Postclassical Narratologies: New Essays*, edited by Jan Alber and Monika Fludernik. Columbus: The Ohio State University Press, 2010.
"The Lydgate Storyworld." In *Narratology Beyond Literary Criticism*, edited by Jan Christoph Meister. Berlin and New York: de Gruyter, 2005.
"Small Intermental Units in *Little Dorrit*." In *The Literary Mind*, edited by Jürgen Schlaeger. Tübingen, Germany: Gunter Narr Verlag, 2008.
"Social Minds in *Little Dorrit*." In *Theory of Mind and Literature*, edited by Paula Leverage, Howard Mancing, Richard Schweikert, and Jennifer Marston Williams. Lafayette, IN: Purdue University Press, 2010.
"Social Minds in *Persuasion*." In *Characters in Fictional Worlds: Interdisciplinary Perspectives* (Revisionen 3), edited by Jens Eder, Fotis Jannidis, and Ralf Schneider. Berlin and New York: De Gruyter, 2010.
"Storyworlds and Groups." In *Introduction to Cognitive Cultural Studies*, edited by Lisa Zunshine. Baltimore: Johns Hopkins University Press, 2010.

CHAPTER 1

Cognitive Approaches

It is only shallow people who do not judge by appearances. The true mystery of the world is the visible, not the invisible.
—Oscar Wilde

IN MARIA EDGEWORTH'S novel *Helen* (1837), the eponymous heroine attends a dinner party given by the family that she is staying with (General Davenant, Lady Davenant, and their daughter Cecilia):

One day at dinner, Helen was seated between the general and a fine young guardsman, who . . . had made **some demonstrations** of a desire to attract her. He was piqued when . . . **he observed** that **her attention was distracted** by a gentleman opposite . . . Helen **looked** first at Cecilia, who, **as she saw**, heard what was said [about the death of a former lover] with perfect composure; and then [**looked**] at Lady Davenant, who had meantime **glanced** imperceptibly at her daughter [i.e., Cecilia], and then upon Helen, **whose eyes she met**—and Helen **coloured** merely from association . . . Helen had left the guardsman in the midst of his sentence, discomforted, and **his eyes were now upon her;** and in confusion she turned from him, and there were **the general's eyes** . . . The general now exerted himself to occupy the guardsman in a conversation about promotion, and drew **all observation** from Helen. Yet not the slightest indication of having seen, heard, or understood, appeared in his countenance . . . Of one point Helen was however intuitively certain, that

1

> **he had noticed** that confusion which he had so ably, so coolly covered. **One ingenuous look** from her thanked him, and **his look in return** was most gratifying; she could not tell how it was, but **it appeared** more as if he understood and liked her than **any look** she had ever seen from him before. They were both more at their ease. (33)

Notice how much of the cognitive functioning described in this passage is being shared between these characters without the use of words. Although people are, in fact, speaking, it is only social chitchat. As the emboldened phrases show, the real communication is going on by means of looks, body language, and gestures. Five characters—Helen, the guardsman, Cecilia, Lady Davenant, and the general—are all engaging in the most complex and subtle mind reading, and all without saying a single word. These are *social minds* in action because they are public, embodied, and so available to each other without the need for speech. Helen's mind is visible: the guardsman can see that she is distracted and the general can see that she is discomforted. In turn, Helen can see the workings of Cecilia's and Lady Davenant's minds: Cecilia's determination not to show her emotions and Lady Davenant's concern for her daughter. In particular, Helen acquires a lot of knowledge of the general's mind: she knows that he knows that she needs help; and she also knows that he understands and likes her.

It is a cliché of literary studies that, whereas novels can give us direct access to the minds of characters, by contrast, in reality, we can never really know what other people are thinking. This is the sort of thing that sounds true while it is being said within that context, but, in other contexts, can sound like complete nonsense. To believe it requires a considerable degree of cognitive dissonance in order to contradict the weight of evidence of our everyday experience. All of us, every day, know for a lot of the time what other people are thinking. This is especially true of our loved ones, close friends, family, and work colleagues. It is also true of our encounters with total strangers. How could it be possible for two people to hold a coherent conversation without at least some knowledge of the other person's thought processes? I am not saying that we *always* know *all* of what other people are thinking. That would be as silly as the cliché that we can *never* really know. Sometimes, as in the quote with which I began, we know what other people are thinking without them having to say anything; at other times we do not know what they are thinking even though they are trying to tell us. Sometimes we have secret thoughts that no one else will ever know about; at other times, other people, especially those close to us, will know better than we do what we are thinking.

The passage just quoted is an example of the *externalist perspective*. For a contrasting illustration of the *internalist perspective* (the theoretical background to both of these terms is explained at the beginning of chapter 2), consider the scene in Walter Scott's *Waverley* (1814) in which Waverley is interviewed by a local laird, together with a clergyman, about his supposed Jacobite activities.

> When Waverley retired, the laird and clergyman sat down in silence to their evening meal . . . Each mused over the particulars of the examination, and each viewed it through the medium of his own feelings . . . The wide difference of their habit and education often occasioned a great discrepancy in their respective deductions from admitted premises. (250–51)

As a presentation of mental functioning, what is striking about this passage is its emphasis on the *differences* between the two minds. It presents characters who have completely opposed ways of thinking and so widely divergent views on another mind: Waverley's. The ensuing discussion makes it clear that the laird is of a dour and suspicious cast of mind and so sees the young man as a violent and dangerous rebel; the clergyman is more trusting and optimistic by nature and so regards him (more accurately, as it turns out) as a decent young innocent abroad. In effect, they are constructing utterly different minds for the same character. Significantly, the two men have great difficulty in understanding each other's thought processes. There is no meeting of minds. This is a picture of consciousness as private, solitary, and inaccessible to others. The emphasis is on the gaps between people, the difficulties that we all sometimes experience in understanding the thought processes of others, the barriers that make it difficult for people to think together or in cooperation with each other.

To take us back to the externalist perspective, have a look now at these three examples. In Charles Dickens's *Little Dorrit* (1857), the villain, Blandois, arrives one evening at a French inn. As he walks in, the narrator remarks, "There had been that momentary interruption of the talk about the stove, and that temporary inattention to and distraction from one another, which is usually inseparable in such a company from the arrival of a stranger" (167–68). Later in the same novel, Mr Meagles admits to Arthur Clennam that "we do, in families, magnify our troubles and make mountains of our molehills in a way that is calculated to be rather trying to people who look on—to mere outsiders" (370). Mr Meagles also explains that "There is one of those odd impressions in my house, which do mysteriously get into houses sometimes, which nobody seems to have picked up in a distinct form from anybody, and yet which everybody seems to have got hold of loosely from somebody and let go again, that she [Miss Wade] lives, or was living [near Park Lane]" (373).

Like the passage from *Helen,* these three statements are examples of the workings of social minds in the novel. Specifically, they describe *intermental thought,* which is joint, group, shared, or collective thought, as opposed to *intramental,* or private, individual thought. (Again, more background on this concept is given in the next chapter.) The minds of the group of people in the inn share a sense of intrusion. And, as the narrator points out, this shared sense of discomfort at the arrival of a stranger is common in such situations. Mr Meagles makes a general point about how families typically behave (making mountains out of molehills) that is also true of his family. Mr Meagles, again, describes the intermental functioning of his family (a shared knowledge of Miss Wade's whereabouts but no knowledge of how this information was acquired) and points out that this sort of thought is typical of families. In all three cases, minds are working in the same way, and the thought being described here is, to some extent, collective. There is one important difference between, on the one hand, the Helen quote and the quote about the French inn, and, on the other hand, the two statements about the Meagles family. The first two are descriptions of social minds by heterodiegetic (or third-person) narrators. The other two are claims by a particular character, Mr Meagles, about the group mind of which he is a part.

This last-mentioned relationship—the one between intra- and intermental activity, between social minds and individual minds, between the internalist and the externalist perspectives—is a complex and fascinating one. It is central to narrative fiction, and it is the subject of this book. My purpose is to put statements such as those discussed above, and the many other examples presented in later chapters, at the heart of narrative theory. Fictional social minds are not of marginal interest; they are central to our understanding of fictional storyworlds. This is because real social minds are central to our understanding of, and ability to operate in, the actual world. My thesis is that social minds are possible because much of our thought is *visible,* which is why Oscar Wilde said that it is only shallow people who do not judge by appearances, and that the true mystery of the world is the visible, not the invisible.

A fierce debate took place within the nineteenth-century novel in particular on the nature of social minds. It had two sides. One was epistemological: To what extent is it possible to have knowledge of the workings of other minds? The other side of the debate was ethical: To what purposes should our knowledge of other minds be put? The epistemological dispute was surprisingly explicit; narrators and characters frequently refer to it. The ethical side was also ever present; there are many occasions on which sharp and painful moral dilemmas arise from the control that characters try to exercise over other minds. In literary studies it is usually unwise to specify the precise point at which a historical phenomenon begins. Your readers will then feel challenged to find earlier examples and you are left looking rather underread. Nevertheless, in the interests of scholarship, I am going to take that risk and propose that this debate began in 1816 on Box Hill, the famous beauty spot in Surrey that is the site of the picnic outing in Jane Austen's *Emma* (1816). You may remember that the expedition party never quite gels. "There seemed a principle of separation" (361) and "a want of union" (361). In order to rouse the party and provoke some witty repartee, to reduce the separation and increase the union, Frank Churchill exclaims, "I am ordered by Miss Woodhouse . . . to say, that she desires to know what you are all thinking of" (363). Mr Knightley sees that she is playing with fire and cautions her by asking, "Is Miss Woodhouse sure that she would like to hear what we are all thinking of?" (363). Emma ignores the warning, plows on with her conceit, inadvertently humiliates Miss Bates, and later incurs Mr Knightley's stinging rebuke. She is made to feel painfully aware of the emotional consequences of the pursuit of knowledge about other minds.

First, though, before going into more detail about social minds in the next chapter, I would like to say a little about the context within which this book has been written. This is the cognitive turn in the humanities, or, more specifically, what has come to be known as *cognitive approaches to literature*. I will then recap on some of the concepts that were introduced in my first book, *Fictional Minds* (2004), because they recur throughout this one, before explaining the ways in which the two books differ from, but are also complementary to, each other. Next, I will briefly introduce the concept of *attribution theory*. After discussing the issue of characterization theory and, in particular, the key notion of *dispositions,* this chapter ends with a brief outline of the structure of the rest of the book.

COGNITIVE APPROACHES

The background to this study is the widespread cognitive turn in literature studies in the 1990s that followed the linguistic turn of the 1960s and 1970s. (I cannot guess what the next turn will be, but, as part of the cognitive turn myself, I am in no hurry for it.) As I see it, there are three important new developments in research in my field: *cognitive narratology, cognitive approaches to literature,* and *cognitive poetics*. At one point, there seemed to be a danger that a researcher in one of these areas might not be aware of similar work being done by people in the others. However, thanks to the invaluable efforts of scholars such as Monika Fludernik, David Herman, and Lisa Zunshine, this danger has been averted. Many lines of communication are now open. The barriers are now breaking down to the extent that the boundaries between the three areas are becoming rather blurred. Nevertheless, their outlines can still be discerned.

The first, cognitive narratology, has applied the findings of the various cognitive sciences, for example the insights of philosophers of mind, psychologists, and cognitive scientists such as Antonio Damasio, Daniel Dennett, and Steven Pinker, to a number of different aspects of the narrative comprehension process. Notable examples of the success of this approach include *Towards a "Natural" Narratology* (1996) by Monika Fludernik, David Herman's *Story Logic* (2002), and Marie-Laure Ryan's *Possible Worlds, Artificial Intelligence, and Narrative Theory* (1991). In fact, David Herman (2003b) argues that, as narrative is a key cognitive tool and a central and indispensable way of making sense of the world, the discipline of narratology itself should be considered as one of the cognitive sciences. As Herman's claim implies, cognitive narratology takes narrative in general as its object of study—it is as interested in film as in print, as interested in nonfiction as in fiction—but most of its work up to this point has focused on novels and short stories. The second new development, cognitive approaches to literature, differs from the first in that it has emerged from literary criticism generally, rather than from narrative theory, and has drama and poetry as its subject matter too. One of its particular areas of interest is the analysis of metaphor. Important works in this field include *Dreaming by the Book* (1999) by Elaine Scarry, Mark Turner's *Reading Minds* (1991), and Lisa Zunshine's *Why We Read Fiction* (2006). The third field, cognitive poetics, is a type of applied linguistics that, like the previous area, is concerned with poetry and drama as well as the novel and also with the role of metaphor. It differs from the other two in its use of specifically linguistic tools for the analysis of texts. Leading works in this field include Catherine Emmott's *Narrative Comprehension* (1997), Elena Semino's *Metaphor in Discourse* (2008), and Peter Stockwell's *Cognitive Poetics* (2002).

All three of these approaches have made a number of important contributions to our understanding of the reading process. In particular, their illuminating research findings have great heuristic and pedagogical value. Although I am not a teacher myself, I have noticed that this work is gradually filtering down into teaching courses at both the postgraduate and undergraduate levels. Cognitive approaches can initially sound intimidating to students, but it is perfectly possible to make the subject highly accessible to, and surprisingly enjoyable for, those who are new to it. Of particular benefit is the potential versatility of this new subject area. To talk of a cognitive approach to literature can be rather misleading if it gives the impression that it is simply one alternative among a range of others: historical and cultural, Marxist, feminist, rhetorical and ethical criticism, and so on. I do not see it like that. In my view, the cognitive approach is the *basis* of *all* the others. It does not stand alongside them; it sits underneath them. It is the means by which critics gather the evidence that allows them to make their various judgments. It follows then that the cognitive approach is not necessarily an end in itself and so its analyses will naturally tend to drift into these other fields. Significantly, a recent collection of essays edited by Lisa Zunshine is titled *Introduction to Cognitive Cultural Studies* (2010), and it applies cognitive insights to a range of historical, social, and cultural concerns.

As my interest is in the fictional minds of characters in novels, it seems to me to make sense to explore the various cognitive sciences concerned with the study of real minds such as the philosophy of mind; social, cognitive, and discursive psychology; neuroscience; and psycholinguistics. My cognitive approach is a pragmatic, undogmatic, and unideological one. If these real-mind disciplines can assist our study of fictional minds, then that is fine; if they cannot, then there is no reason to use them. However, it has been my experience that we understand fictional minds much better when we apply to them some of the work done on real minds by psychologists, philosophers, and cognitive scientists. In fact, I would go further and argue that, from my perspective, all serious students of literature are cognitivists, whether they like it or not. We all study the workings of fictional minds and think of novels in terms of the mental functioning of characters. So the divide is not between cognitivists and noncognitivists; it is between those who *explicitly* see themselves as cognitivists and make use of real-mind discourses to study literary texts, and those who do not. I can understand the concerns of what may be termed *implicit* cognitivists who are skeptical about the value of explicitly cognitive approaches to literature. They may suspect, for example, that these approaches erect a huge and unwieldy conceptual apparatus with disappointing results, that they are unconvincing, that they simply tell us what we already know, and that they tell us only a small part of the story because they divorce mental functioning from its social and physical context.

I hope that this book may help a little to allay these concerns by showing that, with the minimum of theoretical scaffolding, original, illuminating, and convincing results can be obtained. The cognitive conceptual apparatus in this book is intended both to call attention to overlooked phenomena in novels and to offer some new ways of talking about them. I am interested in particular in the last of the concerns listed in the previous paragraph (that the social context is left out of account) because it is also felt by many psychologists, philosophers, and scientists in relation to the study of real minds. I want to stress emphatically that *an interest in the mind does not necessarily entail a lack of interest in the social mind.* My own experience has been the precise opposite. Fictional mental functioning should not be divorced from the social and physical context of the storyworld within which it occurs. In the view of the philosopher Brian Cantwell Smith (1999, 769), the classical (or internalist) view of the mind sees it as individual, abstract, detached, and general, while the new (or externalist) view sees it as social, embodied, engaged, and specific. It is this new cognitive perspective that underpins this book. I have found it disappointing that, although many literary theorists have made good use of what may be termed the "hard" cognitive sciences such as neuroscience, much less use has been made of the "soft" sciences such as social psychology, discursive psychology, sociolinguistics, and anthropology. Some scholars have studied the workings of fictional minds within their social and physical context by making illuminating use of these soft sciences, for example David Herman (2007b) and the literary critic John V. Knapp (1996), but there is still much more to do.

FICTIONAL MINDS

There has always been a good deal of interest within traditional narratology in the presentation of consciousness in the novel. See especially *Transparent Minds* by Dorrit Cohn (1978), and also the excellent studies by Mieke Bal (1997), Seymour Chatman (1978), Monika Fludernik (1993), David Lodge (2002), and Shlomith Rimmon-Kenan (1983). *Fictional Minds* was, in part, a critique of this tradition. In it, I argued that these writers provide only a partial and misleading picture of fictional minds because they tended to limit the scope of their analyses to the part of the mind known as inner speech. I therefore proposed a much fuller, more holistic, and more informative view of the subject. The book was based on the following five basic arguments (some of which have already been mentioned).

1. Classical methodologies such as *the speech category approach* (the discourse analysis of thought presentation that employs such concepts as free indirect discourse, stream of consciousness, interior monologue, and so on), story analysis (the study of characters as actants, functions, et cetera), the concept of focalization or point of view, and the study of characterization do not add up to a complete and coherent study of all aspects of the minds of characters in novels.

2. Traditional narratology neglected the whole minds of fictional characters in action by giving undue emphasis to private, passive, solitary, and highly verbalized inner thought at the expense of all the other types of mental functioning.
3. In studying fictional minds, we should make use of what I called the *parallel discourses* on real minds, such as neuroscience (Antonio Damasio [2000]), psycholinguistics (Steven Pinker [1994, 1997]), psychology (Edwin Hutchins [1995] and James Wertsch [1991]), and the philosophy of mind (Daniel Dennett [1991, 1996] and John Searle [1992]), to study the whole of the mind in action in the novel. They are parallel discourses because they contain a different kind of picture of consciousness from the one that is characteristic of classical narratology and so can provide explanations that are fuller than those that are currently available as to how readers are able to reassemble fictional minds from narrative texts.
4. The constructions of the minds of fictional characters by narrators and readers are central to our understanding of how novels work, because readers enter storyworlds primarily by attempting to follow the workings of the fictional minds contained in them. Fictional narrative is, in essence, the presentation of mental functioning. The term *plot* is generally defined as a chain of causally connected events in a story. (For a very helpful analysis of the various usages for this difficult term, see Abbott [2008, 240]. For illuminating work on narrative causality generally, see Kafalenos [2006] and Richardson [1997].) But what are these causal connections in practice? Generally, events in the storyworld are of little importance unless they become the *experiences* of characters. Events can occur independently of characters, but they will, on the whole, have a significance for the narrative only because of their effect on those characters' minds. Descriptions of novels by actual readers tend to focus less on events themselves than on characters' reactions to those events, what they were thinking and feeling, their beliefs and desires, and so on. These descriptions will usually include actions but, typically, will also refer to the mental network behind them—the intentions, purposes, motives, and reasons for the actions. A plot summary is often of the following form: character A performed action B *because of* their belief C and their desire D. This is a causal network because action B was caused by the mental events C and D. We follow the plot by following the workings of fictional minds. These beliefs, desires, and other thought processes to a great extent *compose* the plot. To put the point another way, a description of a plot is an exercise in attribution. There is more on this in the later section of this chapter on attribution theory.

To say this is not to conflate thought and action, or to privilege thought over action. It is simply to say that the concept of action necessarily requires the presence of thought. Neither is it to flatten out the undeniable differences between novels, or to make impossible any worthwhile distinctions between them. To say that the reader can follow the actions of the characters in Henry Fielding's *Tom Jones* (1749) only by following the thought processes behind those actions is certainly not to say that it is the same sort of novel as James Joyce's *Ulysses* (1922). Of course the two are different. Fielding gives us much less of the workings of characters' minds than does Joyce, and so events are more central to the plot of the former's novel and thoughts more central to the plot of the latter's. The two novels are at very different points on the thought-action spectrum, but my point is simply that it *is* a spectrum. There is no unbridgeable dichotomy between events/actions and thoughts/feelings. I say more about what I call the "thought-action continuum" in the discussion of action in *Little Dorrit* in chapter 4.

5. When the traditional narratological approaches referred to in point 1 above are brought together within a new theoretical perspective, the study of fictional minds can then be established as a clearly defined and discrete subject area in its own right within the discipline of narratology. *Fictional Minds* was intended to give an indication of what this new subject area might look like.

I will now provide brief explanations of three of the concepts that were introduced in that book because they recur throughout this one. These are the continuing-consciousness frame, what I referred to then as "embedded narratives," and situated identity.

Readers are able to follow the workings of characters' minds by applying what I call the *continuing-consciousness frame*: the ability to take a reference to a character in the text and attach to it a presumed consciousness that exists continuously within the storyworld between the various, more or less intermittent references to that character. To make sense of a text, the reader has to collect together all of the isolated references to a specific proper name and construct a consciousness that continues in the spaces between all of the mentions of the character with that name. The reader strategy is to join up the dots. In particular, the reading process is creative in constructing coherent and continuous fictional consciousnesses from what is often a bare minimum of information. We frequently finish novels with a strong sense of the individual personality of a particular character. If, however, we were to take the trouble to count up the specific references to that character, we might be surprised at how little there is in the text from which we derive our vivid impressions. When I reread George Eliot's *Middlemarch* (1872) a while ago, I was surprised to find that the famous scene in which Lydgate finds himself unexpectedly engaged to Rosamond occupies less than one page (208) in the Norton edition. It is the continuing-consciousness frame that enables readers to generate so much information from so little source material.

The reader uses existing or prestored knowledge of other minds in the *actual* world in order to process the emergent knowledge that is supplied by fictional-mind presentations. The everyday work we put into constructing other real minds prepares us, as readers, for the work of constructing fictional minds from the text. Because fictional beings are necessarily incomplete, cognitive frames such as the continuing-consciousness frame are required to supply the defaults that fill the gaps in the storyworld and provide the presuppositions that enable the reader to construct continually conscious minds from the text. One key default setting is the assumption that a consciousness will continue throughout the text until interrupted, as in life, by death or absence. Another is that characters will think and act in certain fundamental respects like real people. I will say more about cognitive frames when I discuss characterization theory below. A number of narrative theorists have referred to aspects of the continuing-consciousness frame from within their own theoretical frameworks. Monika Fludernik (1996) puts the notion of *experientiality* at the center of her perspective on narrative. Mieke Bal explains the difference between the two editions of her book *Narratology* (1985) and (1997) in terms of a new and growing emphasis on subjectivity: "This attention paid to subjectivity is, indeed, the basic tenet of the theory presented in this book" (1997, 11).

Another key tool for the study of fictional minds is Marie-Laure Ryan's notion of embedded narratives (1991), which I extended in *Fictional Minds* to mean the whole of a character's mind in action: the total perceptual and cognitive viewpoint, ideological worldview, memories of the past, and the set of beliefs, desires, intentions, motives, and plans for the future of each character in the story as presented in the discourse. My use of the term was intended to convey that, when we examine these embedded narratives, we see storyworlds from the limited and aspectual viewpoints of their inhabitants. The results of an analysis of a single fictional mind can then be enmeshed with those of the other minds in the storyworld, with their own embedded narratives, their own motives, intentions, and plans. The combination of all of these forms the plot of the novel. A complete picture of an aspectual, subjectively experienced storyworld results. (This requires skill on the part of the novelist. As the narrator of Ford Madox Ford's *The Good Soldier* [1915] remarks of the narratorial role, "It is so difficult to keep all these people going" [200]). The storyworld is aspectual in the sense that its characters can only ever experience it from a particular perceptual and cognitive aspect at any one time. As John Searle explains, "Whenever we perceive anything or think about anything, we always do it under some aspects and not others" (1992, 156–57). Aspectuality is another concept that will crop up regularly in the pages to come.

My use of the term *embedded narrative* was, in a sense, simply a label for an approach that has always been used by literary critics in practice, but which has not yet been sufficiently theorized. Some, but only some, of the material that is covered by the term has been categorized separately within narratology under the various headings I mentioned earlier: consciousness representation, story analysis, focalization, and characterization. The usefulness of the label is that it encourages a detailed, precise, functional, and inclusive approach toward the whole of a fictional mind in its social and physical context. It clarifies the process by which the reader constructs a series of encounters with a particular fictional mind into a narrative that is coherent and continuous. At the time, I thought that it was the best term available to convey the fact that fictional minds are, literally, narratives. As I aim to show in chapter 3, Lydgate's mind, like the minds of all the other characters in *Middlemarch,* is a narrative that is embedded within the whole text. However, the disadvantage in using the term is that it already has a meaning: it is usually used to describe the narratives that are embedded in so-called *frame narratives*. The tales that Scheherazade tells in *The Arabian Nights* are embedded narratives that occur within the frame narrative of her attempts to escape execution. Nelly Dean's story in Emily Brontë's *Wuthering Heights* (1848) is embedded within Lockwood's frame narrative. I thought that the context would always make clear which meaning was being employed, but narratological colleagues have persuaded me that this is not the case and that there is too much room for confusion. I have therefore abandoned the term and will, in this book, use the label *cognitive narratives* instead.

The relationship between the continuing-consciousness frame and the notion of cognitive narratives is this: the former is the means by which we are able to construct fictional minds; the latter is the result of that construction. Cognitive narratives are the product of the application of the continuing-consciousness frame to the discourse. I will use the term *double cognitive narratives* to refer to the versions of characters' minds that exist in the minds of other characters, the presence of one person's mind within the mind of another, or, in my terms, the construction of a double cognitive narrative for one character within another character's cognitive narrative.

It is important that I distinguish my use of the new term *cognitive narrative* to describe a character's mind from the much wider debates about the nature of consciousness and, in particular, whether people in real life regard their lives as narratives. Daniel Dennett stresses the essential "gappiness" and discontinuity of the various "multiple drafts" of consciousness. According to him, it is an illusion that we experience a full, unified, and uninterrupted stream of consciousness: "Consciousness is gappy and sparse, and doesn't contain half of what people think is there!" (1991, 366). Dennett criticizes the view of Gerald Edelman that "One of the most striking features of consciousness is its continuity" (1989, 119; quoted in 1991, 356). Dennett's typically robust response is that "This is utterly wrong. One of the most striking features of consciousness is its *dis*continuity" (1991, 356). He reinforces the point and relates it to the question of identity by commenting that "while consciousness appears to be continuous, in fact it is gappy. A self could be just as gappy . . . Are you the very person whose kindergarten adventures you sketchily recall (sometimes vividly, sometimes dimly)? . . . Is (was) that child you?" (1991, 423). Dennett comments that his multiple-drafts model of consciousness is "initially deeply counterintuitive" (1991, 17). According to the science writer Susan Blackmore, "Every time I seem to exist, this is just a temporary fiction and not the same 'me' who seemed to exist a moment before, or last week, or last year. This is tough, but I think it gets easier with practice" (2005, 81). It may well be that part of the required practice that Blackmore refers to is the reading of postmodern novels.

The philosopher Galen Strawson (1997, 2004) has a similarly "gappy" view of consciousness and, in addition, resists attempts to bind the notion of the self together by means of the concept of narrative. Strawson criticizes in refreshingly blunt terms what he calls the *psychological Narrativity thesis* and the *ethical Narrativity thesis*. The former is the "widespread agreement that human beings typically see or experience their lives as a narrative or story of some sort, or at least as a collection of stories" (2004, 428). It is associated with such thinkers as the psychologist Jerome Bruner (1986). The latter is the connected view that "experiencing or conceiving one's life as a narrative is a good thing; a richly Narrative outlook is essential to a well-lived life, to true or full personhood" (2004, 428). A well-known advocate of this position is the philosopher Alasdair MacIntyre (1981). In Strawson's opinion, both these arguments are wrong. They hinder human self-understanding, close down important avenues of thought, impoverish our grasp of ethical possibilities, needlessly and wrongly distress those who do not fit their model, and are potentially destructive in psychotherapeutic contexts (2004, 429). In Strawson's view, we would do better to accept the gappy nature of consciousness and the transitory, ephemeral, and nonnarrative nature of the self.

In his perceptive commentary in the Editor's Column of the journal *Narrative* (October 2005), James Phelan welcomes Strawson's intervention in this debate, despite having some reservations (which I share) about his position. Phelan then discusses what he calls *narrative imperialism*—"the impulse by students of narrative to claim more and more territory, more and more power for our object of study, and our ways of studying it" (2005, 206). He argues that "now that so many disciplines have made the narrative turn, now that narrative and narrative theory are so firmly established as important objects of study, the accompanying overreaching, unsustainable, and extravagant claims may be more harmful to our field than the misplaced humility accompanying overly modest ones" (2005, 210). Strawson's position is a provocative and bracing onslaught on what has become a rather stifling orthodoxy. If his relentless probing forces people to say precisely what they mean by statements such as "our lives are narratives," then that can only be a good thing. I am skeptical about some aspects of Strawson's arguments (are there really people who do not see their lives as narratives, at all, in any way, ever?), but I think that the more important point is that he is right that much of the "life is a narrative" rhetoric of present-day cultural studies is unthinkingly flabby. In saying so, I am acutely conscious of potential charges of inconsistency, given the fact that I refer to fictional minds as cognitive narratives. My defense is that I am talking about fictional, not real minds, and these sorts of minds are narratives in a literal sense. Calling fictional minds narratives does not have any relevance to the entirely separate point about whether or not real minds can be regarded as narratives.

When I refer to fictional minds, I mean those of *characters*. The enmeshing of the workings of these minds is often framed within a larger perspective: that of the narrator, and also, especially in novels with unreliable narration, that of the implied author. Obviously, the readers' awareness of the workings of characters' minds is determined, or at the least heavily influenced, by their presentations by narrators and implied authors. It might be a plausible next step, therefore, to refer to the narrators of novels such as *Helen* and *Little Dorrit* as having social minds because of their sensitivity to the presence of minds of this sort within the storyworlds they have created. This is, however, for me, a step too far. The most urgent need is to establish the existence of social minds *within* storyworlds. I do not wish to get drawn into the fascinating and intricate disputes that surround the status of narrators and implied authors by referring to their minds. It seems to me to be better, therefore, to make characters' minds the main focus of this book. I will, of course, refer to narrators and implied authors where appropriate; it is just that I will not talk about them as having minds.

Analyses of concepts such as *identity, self,* and *subjectivity* sometimes focus in restrictive and unhelpful ways on individuals divorced from their social context. My term *situated identity,* by contrast, is intended to convey a balance between the perceptions of individuals regarding themselves and the perceptions of others regarding those individuals. If an aspect of our identity is under consideration, how is it to be determined? Which is more reliable: our own first-person attribution of various qualities to ourselves, or the third-person attributions of others? Where is our identity situated? If you want to find out about an aspect of someone's mind and make an attribution to them of a particular disposition, say selfishness, whom do you ask? Certainly not just them, because you know that you cannot be sure that you will get a complete answer. Selfish people may not admit to being selfish. For reasons of this sort, we are all reluctant to take somebody's word for the workings of their own mind, and this seems to me to be a tacit admission that there is a strong sense in which our mind is distributed among those other people who have an image of us in their minds. How else can we say that someone is selfish when there is no representation of selfishness in their mind? This image is contained in the minds of others but we are attributing it to this particular mind. Surely, then, our identity is situated among the minds of others. Furthermore, we behave in different ways with different people. Someone seeing you in an unfamiliar context might easily say, "You've become a different person!" As Walt Whitman said, we "contain multitudes." And the situating of identity between individuals and others requires endless negotiation. As the wife says to her husband in the *New Yorker* cartoon as they go into a dinner party, "Remember—just *don't* be yourself!"

Lisa Zunshine approaches this issue from a different direction in her discussion of the concept of *metarepresentation* (the representation of a representation) in *Why We Read Fiction*. She points out that many of the statements to be found in fictional texts must be taken "under advisement," as U.S. lawyers say. A character proclaiming that she is a generous person and that another character is selfish does not, of itself, guarantee the truth of either statement. Zunshine makes brilliant use of a literary example of metarepresentation that has great relevance to the subject of this book. Everyone knows the famous first sentence of Jane Austen's *Pride and Prejudice* (1813): "It is a truth universally acknowledged, that a single man in possession of a fortune, must be in want of a wife" (5). Quoted in isolation as a flat assertion, it does not look like a very promising example of metarepresentation. However, as Zunshine explains, it is transformed when viewed in the context of the overlooked second sentence: "However little known the feelings or views of such a man may be on his first entering a neighbourhood, this truth is *so well fixed in the minds of the surrounding families,* that he is considered as the rightful property of some one or other of their daughters" (quoted in Zunshine 2006, 62; her emphasis). The italicized phrase points out that this is no universally acknowledged truth at all, merely a collective belief held by a specific group of people. The reader will have to take the initial statement under advisement while following the rest of the narrative. There is a striking similarity between the language used here and that to be found in the first few pages of *Middlemarch*. For example, the Austen sentence is a statement of the views of "surrounding families" while the passage from the Eliot novel that is analyzed at the beginning of chapter 3 is about the attitudes of "neighbouring families" (4).

RELATIONSHIP BETWEEN THE TWO BOOKS

I would now like to say a little about the relationship between this book and *Fictional Minds* and also about some of the reactions to the earlier book that are relevant to this one.

As I have said, *Fictional Minds* used the real-mind discourses of philosophy, psychology, psycholinguistics, and the other cognitive sciences to construct a theoretical framework for the study of characters' minds. The purpose of this book is to put that framework into practice. This time, therefore, the primary focus is on fictional-mind rather than real-mind texts. This study will be more "literary" than the first one and will consist of sustained close readings of a small group of novels. From chapter 3 onwards, there will be few explicit references to such figures as Antonio Damasio, Daniel Dennett, and John Searle. The same is true of the great Russian narrative theorist Mikhail Bakhtin, another all-pervasive influence on everything that follows. The rather paradoxical reason is that the only alternative is to refer to them continuously, and so the relative absence of their names and the names of other, similar theorists should be regarded as a kind of backhanded compliment to them. However, I should stress that *Social Minds in the Novel* is completely self-contained, and an understanding of it does not depend in any way on a prior knowledge of *Fictional Minds*. In her review of that work in the journal *Anglia*, the narratologist Jarmila Mildorf suggested that "the question arises to what extent this new approach is applicable in actual analyses of narrative texts" (2006, 776). This book is intended to provide an answer to that question. She also expressed a concern that my approach "involves the danger of making narrative analysis fuzzier and perhaps less reliable" (2006, 776) than traditional narrative approaches. I hope that the chapters that follow will meet this concern by displaying a precision and reliability that is equal to, albeit very different from, traditional narrative theory.

I now have a confession to make. I said at the end of *Fictional Minds* that it was the first of a pair. The second book would look at the historical development of constructions of fictional minds over a long period of time and a wide range of narratives in order to see what similarities and differences could be found between these various constructions. As you can see from a glance at the contents page of this book, I have broken my promise. My excuse is that, on reflection, I regretted being so headstrong, and decided that the original intention was wildly overambitious. I had missed a stage, and another book was required first. What was needed initially was a study that would focus specifically on social minds in the novel. Only then, I now think, would it be the right time to implement a fully historicized approach. In any event, luckily for me, a book is now available that is precisely what I had in mind. Indeed, it is a far more comprehensive treatment of the subject than I could have produced. It is David Herman's excellent edited collection *The Emergence of Mind: Representations of Consciousness in Narrative Discourse in English* (2010), which covers the period 700 to the present day.

Now for the reactions to *Fictional Minds*. I have been asked whether fictional minds form part of the story level (the content plane, the narrated, the "what," the *fabula*) or the discourse level (the expression plane, the narrating, the "how," the *sjuzhet*). The answer is that the detailed discussions in the chapters that follow will consider two separate but related issues. One is the story-level issue of the nature of the fictional minds constructed by the texts, the *what* that is the content of those minds. The other is the discourse-level issue of the techniques used to represent consciousness in narrative, *how* minds are presented in the discourse. It will, however, soon become apparent that it is difficult in practice to maintain a distinction between the two. I will focus primarily on the first issue, the *what,* but it is impossible to talk about the *what* without detailed consideration of the *how*. To describe the contents of fictional minds is to focus on how those minds are presented in the text. Also, the techniques that are used for fictional-mind presentations will determine, to a certain extent, what thoughts are described. The workings of minds in nineteenth-century novels, for example, are shaped, colored, and limited by the heterodiegetic narration in which many of them are presented.

Another question that has been asked is this one: Am I saying that the process of following characters' fictional mental functioning is both a necessary and a sufficient condition for narrative comprehension? This is not an easy question to answer in those terms. My preferred formulation would be to say that it is the fundamental and principal way by which we understand narrative. In the terms of the question, my feeling is that it is too weak to say that it is necessary and certainly too strong to say that it is sufficient, because there are several other features that are also necessary for narrative comprehension. These include a good understanding of the physical makeup of a storyworld and the events that occur in it, and a sensitive appreciation of the thematic component of narrative. On the other hand, I do not wish to compromise on the claim that the ability to follow fictional mental functioning is *always* necessary for narrative comprehension. I would concede too much by saying, for example, that it is only *typically* necessary. As I said earlier, an understanding of characters' thought processes is as necessary for *Tom Jones* as it is for *Ulysses*. I cannot find any way of retreating from the universality of my claim. Equally, I do not see any way in which this claim is a refusal to acknowledge the astonishing and endless variety of narrative. To say so would be like suggesting that I am trying to flatten out fictional variation by pointing out that *Ulysses* and Dan Brown's *The Da Vinci Code* use exactly the same 26 letters of the alphabet.

Am I talking about how readers in fact read novels, or am I attempting to advance a radically new way of reading? The answer is the former—I aim to show how readers make sense of fiction, to explain the processes that we all engage in, to make explicit what we all intuitively do in practice. In addition, though, I hope to offer a radically new way of *studying* novels. These two aims are not as contradictory as may at first appear. The reason why they are consistent with each other is that, in my view, narrative theory has in this respect taken insufficient account of the practice of actual readers.

One question that I ask myself occasionally, and I am surprised that no one else has, is this one: Can the approach that I have outlined above be described as *behaviorist*? The unsurprising and rather dull answer is: It depends on what you mean. If you mean what may be called *strong behaviorism*—the discredited doctrine of early behaviorist psychologists such as B. F. Skinner who appeared to argue that there are no mental processes, there is no consciousness, there are only dispositions to behave in certain ways—the answer is: Of course not. If, however, you are referring to what may be termed *weak behaviorism*—the argument that a surprisingly large number of statements about minds are, in fact, statements about dispositions and behavior—the answer is: Yes. (Incidentally, this discussion is an illustration of a widespread problem with "isms" such as behaviorism and poststructuralism. They often take two forms: a strong form that is heavily counterintuitive and unsustainable, and a weak form that is simply a restatement of the obvious. Confusion reigns when proponents and opponents argue over different forms without realizing it. This frequently happens because proponents start with the strong form and then retreat to the weak one under pressure, but without telling their opponents that they have done so.)

The next question ("Am I saying that fictional minds are the same as real minds?") is so important that I am going to put my answer to it in italics: *I am not saying that fictional minds are the same as real minds. I am saying that fictional minds are similar to real minds in some ways and different from them in other ways. We will not understand fictional minds unless we understand both of these aspects: both their similarities to, and their differences from, real minds.*

My first book focused on the similarities for two reasons: one was that they had been neglected by traditional narrative theory; the other was that I am particularly interested in them. This emphasis may have given the unfortunate impression that I was arguing that fictional minds are the same as real minds. I emphatically do not believe this. Indeed, I believe that to say so makes no sense. It seems obvious to me that fictional minds are similar to real minds in some ways but profoundly different from them in other ways. Equally, though, to go to the other extreme and argue that fictional minds are semiotic constructs and are therefore utterly and unbridgeably different from real minds does not work either. Fictional minds are certainly semiotic constructs, but many of the semiotic operations that are necessary to recover meaning from them involve their similarity to real minds. Some of these operations are the subject of this book. It is, however, true to say that, when examining challenging and experimental postmodern novels (as well as other "unnatural narratives," as Brian Richardson [2006], Jan Alber [2009], and others term them), the emphasis will change. The stress will probably then be more on the differences. I welcome the challenge provided by texts that defamiliarize, question, modify, complicate, distort, subvert, or contradict our default assumptions about the similarities between fictional minds and real minds. We find out more about the semiotics of fictional minds by taking up, rather than avoiding, this challenge. These narratives derive their power to shock precisely from their attempts to withhold what we take for granted in the presentation of consciousness in fiction. But the norms have to exist, and they have to apply to the majority of novels, and they have to be well studied and well understood, for the transgressions to have any impact.

In a famous essay, "The Hedgehog and the Fox" (1953), Isaiah Berlin muses on the remark of the Greek poet Archilochus that while the fox knows many things, the hedgehog knows one big thing. More recently, Stephen Jay Gould wrote a book called *The Hedgehog, the Fox, and the Magister's Pox* (2003). The remark is gnomic enough to be capable of different interpretations. What it suggests to me is a continuum in which, at the fox end of the scale, can be found those scholars who, within a particular field such as narratology, are able to turn their hands to a number of different issues and achieve a broad mastery over the whole area. At the hedgehog end are those who are content to plow a deep furrow, and pursue a single issue. It is then possible to discern a logic or a thread that ties together all of the work of hedgehog scholars and gives their books and essays a satisfying sense of coherence. Most people, of course, are in the middle of the spectrum, combining particular interests with a broad knowledge. On the evidence of the previous few paragraphs, it seems to me that I must be a hedgehog.

ATTRIBUTION THEORY

A key tool for analyzing the process of recovering and reassembling fictional storyworlds is the application of *attribution theory:* the study of how we ascribe states of mind to others and also to ourselves (Heider 1958, Kelley 1973, Wilson 2002). In relation to real minds, when we are coming to a view on why someone acted as he or she did in a particular situation, we ask ourselves such questions as: Would other people have acted in the same way in this situation? Did this individual act in the way that they would normally do in similar situations? Would this person have acted in the same way if some of the circumstances had been different? Attribution theory can be used to formulate tentative answers to questions such as these: How do readers attribute states of mind such as emotions, dispositions, and reasons for action to characters? What, in precise terms, do readers do with the explicit evidence that is made available to them in texts, together with any implicit or inferential evidence that they might have on characters' patterns of behavior? How do heterodiegetic narrators attribute states of mind to their characters? By what means do homodiegetic (or first-person) narrators attribute states of mind to themselves and also to other characters? How do characters attribute mental states to themselves and to other characters? With regard to the issue of characterization, how does an attribution of a mental state help to build up in the reader a sense of the whole personality of that character? And, finally, a question that forms the subject matter of this book: How do readers, narrators, and individual characters attribute mental functioning to groups?

Attribution theory rests on the concept of *theory of mind,* the term used by philosophers and psychologists to describe our awareness of the existence of other minds, our knowledge of how to interpret our own and other people's thought processes, our ability to make sense of other people's actions by understanding the reasons for those actions. (Philosophers and psychologists also use the terms *folk psychology* and *intersubjectivity* to refer to this ability.) We are able to attribute states of mind to others because we have a theory of mind. Readers of novels have to use their theory of mind in order to try to follow the workings of characters' minds by attributing states of minds to them. In particular, readers have to follow the attempts that characters make to read other characters' minds. Anyone who has a condition such as autism or Asperger syndrome, and who therefore suffers from what is called *mind blindness*, will find it difficult to understand a novel. Novel reading is mind reading. (However, it should be borne in mind that there are different sorts of autism spectrum disorders and the degree of difficulty with theory of mind will vary greatly between disorders.) There is now a lot of interest in narratives about autism and Asperger syndrome. Mark Haddon's novel *The Curious Incident of the Dog in the Night-Time* (2003) is a well-known example. (For more on theory of mind and the novel, see the compelling accounts by Lisa Zunshine [2006, 2008]).

The philosopher Peter Carruthers has put theory of mind into a historical context by emphasizing the importance of the tracking function in the evolution of human consciousness. He points out that the "early hominids [who] engaged in hunting and gathering . . . would have needed to keep track of the movements and properties of a great many individuals—both human and non-human—updating their representations accordingly" (2000, 272). He then links this tracking argument to the development of a theory of mind. "The central task of the mind-reading faculty is to work out and remember who perceives what, who thinks what, who wants what, who feels what, and how different people are likely to reason and respond in a wide variety of circumstances" (2000, 273). I mention his argument because it seems to me that it also works perfectly as a description of the reading process. We comprehend narrative by working out and remembering which character perceives, thinks, wants, and feels what, and how the different characters are likely to reason and respond to the circumstances of the storyworld in which they find themselves.

Theory of mind is as relevant to first-person as to third-person attribution, and first-person attribution plays an important role in the philosophical concept of action. (There is more on this in chapter 4.) We sometimes find it difficult to know exactly why we have acted in the way we have. We ask ourselves, "What made me do that?!" In other words, our first-person theory of mind is not as efficient as we often assume it to be. Nevertheless, a certain minimal level of reading of one's own mind is necessary for us to take responsibility for our actions. A valuable perspective on this issue has been provided by the well-known American socialite Paris Hilton. In a characteristically oblique intervention in debates in the philosophy of action, she once remarked, "In the future, I plan on taking more of an active role in the decisions I make." There is much food for thought there, I think you will agree. However, this rich and subtle reference to the mental network of causes, reasons, motives, and intentions that lies behind our actions (provocatively hinting, even, at the possibility of the *absence* of this network in this case) cannot be pursued further here. Within Zen Buddhism, a kōan is a story, question, or statement that is inaccessible to rational understanding but may be accessible to intuition. The one that everyone knows is "What is the sound of one hand clapping?" To me, Hilton's statement has some of the quality of a kōan. Whenever I think that I have fully grasped its meaning, I find that it eludes me still.

There are two rival explanations for our theory of mind: the oddly termed *theory-theory* holds that we all have a theory of sorts about the nature of behavior, albeit not a full-fledged scientific one. The *simulation theory*, by contrast, maintains that we simply simulate the thinking of others by trying to imagine what it would be like to be them in particular circumstances. However, some philosophers and psychologists have recently made a commendable effort to go beyond the theory-theory/simulation theory debate. In fact, some use the term *intersubjectivity* in preference to *theory of mind* because they feel that the latter term is misleading. A summary of the latest thinking on the subject can be found in *The Shared Mind: Perspectives on Intersubjectivity*, edited by Jordan Zlatev et al. (2008). The philosopher Daniel Hutto, in *Folk Psychological Narratives* (2008), suggests that, for most of the time, when we understand the actions of others we are not employing a theory of mind at all. Nor are we mind reading. And both the standard explanations of our ability to understand others (theory-theory and simulation theory) are, he thinks, misconceived. Hutto argues that our capacity to understand the actions of others in terms of their reasons has a sociocultural basis. Because many of the social roles and rules governing our routine encounters are well-established in standard narrative patterns of human behavior, folk psychology, theory of mind, and mind reading are usually unnecessary. We have many other, more basic and embodied means than mentalistic predictions or explanations. We generally do not need to speculate on the innermost thoughts of others because their behavior is immediately explicable by means of the expectations and scripts that are provided by cultural practices.

Hutto thinks that children develop their interpretative skills not by means of a theory, but by being exposed to and engaging in stories about persons who act for reasons. These narratives serve as exemplars and teaching tools. In their guided encounters with stories, children come to understand the relations that hold between beliefs, desires, reasons, and actions. As a result, children acquire not the set of abstract rules implied by the term *theory of mind,* but an appreciation of how actions actually occur in sociocultural contexts. He calls this argument the *narrative practice hypothesis.*

According to this view, use of a theory of mind is a supplementary method that only comes into play on those comparatively rare occasions when the actions of others *do* require explanation and we do not have direct and reliable access to their narratives, for example by asking them. In those cases, we construct narratives for others. Hutto calls these *folk psychological narratives*. Folk psychology, for Hutto, is essentially a distinctive kind of narrative practice.

Hutto is certainly to be commended for his radical and challenging thesis. Die-hard cognitivists may not be totally convinced, of course, and may insist that all he has done is to show that narratives play a key role in the acquisition of a theory of mind. Hutto meets this objection head on, but I suspect that his book is not the last word. For example, a significant issue here is the quantity and quality of narrative that children are actually exposed to. Some people may not be as sanguine as Hutto is that children typically get sufficient acting-for-reasons roughage in their narrative diet. As Hutto is a philosopher and not a narratologist he does not explore the implications of his work for the study of *literary* narratives. However, he defines the narratives told to children as stories about people who act for reasons, and this sounds to me like a good definition of adult novels too.

Hutto is unusual in drawing attention to the importance of what people say as a source of information about what they think. He stresses that these *second-person* explanations are at least as common as the third-person kind and may be more reliable. In Anthony Trollope's *The Warden* (1855), Mr Harding quotes an old proverb: "Every one knows where his own shoe pinches!" (175). This is an internalist motto because it is a vivid way of expressing the apparent truth that we cannot know what another person is experiencing. But suppose that you are out walking with someone and you notice that they are hobbling. They stop, take their shoe off and inspect it, rub their foot in a particular place, put a plaster on it, and so on. That is fairly close to knowing where their shoe is pinching, is it not? In addition, as Hutto says, information can be obtained directly from the other person. Your companion might simply *tell* you where their shoe is pinching. This perspective on mental functioning raises issues of authority and reliability that go to the heart of our experience of reading novels. You may say that people lie, just as characters do. Well, they do, sometimes. Or that they are unreliable, just as narrators can be. Well, they are, sometimes. But how likely is that, in this case? Obviously, you can make up scenarios based on pretence, perhaps caused by a reluctance to walk any further, but would you not be likely to spot subterfuges of that sort? People often tell the truth about what they are thinking, just as characters do, and it is often perfectly possible to know when they are not doing so. We should not apply standards to second- and third-person knowledge about mental states that are unreasonably and inconsistently higher than the standards we require for other areas of knowledge.

Although I find Hutto's approach completely convincing, I intend to continue to use the term *theory of mind* for three reasons. First, it is here to stay, especially now in literary studies, and to avoid it would cause unnecessary confusion. Next, he appears to use the term in a fairly narrow sense by tying it closely to the two rival explanations for it (theory-theory and simulation). That is, in asserting that we rarely need to use our theory of mind, he often seems simply to be rejecting the two rival explanations. I see no harm, then, in continuing to use the term, but in a more general sense, as a kind of umbrella or generic label for our ability to understand others. Used in this way, it would not necessarily commit us to either of the previous rival explanations, and would leave open the possibility of adopting Hutto's alternative sociocultural and narrative approach. However, anyone employing this inclusive use of the word *theory* should make every attempt not to give the mistaken impression that we are self-consciously employing a fully worked-out theoretical position whenever we try to work out what someone else is thinking. Finally, as Hutto admits, we do use our theory of mind (in the narrow or restrictive sense) for particularly puzzling examples of behavior that are not amenable to fast, easy explanations by means of sociocultural scripts. This is just the sort of behavior that is characteristic of people in novels. Fictional mind-reading tends to involve characters, often in moments of crisis, who are self-consciously using complex theory of mind to try to interpret the opaque intentions and motives of another.

CHARACTERIZATION

Characterization theory is based on the insight that a reader's construction of a character in a novel is a process that is both frame-driven (top-down in direction) and data-driven (bottom-up). As is now well known, frames or schemas are cognitive structures or mental templates that represent generic concepts stored in our memory (Schank and Abelson 1977). They are arrangements of knowledge about objects, people, or situations that are used to predict and classify new data. We use frames to simplify reality, organize our knowledge, assist recall, make sense of our current experiences, guide our everyday behavior, and predict likely happenings in the future. By capturing the essence of stereotypical situations such as being in a living room or going out for dinner, frames allow us to use default assumptions about what is likely to happen in those situations. That way, it is only when our assumptions are proved wrong that we have to improvise. Frames are hierarchical arrangements that have slots for variables. Once the most appropriate frame (say, a cat) has been activated, some slots are filled with compulsory values (a cat is an animal), or with default values (a cat has four legs), or are empty until filled with values from the current situation (the cat is black). Frame processing is top-down, in that it guides a selective search for data relevant to the expectations set up by the frame, and also bottom-up, because the data contained in an actual situation will often lead to the modification of the frame, or even the generation of a new frame. The concept of *homeostasis,* as used in the social sciences, has marked similarities. It refers to the predicable and expected patterns of behavior to be found in, for example, restaurants and theaters, and also to the maintenance of the specific roles assigned to individuals in families and other social groups.

Narrative theorists such as Monika Fludernik (1996), David Herman (1997), and Manfred Jahn (1997) have used frame theory to illuminate precisely how readers are able to follow narrative texts. They have shown that story frames are sets of expectations about the internal structure of stories that enable readers to recognize a text as a narrative. Comprehension of a story means building a representation of the text by using the prototypical structural patterns that are stored in memory. We acquire the textual frames relating to our knowledge of genre and other narrative conventions primarily by reading a wide range of stories, and our resulting awareness of the appropriate genre prefocuses our understanding of, and response to, a particular text. During the reading process, events in the story are marked as salient and acquire significance because of the expectations that are defined by frames. In particular, we use frames as part of our literary competence and performance to reconstruct from fictional narratives the storyworlds that are described in those narratives. Frames allow readers to fill in the gaps in storyworlds because the appropriate ingredients for extracting the meaning of a sentence in a narrative are often nowhere to be found within that sentence. This sort of gap-filling helps readers to track the movements of characters and objects through storyworld time and space. (For more detail on tracking of this sort, see Emmott 1997.)

Frame theory evaluates how incoming data are put into the relevant slots, the order in which slots are filled, the classification of the information contained in the slots (into, say, rules, events, and characters), how stories can be broken down into component parts, the types of causal relations that connect these components, and, importantly, how we repair unfounded assumptions about the direction of the story. As with our use of real-life frames, this is both a top-down and a bottom-up process. It is also dynamic in that when a reader fills a new slot, changes to existing slots may be required.

A reader's attention does not spread equally and evenly throughout a text, but continually works forwards and backwards to make adjustments to frames. Novels often challenge readers' expectations and thereby force them to abandon established frames in favor of new, refreshed ones. Specifically, cognitive frames are essential to the construction of fictional minds. As discussed earlier, when a reader meets or hears of a character for the first time, a continuing-consciousness frame is established (top-down) which is then fed (bottom-up) by specific information about the character from the text, and so on. These initial character frames usually involve stereotypes: either those that are based on real-world knowledge, or those that are to be found in various literary genres, or a combination of the two. As more bottom-up information on a particular character is processed, frame refreshment or subcategorization may take place. More radically, frame disruption, decategorization, invalidation of previous inferences, or even a focused search for a new, more adequate character category might occur. (For an illuminating application of this sort of approach to drama, see Jonathan Culpeper's book *Language and Characterisation: People in Plays and Other Texts* [2001]).

It seems to me that this characterization process has been interpreted up until now in a rather constrained and limiting way. In particular, it has been generally assumed that the character frames that are used in the ways described above consist only of the cultural and literary stereotypes that relate to *individual* types such as the rake, the fallen woman, and the braggart. I will try to extend in some new and possibly unexpected directions our understanding of character theory by examining some of the different sorts of cognitive frames that are also used by the reader in the construction of character. This can be done by making use of the insights relating to the *social* nature of cognition that have emerged from the soft cognitive sciences of social and discursive psychology, philosophy of mind, and theoretical anthropology.

The aim of deepening and widening characterization theory in order to provide a richer and fuller account of how readers actually construct characters can be achieved in two stages. The first stage (the subject of the next chapter) is to recognize that the minds belonging to characters in novels do not function in a vacuum. As with real minds, fictional minds are only partially understood if only an internalist perspective is applied to them. Characterization theory will always be incomplete until it also takes account of the externalist aspects of the character construction process. Fictional minds, like real minds, form part of extended cognitive networks. We will never understand how individual minds work if we cut them off from the larger, collective units to which they belong. To adapt the title of Edwin Hutchins's important book *Cognition in the Wild* (1995), we need to study fictional cognition in the wild. The study of the presentation of consciousness in fiction should take place not only *within* individual characters but also in the spaces *between* them.

The second stage is to recognize that there is a deep fault line within narratology between the theories relating to characterization and the theories relating to the representation of consciousness, and that the existence of this fault line has seriously distorted our understanding of fictional mental functioning. The theory of social minds presented in this book is intended to be a contribution as much to characterization theory as to the theory on the representation of consciousness. The gap that currently exists between the analyses of characterization and consciousness is particularly difficult to understand since a good deal of fictional discourse is, in my experience, situated precisely within this theoretical hole. Future chapters will analyze the process of characterization by discussing the representation of the consciousnesses of Tertius Lydgate in *Middlemarch,* Anne Elliot in Jane Austen's *Persuasion* (1818), and Joe and Clarissa in Ian McEwan's *Enduring Love* (1997). There are several strategies, it seems to me, for bringing characterization and consciousness together. In this book, I shall discuss three: dispositions (that is, a person's abilities and inclinations to act in certain ways), action, and emotions. Action is investigated in chapter 4 (using a passage from *Little Dorrit* as an example text) and emotions in chapter 5 (looking at chapter 23 of *Persuasion*). Dispositions are the subject of the following section.

DISPOSITIONS

A good deal of illuminating work has been done on characterization by narratologists and literary theorists such as Mieke Bal (1997), Jonathan Culler (1975), Umberto Eco (1981), Uri Margolin (1995, 1996a), and Shlomith Rimmon-Kenan (1983). However, despite the first-rate quality of this research, a serious concern remains. It is the fault line mentioned just now that has developed within narrative theory between the study of characterization and the study of the presentation of consciousness. It is my contention that the introduction into narratology of the concept of *dispositions* will help to some extent to mend this fault line.

Consider this sentence from Henry James's *The Portrait of a Lady* (1882): "Isabel felt some emotion, for she had always thought highly of her grandmother's house" (81). Is this not the sort of sentence that readers frequently encounter in fictional texts? It reports a single mental event—Isabel feeling emotion—but, at the same time, it puts this single event into the context of Isabel's personality, her character, her self. As readers, we accept this sentence as a whole, as a gestalt, as a coherent explanation of a single aspect of Isabel's whole mind. We do not think to ourselves, "That's a strange sentence—yoking together two completely separate classes of statements!" However, look at any of the excellent introductions to narrative, new and old. Narratology is well served by having several, really first-class introductory teaching texts by Shlomith Rimmon-Kenan (1983), Mieke Bal (1997), Jacob Lothe (2000), Suzanne Keen (2003), Luc Herman and Bart Vervaeck (2005), Porter Abbott (2008), and Monika Fludernik (2009). Unfortunately, though, I have been unable to find any evidence that they have anything to say about that sentence *as a whole*. They typically contain a chapter about the representation of speech and consciousness, and a completely separate chapter about characterization. As a result, what you find, in effect, is that the first half of the sentence is classified under one category, as the representation of consciousness, while the second half is classified under another, as characterization. And, to make the division even deeper, the chapters that are devoted to characterization will rarely refer to consciousness, and the chapters on consciousness have almost nothing to say about characterization. This wholly artificial and arbitrary division completely fails to capture the readers' experience of that completely typical sentence about Isabel.

This seems strange. Narrative texts are full of statements such as the one just quoted that present an episode of immediate consciousness within the context of the character's dispositions. These statements often fulfill a pivotal role in guiding the direction of the narrative by showing that a particular mental event is a manifestation of a disposition and that the disposition is a causal factor in the event. The event and the disposition are linked together. It is by interpreting episodes of consciousness within a context of dispositions that the reader builds up a convincing and coherent sense of character. It is through the central, linking concept of dispositions that characterization and thought presentation can be seen as different aspects of the same phenomenon. However, within narrative theory, character traits belong to the subject area of characterization, and mental events belong to the subject area of thought presentation. The absence of a holistic approach makes a recognition of the whole fictional mind difficult to achieve.

In making this criticism, I need to stress emphatically that I am not talking about the *practice* of nonintroductory narratology texts, such as those on the representation of consciousness (Dorrit Cohn's *Transparent Minds* [1978]) and those about character (James Phelan's *Reading People, Reading Plots* [1989] and Alex Woloch's *The One vs. the Many* [2003]). For example, although Phelan's book is about characterization and does not explicitly address the relationship between that topic and the representation of consciousness, it does sometimes draw on representations of characters' minds in its discussions of their mimetic functions. My argument is that there is a problem with the standard *introductions* to narratology. This problem is less obvious in other work in the field because, *in practice,* it is not possible to draw a coherent distinction between character and consciousness. However, the distinction is still being made in the introductory *theory.*

Now let us look at the solution—dispositions—from a number of different angles: real minds, theories about real minds, actual fictional narratives, and theories about fictional narrative. I will then go on to a brief discussion of some of the statements about dispositions to be found in a chapter from *The Portrait of a Lady.*

First, our experience of real minds, both our own and others'. Appeals to introspection are always dangerous because people's minds work in different ways, but I will take the risk anyway. When you become self-consciously aware of having had a particular mental event—a thought, sensation, emotion, or feeling—do you find that you often tend to link it to your character traits, your habits of thought, your dispositions? You may experience a single feeling of irritation with someone and then think, "he really does annoy me when he starts talking like that!" You notice a recurring pattern there regarding your reactions to his behavior. Or you have a memory of an embarrassing moment and think, "I really do wish I could stop remembering things like that and think more positively!" In other words, are you inclined to locate your current thought processes within the context of your *whole* mind? Here is another question: Do you do the same to other people? That is, when you are engaged in third-person, rather than first-person attribution? A colleague suggests moving a meeting from Friday afternoon to earlier in the week and you think, "That's only because he likes to get away early on Fridays to have a long weekend!" You are linking the assumed mental event behind his action to an assumed disposition to act in a certain way.

The answers that I am hoping for, by the way, are "yes" in every case. And assuming they really *are* yes, the conclusion that we can draw is that a person's dispositions are important to the workings of their mind. They form the links between the aspects that endure over time—their beliefs and attitudes, their personality, their character, their self—and the immediate mental events of their consciousness. Most mental events—admittedly not all, but most—are manifestations of a person's dispositions. And a person's actions and behavior, how they interact with their physical and social environment, will also arise out of their dispositions. Let us look again at the notion of the self in this context. What tools should we use to measure the self that is located between the individual and others? On the one hand, individual mental events are too small-scale. We need a concept to link individual mental events together. On the other hand, the concepts of character or personality are too large-scale and too contestable to do the job either. As I said earlier when introducing the concept of situated identity, think how much disagreement there often is over someone's personality. What is most help, I suggest, is the medium-sized area in the middle—dispositions.

Now to turn to formal theories about real minds. That dispositions play such a central role in considerations of a person's whole mind is the reason why they are so important in both philosophy and psychology. In chapter 5 of his *Principles of Psychology*, the psychologist William James (the brother of Henry) called them *bundles of habits* (1983, 109). In a particularly evocative phrase, the philosopher Daniel Dennett terms them *mind-ruts* (1991, 300). The concept has great explanatory power within the behaviorist perspective of such philosophers as Gilbert Ryle and Ludwig Wittgenstein. According to Ryle, "to talk of a person's mind is . . . to talk of the person's abilities, liabilities, and inclinations to do and undergo certain sorts of things, and of the doing and undergoing of these things in the ordinary world" (1963, 190). He also suggested that a "number of the words which we commonly use to describe and explain people's behavior signify dispositions and not episodes" (1963, 112). The philosopher Stephen Priest explains that, for Ryle, "it is a mistake to think of a belief as any kind of occurrence at all. Beliefs are dispositions. According to Ryle's account, a person has a disposition if he or she has a tendency or propensity to behave in a particular way" (1991, 48). This emphasis by philosophers and psychologists on the importance of dispositions is shared by scholars in other disciplines. The anthropologist Clifford Geertz maintains that "the term *mind* denotes a class of skills, propensities, capacities, tendencies, habits" (1993, 58)—another list of dispositions. Antonio Damasio believes that "What we usually describe as a 'personality' depends on multiple contributions . . . anything from trivial preferences to ethical principles" (2000, 222). In the first book on cognitive science that I read after drafting this passage (Merlin Donald's *A Mind So Rare* [2002]) I had to wait until only the second page before coming across a reference to dispositions. I may have been lucky, but I do not think so.

All these theorists are saying that when we talk about a mind, we are talking in the main about dispositions. They argue that our emphasis should not be on specific mental occurrences such as single thoughts, but on states of mind that exist over time. We often think that we are talking about mental *events* when what we are really talking about is mental *states*. You may find some of this implausible, but it is salutary at the very least, I think, to be aware of a discourse about minds that is so different from what we are used to as narrative theorists.

So, dispositions are as important in theories about real minds as they are in our folk psychological beliefs about ourselves and others. Are they important in fictional narrative too? Surely they are. As I have already suggested, narrative texts are full of statements that present an episode of immediate consciousness within the context of a character's dispositions. Consider again the example that I used earlier ("Isabel felt some emotion, for she had always thought highly of her grandmother's house") in the light of my comments on real minds. This statement places the single mental event of Isabel feeling emotion within the context of Isabel's disposition to think highly of her grandmother's house. The second half of the sentence is given as an explanation for the first. The mental event occurs, in part, because of the disposition. That is the force of the word "for" in that sentence. It is by means of frequently encountered sentences such as these that we are able to build up a sense of Isabel's *whole* mind—her consciousness, her emotions, her beliefs, her personality, her self, her character.

But what happens when we leave behind the real minds of both folk and academic psychology and the fictional minds of narratives and turn to narrative theory? Well, in my experience, a strange thing happens: dispositions disappear. It is rare indeed for works of narrative theory even to mention the word. Obviously, discussions of character traits arise within the passages of practical criticism that are contained in theoretically oriented works, but the notion of dispositions has, as far as I am aware, never been *explicitly theorized*, either in relation to characterization or to the representation of consciousness. But if dispositions are so important to the theory and practice of real minds and to the actual constructions of fictional minds, why are they so neglected when it comes to theories of fictional minds? My guess is that it is because characterization theory began life as a *semiotic* study, a specific area of inquiry with a conceptual apparatus of intertextual stereotypes, actants, functions, and so on. Meanwhile, the representation of consciousness developed along parallel lines as a *linguistic* study, a completely separate subject area with a different conceptual apparatus of free indirect discourse, stream of consciousness, interior monologue, et cetera. As neither semiotics nor linguistics is comfortable with the concept of dispositions, what is needed is a *cognitive* study of fictional minds that is.

John V. Knapp is absolutely right to say that "the application of dispositional research to literary study . . . will in its own right open new and, I hope, fertile ground for literary criticism and the teaching of literature" (1996, 16). To show what the study of fictional dispositions might look like, I have listed below some of the statements about them that are to be found in chapter 3 of *The Portrait of a Lady*. Although this is a short chapter, I found in it so much material that I was obliged to use only a selection. There is a gloss for each disposition-description that explains its function. Many of the sentences describe actions too and are also presentations of social minds.

> Being a high-tempered man he had requested her to mind her own business. (80)
> *The disposition (being high-tempered) is given as the reason for the action (the request).*

> Mrs Touchett's behavior was, as usual, perfectly deliberate. (80)
> *The phrase "as usual" shows that her deliberate behavior on this occasion arises from her disposition to behave in this way.*

> To say [Isabel] was so occupied is to say that her solitude did not press upon her; for her love of knowledge had a fertilising quality and her imagination was strong. (76)
> *The two dispositions (love of knowledge and strong imagination) are the reasons for her current state of mind (solitary occupation). The word "for" establishes the connection.*

> There was no need of writing, for she should attach no importance to any account of them she should elicit by letter: she believed, always, in seeing for one's self. (80)
> *Mrs Touchett's general background disposition (wanting to see for oneself) explains a current, hypothetical one (attaching no importance to accounts of others). The causal connection is made clear, very concisely, by a colon.*

> She was not fond of the English style of life, and had three or four reasons for it to which she currently alluded; they bore upon minor points of that ancient order, but for Mrs Touchett they amply justified non-residence. (76)
> *The statement presents a character's self-conscious awareness of her own motive (disposition to dislike the English way of life) for her action (non-residence).*

> The opportunity of listening to the conversation of one's elders (which [for] Isabel was a highly-valued pleasure) [was] almost unbounded. (77)
> Even as a child she thought her grandmother's home romantic. (77)
> *These two descriptions explain the background to the workings of Isabel's mind by describing her childhood dispositions.*

Isabel felt some emotion, for she had always thought highly of her grandmother's house.
But the emotion was of a kind which led her to say: "I should like very much to go to Florence." (81)
As discussed earlier, the first sentence relates a specific and current mental event (feeling emotion) to the background disposition (thinking highly). Then the disposition and the mental event are used to explain the action (making a statement). Again, the word "for" has an explanatory role.

She was as eccentric as Isabel had always supposed; and hitherto, whenever the girl had heard people described as eccentric, she had thought of them as offensive or alarming . . . But her aunt made it a matter of high but easy irony . . . (82)
This illustrates Isobel's evolving character and personality as she finds that her previous disposition (to find eccentric people offensive) was mistaken. The development of dispositions has a role in the explanation of character change.

[Mrs Touchett] was virtually separated from her husband. . . . This arrangement greatly pleased her; it was so felicitously definite. It struck her husband in the same light, in a foggy square in London, where it was at times the most definite fact he discerned; but he would have preferred that such unnatural things should have a greater vagueness. (75–76)
This is the background to the characters' joint disposition to live apart. It also explains the different attitudes of Mr and Mrs Touchett toward their shared decision.

She had her own way of doing all that she did, and this is the simplest description of a character which, although by no means without liberal motions, rarely succeeded in giving an impression of suavity. Mrs Touchett might do a good deal of good, but she never pleased. (75)
This statement describes other characters' perceptions of Mrs Touchett's dispositions.

She was usually prepared to explain [her motives]—when the explanation was asked as a favor; and in such a case they proved totally different from those that had been attributed to her. (75)
Mrs Touchett's disposition to explain her motives makes clear the substantial differences between her constructions of her own mind and other characters' constructions of it.

> Mrs Touchett was certainly a person of many oddities, of which her behavior on returning to her husband's house after many months was a noticeable specimen. (75)

A specific action (returning home) is put in the context of her "odd" dispositions.

> It had lately occurred to her that her mind was a good deal of a vagabond, and she had spent much ingenuity in training it to a military step and teaching it to advance, to halt, to retreat, to perform even more complicated maneuvers. (79)

This sentence illustrates Isabel's highly self-conscious awareness of her habits of thought.

Despite, I hope, finding this exercise of interest, you may be thinking that the notion of dispositions will be of less value when it comes to the study of the modernist novel, where there is an intense focus on the individual mental events that make up the stream of consciousness. In *Ulysses*, for example, Leopold Bloom's consciousness is directly presented as a stream of thought. Well, up to a point. Recall the famous introduction to Bloom: "Mr Leopold Bloom ate with relish the inner organs of beasts and fowls. He liked thick giblet soup, nutty gizzards, a stuffed roast heart, liver slices fried with breadcrumbs. Most of all he liked grilled mutton kidneys which gave to his palate a fine tang of faintly scented urine" (45). This is a description of a disposition.

I have been talking so far only about *explicit* disposition sentences. I have not mentioned yet the fact that readers are predisposed (note my use of the term) to infer dispositions from statements about individual mental events. The alert reader will quickly notice from the two streams of consciousness that make up the bulk of some, but only some, of the eighteen episodes in *Ulysses* that, despite the fact that it is not openly stated, Bloom has a disposition to think scientifically while Stephen's is to think philosophically.

STRUCTURE OF THE BOOK

The next chapter provides the theoretical context for the detailed work on social minds that will occupy the rest of the book. It goes into more detail on such concepts as the internalist and the externalist perspectives, intermental and intramental thought, and intermental units. The chapter then presents a short taxonomy of intermentality before attempting to justify this potentially unfamiliar way of thinking to any literary scholars who may have reservations about it. To conclude it, I present a case study—a passage from Evelyn Waugh's *Men at Arms* (1952)—in order to give an initial indication of what an analysis of social minds in the novel might look like. This one focuses specifically on the notion of unconscious thought.

Chapters 3, 4, and 5 consist of discussions of the social minds to be found in those magnificent canonical warhorses *Middlemarch, Little Dorrit,* and *Persuasion.* As your heart may well be sinking at the thought of yet more readings of these great, but undeniably well-studied, novels, I think I should explain my choice of texts. I wish to show that cognitive analyses really can reveal fresh insights, even into apparently overanalyzed novels such as these. My aim is to ensure that the next time you read these three novels with which you thought you were completely familiar, you will read them differently.

In chapter 3, I argue that *Middlemarch* is a mosaic of intermentality. The various intermental units portrayed in it are so integral to the plot of the novel that it would not be possible for a reader to follow that plot without an understanding of them. The chapter is divided into three parts: the initial construction of the Middlemarch mind (in the singular), the subsequent development of (plural) Middlemarch minds, and the Lydgate storyworld. This arrangement is, I think, true to the actual experience of reading *Middlemarch*. The existence of the apparently monolithic, single, large intermental unit that I call *the Middlemarch mind* is established in the first few pages of the novel before it becomes apparent that what appears at first to be a single mind consists in fact of several different Middlemarch minds. In the final section I describe the construction of an individual character, Lydgate, and analyze the most important small intermental unit to which he belongs: his marriage to Rosamond. This section explains how the reader brings together attributions from various sources in order to construct a single, easily identifiable fictional mind. This section is placed last because I think that the individual characters and small units in the novel are best understood within the wider intermental context that is established by the first two sections of this chapter.

The discussion of *Little Dorrit* in chapter 4 starts with some general issues such as the importance of the externalist perspective on private thought and the concept of physically distributed cognition. It then looks at three of the ways in which the social minds in the novel communicate with each other: the face, nonverbal communication, and the look. I go on to scrutinize the workings of some large, medium, and small intermental units, the last-named starting with the Dorrit family and including some of its individuals (such as Mr Dorrit and Fanny) as well as its subunits (for example, Little Dorrit and Mr Dorrit, and Little Dorrit and Fanny). Next, I look at the most important intermental pairing in the novel—the relationship between Little

Dorrit and Clennam—first from the point of view of Clennam's knowledge of Little Dorrit's mind and then of her knowledge of his. This is followed by a discussion of some other small units such as Clennam and Mrs Clennam, Mrs Clennam and Flintwinch, and Little Dorrit and Pet. The chapter then makes use of attribution theory in relation to a key element of narrative fiction, action, by analyzing a short passage from the novel. I aim to show how the presentations of actions contained in novels are extremely informative about the mental functioning of fictional characters. In particular, I will discuss what discursive purposes are served by these presentations. By looking at an apparently internalist issue such as action within an externalist context, I reveal that some of the actions described in this passage are undertaken by groups and that Clennam's actions can best be understood as a response to their intermental behavior.

Chapter 5 consists of four parts, the first two of which relate to *Persuasion*. In the first, I focus on Anne Elliot's social mind by examining some of the small intermental units to which she belongs, in particular her relationship with Wentworth. In its second part, the chapter will follow the same pattern as the two previous ones in placing an apparently internalist narrative feature after the analysis of social minds. In this case it is emotions. I argue that much of the mental functioning in novels consists of emotions and feelings. Emotions drive narratives. A novel with all of the emotions and feelings taken out would not make much sense. Then, after commenting briefly in the third part of the chapter on some other nineteenth-century novels such as Charlotte Brontë's *Shirley* (1849), Elizabeth Gaskell's *Wives and Daughters* (1865), and *The Warden* in order to widen the perspective a little, I return in the fourth part to the three main texts in order to summarize some of the similarities and differences in the social minds contained in them.

Chapter 6, the final chapter, is again divided into four parts. In the first, I discuss the need for a rigorously diachronic approach to the study of social minds in the novel and comment briefly on some of the issues that would arise from the writing of such a history. The second part consists of an analysis of the intermental thought to be found in *Enduring Love* (together with a brief mention of another of Ian McEwan's novels, *Atonement* [2001]). This discussion is placed at this point in the chapter in order to give a brief indication of what a social-minds perspective on the modern novel might look like. The book is undeniably "nineteenth-century-centric" and I even thought about making this bias explicit by calling it *Social Minds in the Nineteenth-Century Novel*. However, on reflection, I decided to stay with the more general title. Although my sort of approach is particularly suited to the novels of that century (as well as the eighteenth century), I believe that it can also be productively applied to the twentieth- and twenty-first-century novel too, the experimental as well as the formally conservative kind. The discussion of fractured, dislocated intermentality in *Enduring Love* is an attempt to "moderate [this book's] implicit nineteenth-century-novel-centric vision of the 'natural' narrative transaction" (I owe this splendid formulation to Porter Abbott [personal communication]). In the third section of this chapter I discuss possible future developments in the study of social minds in other narrative media such as film. The fourth and final section is a rhetorical flourish.

As you will see from a glance at the contents page, this book is not systematically chronological. It is not possible for a single study to be exhaustive in its analyses of the workings of social minds in even a few case studies. The subject is simply too big. What I do, therefore, in chapters 3 to 5 is to highlight different aspects of the three texts under discussion. The decisions as to which aspects to highlight in which novels were evidence-led rather than theory-imposed, bottom-up rather than top-down. In each case, the evidence took me in directions that differed markedly from those indicated by the other two novels. Every text established its own, distinctive intermental personality. However, it would not be true to say that the aspects of social minds that are highlighted in one text never occur in another. Quite the contrary. This is why, at the end of chapter 5, I summarize some of the shared features of the three texts.

I start with *Middlemarch* because it is the best way into the subject of social minds in the nineteenth-century novel. It is the fulcrum around which the subject turns. In particular, an analysis of its opening few pages is an excellent introduction to the study of social minds in practice. It is also a good place to begin because its language is more obviously cognitive than any other novel of the period. Finally, it is an opportunity to show how the identity of an individual character (my example is Lydgate) is constructed in terms of a socially situated and distributed network of other minds. Individual characters and small units are investigated in this chapter within the context of the large unit of the whole Middlemarch mind and the medium-sized units of the various town minds. The emphasis in the analysis of *Little Dorrit* is rather different. There, I focus much more on the mechanics of small intermental units such as the look, facial expressions, and bodily movement. The chapter also goes into some detail on the dynamics of several small intermental units such as the Dorrit family and the relationship between Clennam and Little Dorrit. I then go back in time to *Persuasion* to return to the key issue of how a character (Anne Elliot being the example in this case) is necessarily embedded within networks of social minds. The treatment of Anne differs, though, from that of Lydgate. With Anne, I focus less on the basics of character construction and more on the role that this kind of approach to character plays in our overall understanding of the whole novel.

To implement the externalist perspective fully, it is necessary to examine within it not only obviously external topics such as social minds and intermental thought but also some apparently more internalist issues. To achieve this aim, it is necessary to establish the externalist perspective first. In *Fictional Minds,* I adopted the usual order of internalist first and externalist second. For this book, I have made a conscious decision to work in the reverse direction. This is why chapters 3 to 5 start with social minds before going on to three concepts that are generally thought of as belonging more naturally within the internalist perspective: the construction of character in *Middlemarch,* action in *Little Dorrit,* and emotions in *Persuasion.* My aim is to show, in every case, that these issues benefit greatly from being seen from within an externalist perspective.

I have been told that this kind of analysis is "infectious." In other words, after you finish this book you will find social minds at work in whatever novel you next read. I was pleased to hear this and hope that it is always the case. (This process has already begun for me. My holiday reading during a well-earned break from the final revisions for this book included a novel by the excellent Irish writer John McGahern called *Amongst Women* [1991]. I found the following description of three sisters on page two: "Apart, they could be breathtakingly sharp on the others' shortcomings but together their individual selves gathered into something very close to a single presence" [2]). On the face of it, the infectious nature of the analysis might sound like an argument for going easy on the amount of evidence to be presented in this book. I have, however, not done so. I was reluctant to prune the quotations in chapters 3 to 5 and, as a result, a substantial amount of evidence has been assembled in them. The danger is that you may start to think, "OK! We've got the picture, now!" But my intention in quoting so frequently from the texts is to show that social minds are woven into the fabric of their discourses. I hope that the weight of evidence presented in them is sufficient to demonstrate the point. In fact, the following chapters contain only a sample; there was insufficient room to use it all. I would like this book to represent a paradigm shift. I want readers to say of it, "Wow! There was so much of this stuff going on and we never saw it!"

CHAPTER 2

Introduction to Social Minds

> *Mixing blue and yellow which together makes green.*
> —Edith Somerville (describing her writing partnership with Martin Ross)

S PEAKING BROADLY, there are two perspectives on the mind: the internalist and the externalist. These two perspectives form more of a continuum than an either/or dichotomy, but the distinction is, in general, a valid one.

- An internalist perspective on the mind stresses those aspects that are inner, introspective, private, solitary, individual, psychological, mysterious, and detached.
- An externalist perspective on the mind stresses those aspects that are outer, active, public, social, behavioral, evident, embodied, and engaged.

I use the term *social mind* to describe those aspects of the whole mind that are revealed through the externalist perspective.

It seems to me that the traditional narratological approach to the representation of fictional character is an internalist one that stresses those aspects that are inner, passive, introspective, and individual. This undue emphasis on private, solitary, and highly verbalized thought at the expense of all the other types of mental functioning has resulted in a preoccupation with such concepts as free indirect discourse, stream of consciousness, and interior monologue. As a result, the *social* nature of fictional thought has been neglected. But, as Antonio Damasio suggests, "the study of human consciousness requires both internal and external views" (2000, 82), and so an externalist perspective is required as well, one that stresses the public, social, concrete, and located aspects of mental life in the novel.

As table 2.1 shows, a number of the concepts that are used to analyze the workings of fictional minds tend to fit easily into one or other of these perspectives. Some of these pairs oppose each other precisely; other pairings are much looser. The types of relationships within the pairings include opposition, complementarity, and intersection (as, for example, when an interior monologue shows evidence of Bakhtinian dialogicality). The term *aspectuality*, as mentioned in the previous chapter, refers to the fact that storyworlds are always experienced under some aspects and not others by the characters who inhabit them. People experience the same events in different ways. Within the internalist/externalist framework, I see focalization and aspectuality as complementing each other. Focalization occurs when the reader is presented with the aspect of the storyworld that is being experienced by the focalizer at that moment. In this context, the concept of aspectuality serves as a reminder that, meanwhile, the storyworld is also being experienced differently, under other aspects, by all of the characters who are not currently being focalized in the text. Any of those other characters could have been focalized if the author had chosen to do so. The term *continuing consciousness*, as I have said, stands for the process whereby readers create a continuing consciousness for a character out of the scattered, isolated mentions of that character in the text. The idea of continuing consciousnesses links nicely with the concepts of aspectuality and focalization. Other characters'

TABLE 2.1

INTERNALIST PERSPECTIVE	EXTERNALIST PERSPECTIVE
Private minds	Social minds
Intramental thought	Intermental thought
Personal identity	Situated identity
First-person attribution	Third-person attribution
Subjectivity of self	Subjectivity of others
Focalization	Aspectuality
Introspection	Theory of mind
Stream of consciousness	Continuing consciousness
Interior monologue	Bakhtinian dialogicality

consciousnesses are continuing while, at any single point in the narrative, only one consciousness is being focalized.

The internalist/externalist framework is also helpful in expanding our awareness of the implications of the concept of subjectivity. As the list suggests, the term can be used in both a first-person way (subjectivity of self) and a third-person way (subjectivity of others). The term *situated identity* locates selfhood and identity between the two. Aspectuality acts as a reminder here too, this time of the existence of the subjectivity of others, as available to us through the use of our theory of mind. The concept of aspectuality is a way of bringing to center stage previously marginalized characters whose voices may not often be heard. Knapp (1996) has applied the techniques of family systems therapy to D. H. Lawrence's *Sons and Lovers* (1913) in order to reinterpret the emotional landscape of that storyworld from the point of view of Paul's father. This is an unusual perspective because the focalization in the novel (through Paul, who has a difficult relationship with his father and tends to side with his mother) does not encourage it.

An important part of the social mind is our capacity for *intermental thought*. Such thinking is joint, group, shared, or collective, as opposed to *intramental*, or individual or private thought. It is also known as *socially distributed, situated,* or *extended cognition,* and also as *intersubjectivity*. Intermental thought is a crucially important component of fictional narrative because, just as in real life, where much of our thinking is done in groups, much of the mental functioning that occurs in novels is done by large organizations, small groups, work colleagues, friends, families, couples, and other intermental units. Notable examples include the army in Evelyn Waugh's *Men at Arms,* the town in William Faulkner's "A Rose for Emily" (1930), the group of friends in Donna Tartt's *The Secret History* (1992), the villainous Marchioness de Merteuil and the Viscount de Valmont in Laclos' *Les liaisons dangereuses* (1782), and Kitty and Levin in Tolstoy's *Anna Karenina* (1877), who, in a famous scene, write out only the initial letters of the words that they wish to use but who nevertheless understand each other perfectly. However, these are only a few of the most notable examples. My argument is that intermental units are to be found in nearly all novels. It could plausibly be argued that a large amount of the subject matter of novels is the formation, development, maintenance, modification, and breakdown of these intermental systems. As storyworlds are profoundly social in nature (even Robinson Crusoe has his Friday), novels necessarily contain a good deal of collective thinking. However, intermental thought in the novel has been invisible to traditional narrative approaches. Indeed, many of the samples of this sort of thought that follow in later chapters would not even count as examples of thought and consciousness within these approaches.

But shared minds become clearly visible within the cognitive approach to literature that underpins this book.

A good deal of the significance of the thought that occurs in novels is lost if only the internalist perspective is employed. Both perspectives are required, because a major preoccupation of novels is precisely this balance between public and private thought, intermental and intramental functioning, and social and individual minds. Within this balance, I will be emphasizing social minds because of their past neglect. In illustrating the importance of the functioning of the social minds in my main example texts, *Middlemarch, Little Dorrit,* and *Persuasion,* I aim to show that it is not possible to understand these novels without an awareness of these minds as they operate within their storyworlds. They are one of the chief means by which the plots are advanced. If you were to take all of the social thought out of these three novels, they would not be comprehensible. So, given the importance of this subject to the study of the novel, it seems to me that it is necessary to find room for it at the *center* of narrative theory.

I will take one example from many in order to illustrate the issues that may arise from an overreliance by literary critics on the internalist perspective. I have chosen *Reading the Nineteenth-Century Novel: Austen to Eliot* (2008) by Alison Case and Harry E. Shaw, because it is an excellent study that contains many valuable internalist insights. (For example, it points out that Charlotte Brontë's *Jane Eyre* [1847] starts with a tight, uncontextualized focus on Jane's consciousness and explains how revolutionary this decision was within the evolution of the nineteenth-century novel.) But, more troubling from an externalist perspective, Case and Shaw also remark on "how difficult it is for people to be simply themselves in any social setting" (2008, 24). These questions occur to me: Why assume that the self can only be found (or easily found) in solitude? Could it not be the other way round? Is it possible that we are only really ourselves when with others? When we are alone, are we not more easily tempted to construct convenient, comfortable, easy-to-live-with narratives for ourselves that may be distortions of reality? Similarly, Case and Shaw talk about *Wuthering Heights*'s "conflicting fantasies of escape from, or reconciliation with, the multiple *restraints* of selfhood that enable a stable, social world" (2008, 68; my emphasis). (Although this appears to be an objective description of the novel, I sense authorial agreement too.) Well, that is one way of looking at selfhood. Another, more externalist way is to see the social world as providing the *possibilities* for, or *affordances* for, the expression of selfhood.

Within the real-mind disciplines of psychology and philosophy there is a good deal of interest in *the mind beyond the skin* (as opposed to *the mind inside the skull*): the realization that mental functioning cannot be understood merely by analyzing what goes on within the skull but can only be fully comprehended once it has been seen in its social and physical context. Case and Shaw put the point nicely in their otherwise internalist study when they speculate about Walter Scott's wish to "reveal human nature, not from the skin in, but from the skin out" (2008, 37). Social psychologists routinely use the terms *mind* and *mental action* not only about individuals but also about groups of people working as intermental units. So, it is appropriate to say of these groups that they think or that they remember. James Wertsch explains that "the notion of mental function can properly be applied to social as well as individual forms of activity" (1991, 27). As he puts it, a *dyad* (that is, two people working as a cognitive system) can carry out such functions as problem solving on an intermental plane (1991, 27). It is significant that cognitive scientists are now beginning to share the interest of social psychologists in the mind beyond the skin. For an overview of the work being done in the new research area called *social neuroscience*, see *The Neuroscience of Social Interaction: Decoding, Influencing and Imitating the Actions of Others*, edited by Chris Frith and Daniel Wolpert (2004).

You may be asking what is achieved by talking in this way, instead of simply referring to individuals pooling their resources and working in cooperation together. The advocates of the concept of distributed cognition such as the theoretical anthropologists Gregory Bateson (1972) and Clifford Geertz (1993), the philosophers Andy Clark and David Chalmers (1998) and (2009) and Daniel Dennett (1996), and the psychologists Edwin Hutchins (1995) and James Wertsch all stress that the purpose of the concept is increased explanatory power. They argue that the way to delineate a cognitive system is to draw the limiting line so that you do not cut out anything whose absence leaves things inexplicable (Bateson 1972, 465). To illustrate, Wertsch tells the story of how his daughter lost her shoes and he helped her to remember where she had left them. Wertsch asks: Who is doing the remembering here? He is not, because he had no prior knowledge of where they were, and she is not, because she had forgotten where they were and was only able to remember by means of her father's promptings. It was therefore the intermental unit formed by the two of them that remembered (Sperber and Hirschfeld 1999, cxxiv). If you draw the line narrowly around single persons, and maintain that cognition can only be individual, then things remain inexplicable. Neither *on their own* remembered. If you draw the line more widely, and accept the concept of an intermental cognitive system, then things are explained. The intermental unit remembered. The same applies not just to problem solving but also to joint decision making and group action. Here is a simple example from Evelyn Waugh's *Vile Bodies* (1930) that I will use again when explaining the philosophical concept of action in chapter 4: "The three statesmen hid themselves" (86). The decision to hide is an intermental one that is taken together by all three individuals, and the action of hiding is also one that they perform together.

Intermental cognitive systems are, to some extent, independent of the individual elements that go to make them up. This is not to say that the whole is necessarily *greater* than the sum of its parts; it is simply to say that it is *different* from the sum of its parts. One example of this difference is the vivid metaphor with which I began this chapter and which was used by the author Edith Somerville to describe her writing partnership with Martin Ross: a question of "mixing blue and yellow which together makes green." Something similar happened when the poet John Ashbery wrote a novel with James Schuyler in the 1950s, each contributing a line or two at a time. In the diary section of the *Times Literary Supplement* (5 December 2008), the diarist wondered which of the two wrote the line "Why don't you admit that you enjoy my unhappiness?" The following response from Ashbery was published two weeks later: "In regard to the line in question, I can't remember. Schuyler and I were often unable to remember who had written what, as our lines seemed to emerge from an invisible third person" (*Times Literary Supplement* [19 December 2008]). There are musical examples too. Keith Rowe, a member of the free improvisation group AMM, once told me that while the group was playing, he would sometimes not know whether it was he or another member of the group who was producing the sounds that he could hear.

However, in considering the wide-ranging nature of intermental functioning (problem solving, decision making, coming to ethical judgments, and so on), it should be borne in mind that analyses of this sort of thought should involve no preconceptions about its quality. Intermental thought is as beautiful and ugly, destructive and creative, exceptional and commonplace as intramental thought. The communal creativity described in the previous paragraph should be balanced against, for example, the scapegoating tendencies of many groups, and also against Pentagon "groupthink."

An emphasis on social minds will inevitably question these twin assumptions: first, that the workings of our own minds are never accessible to others; and, second, that the workings of our own minds are always and unproblematically accessible to ourselves. This book will, in the main, question the first assumption and will make much less reference to the equally questionable second, although the subject does come up occasionally (as in the *Men at Arms* case study that follows). But in disputing the first-named assumption by discussing the public minds that are to be found in *Middlemarch, Little Dorrit,* and *Persuasion,* I must stress that I am certainly not saying that fictional minds are always easily readable. Sometimes, they are;

sometimes, they are not. In these three novels, I will argue, they frequently are. In other novels, especially those of the twentieth and twenty-first centuries, however, different levels of readability and unreadability will apply. For more discussion on this, see Porter Abbott's "Unreadable Minds and the Captive Reader" (2009).

In an illuminating article titled "Diagramming Narrative," Marie-Laure Ryan uses diagrams as a semiotic tool for the understanding of narrative in relation to three aspects of plot—time, space, and mind. On the question of mind, she refers to the subject matter of narrative as the "evolution of a network of interpersonal relations" (2007, 29) and convincingly shows how diagrammatic representations of these networks can add a good deal to our understanding of the narrative process. She illustrates this approach with two highly technical analyses, one of a minimal, two-sentence narrative and the other of the fable "The Fox and the Crow" (which was also used in Ryan 1991). It seems to me that a modified and necessarily greatly simplified variant of this sort of approach could be used to analyze the workings of social minds in whole novels. For example, the complex interrelations between different intermental units can be thought of as resembling the patterns made by Venn diagrams, in which overlapping circles are used to express the relationships between classes of objects. Such a diagram would show that the memberships of some groups are completely included within larger ones, some might have no overlap of membership with any others, others would have partial membership overlaps, and so on. With at least some of the novels to be discussed later, it would be possible, though difficult, to construct Venn diagrams that could vividly illustrate this complexity in visual terms.

Little narratological work has been done on social minds in the novel. Exceptions include studies of aspects of distributed cognition by John V. Knapp (for example, 1996) and also by the postclassical narrative theorists David Herman (2003a, 2003b, 2007a, 2008, and 2010) and Uri Margolin (1996b and 2000). The exploration of *"we" narratives* (that is, narratives written predominantly in the first-person plural) that was initiated by Margolin and continued by Brian Richardson (2006) has produced rewarding results (see, for example, Marcus 2008). A welcome and related development has been the important work done by the literary critic Susan Sniader Lanser in *Fictions of Authority* (1992), in which she focuses on the concept of *communal voice*. Her use of the term *voice* shows that she is concerned with the relationship between "we" narration and "I" narration in which one speaker represents others. That is to say, she explores the telling, the mode of narration, the discursive practices of the novels that she discusses. Lanser writes persuasively about some of the important issues raised by the notion of communal thought such as the problematic erasure of differences between individuals and the need to make speculative and potentially mistaken assumptions about the thoughts of others. I want to take a more inclusive approach, however, and set these issues as well as some of the more positive ones arising from intermentality into a wider context. Most of the nineteenth-century novels that feature plentiful evidence of shared thought have heterodiegetic narrators and are not therefore examples of a communal *voice*. The studies mentioned above are pioneering, but they have focused in the main only on the relatively small number of narratives written in the "we" form; my point is that little attention has been given to the much larger group of what, in response, I would call *"they" narratives:* that is, narratives that feature social minds.

You may be feeling some doubt about this claim regarding the neglect of intermental thought. Surely we have always known about the importance of groups right from the beginning of Western literature. What about the role of the chorus in Greek tragedy? Well, yes, undoubtedly, but my claim is that this knowledge has not been reflected in the *theory* on mental functioning in narrative. Obviously, we all know about the proverbial *vox populi,* both in literature (especially in drama) and also in our daily lives, but the purpose of the present book is to examine the socially situated or intermental cognition lying at its basis and the various ways in which it is represented in narrative. What about Menakhem Perry's masterly analysis of William Faulkner's short story "A Rose for Emily" (1979), in which the townspeople as a group play such an important role? Perry's article is a groundbreaking contribution to our knowledge of the role of cognitive frames in the reading process, but I do not think that it was part of his intention explicitly to recognize the status of the town as an intermental unit. That is the purpose of this book.

A TYPOLOGY

Obviously the extent, duration, and success of intermental activity will vary greatly from occasion to occasion. Because this is such a wide, relatively uncharted area in the context of literary studies, the following, rather basic typology may be of some value.

1. *Intermental encounters.* At the minimal level, this consists of the group thought that is necessary for conversations between individuals to take place. It is not possible to have a coherent dialogue without at least some intermental communication. A minimal level of mind reading and

theory of mind is required for characters to understand each other and thereby make everyday life possible. It is made easier or more difficult by a variety of factors such as solipsistic versus emotionally intelligent individuals, easily readable versus impenetrable minds, familiar versus unfamiliar contexts, similar versus different sorts of social background, and so on. A heightened awareness of the mental functioning of another can occur within random encounters between people who do not know each other particularly well or even between complete strangers. I am sure that most readers of this book will have had the experience of meeting somebody for the first time and instantly feeling that you are both on the same wavelength. A focus on the workings of long-term, stable intermental units such as couples and families as itemized below can give a misleading impression if it suggests that intermental thought can *only* occur within such units. As we know from our real-life experience, mind reading can occur in a variety of situations. Sometimes, it is what might be called *reciprocal:* there is a conscious and fully intended sharing of thought and so people will know that others know what they are thinking. At other times, it is *inadvertent:* someone may reveal their thoughts without meaning to. In these cases, that person may not know that their mind has been read by another person, or they may notice that it has been, for example by the other's facial expression.

In addition to our various encounters with countless strangers and acquaintances over the course of our lives, we all belong to intermental units. I would define these as stable, fairly long-lasting groups that regularly employ intermental thinking. They vary greatly in size, and I will adopt the rather simplistic approach of referring to them as small, medium, and large units. Obviously, many other, rather more sophisticated typologies are possible. John V. Knapp (personal communication) has suggested one that would measure group membership along a scale of interpersonal intensity. For example, someone may feel an intense involvement in the unit formed by their work colleagues but may have a much more distant relationship with their own family.

2. *Small intermental units.* Characters tend to form intermental pairs and small groups of various sorts such as marriages, close friendships, and nuclear families. It is likely that, over time, the people in these units will get to know quite well what the others are thinking. However, these small groups will obviously vary greatly in the quality of their intermental thought, and readers' expectations may not be met. Many fictional marriages have much less intermental thought than one might think (depending on the level of one's expectations in this matter, of course). For an excellent analysis of the small intermental unit of a mar-

riage, see Elena Semino's "Blending and Characters' Mental Functioning in Virginia Woolf's 'Lappin and Lapinova'" (2006).

3. *Medium-sized intermental units.* The intermentality that occurs between the individuals in medium-sized units such as work colleagues, networks of friendships, and neighborhoods is rather different from the one that arises in random encounters and small units. Here, the emphasis is less on individuals knowing what another person is thinking, and more on people thinking the same way (whether or not they know that others are also thinking that way). Examples that are highlighted in later chapters include some of the subgroups of the Middlemarch mind in chapter 3, the Circumlocution Office in chapter 4, and the party to which Anne Elliot belongs in chapter 5.

4. *Large intermental units.* Individuals are also likely to belong to larger groups that will also have a tendency to think together on certain issues and so produce a collective opinion or consensus view on a particular topic. To pursue this point in greater depth would be to take this study into concepts such as ideology that are well beyond the scope of this book. The dynamics involved in large groups are similar to those that govern medium-sized units. Examples from the novels studied in future chapters include the town of Middlemarch, "Society" in Bath (*Persuasion*), and the important role that the public plays in the passage from *Little Dorrit* that is discussed at the end of chapter 4.

5. *Intermental minds.* These are intermental units, large, medium, or small, that are so well defined and long-lasting, and where so much successful intermental thought takes place, that they can plausibly be considered as group minds. Couples who have been together for a long time, who know each other's minds well, and who are able to work well together on such joint activities as decision making and problem solving are the best examples. However, larger groups may also acquire some of these characteristics. Though well defined, these groups will contain individuals who will often be completely different from each other. Opinions will inevitably differ widely on the point at which a particular collection of people can be regarded as sufficiently stable, well-functioning, and distinctive to be defined as an intermental mind. I will argue that the town of Middlemarch, a large unit, may be called an intermental mind, together with some marriages such as the Crofts in *Persuasion* and the Meagles in *Little Dorrit.*

The simplicity of this typology hardly begins to do justice to the complexity and range of the intermental units to be found in novels. Nevertheless, it does have some value in providing a map, however rudimentary, by which this unfamiliar territory may be initially explored. It is obvious that there is a wide spectrum of phenomena covered by the term *intermental thought* and also by this typology: it ranges from chance encounters between two strangers to the life of a whole town over a long period. I do not see any harm in this, as long as we remain conscious of it. The priority is to establish the viability of the externalist perspective on fictional minds as a whole. Then it will be possible to specify the intricate complexities that can be revealed by that perspective. In his review of Dorrit Cohn's inspirational study *Transparent Minds,* the narratologist Brian McHale said that the "history of our poetics of prose is essentially a history of successive differentiations of types of discourse from the undifferentiated 'block' of narrative prose" (1981, 185). These wise words have guided me throughout my narratological studies. I see the first book as having hacked off a huge, previously undifferentiated block of prose and labeled it *fictional minds.* This current stage involves detaching a smaller but still sizeable chunk (labeled *social minds*) from the fictional-minds block, for the purpose of reducing it further into ever smaller and finer fragments. The intention is that, by these means, the work may eventually, over time, become progressively less industrial and heavy-duty in nature and rather more craftsmanlike.

As with all other aspects of the reading process, we bring our real-world cognitive frames to bear when we encounter fictional intermental units. As I say, these frames will entail the default assumption that our theory of mind works better with spouses, close friends, and immediate family than it does with total strangers. We assume that the attributional success rate will be higher than average in such relationships. Within the externalist perspective, it is not surprising that we often know what other people are thinking. It is not a question of occasional sudden flashes of insight, but of a steady pattern of shared thought processes resulting in fairly accurate prediction rates. This pattern is, of course, regularly disrupted by intermental breakdowns, sometimes serious, and my intention is certainly not to minimize the importance of these breakdowns. As I will repeat at regular intervals throughout this book, it is a balance. Sometimes, as we shall see, the default slots are filled; sometimes, when our assumptions are wrong, they are not. When there are frequent misunderstandings or a fundamental lack of communication, the reader has to reconsider the nature of the relationship and amend the frame. In extreme cases, such as Anne Elliot's relationship with her father and older sister, and Clennam's with his mother, major reconstruction, such as the use of a new, dysfunctional-family frame, is quickly required.

I have found that some literary scholars tend to react with initial skepticism and even hostility to the idea of intermental thought. However, it is my experience that this hostility tends to wear off with time, to be replaced by curiosity and even enthusiasm. Others are interested from the beginning in the concept of intermental *thought,* but resist the concept of an intermental *mind.* It is a step too far. But there is really little difference between what I have in mind for the concept of an intermental mind and what these skeptics are prepared to accept. Intermental minds consist simply of individual minds pooling their resources and producing different results. Have a look again at the definition of an intermental mind that I gave above and ask yourself whether you disagree that couples can get to know each other so well that they are frequently "of one mind" and can solve problems together very efficiently. I doubt that you do. So what we are really talking about is whether the use of the term *mind* is appropriate for this mutual cooperation.

While considering this question, it is worth bearing in mind the *functionalist* perspective on mental life that is characteristic of a good deal of the cognitive sciences and that asks what thinking *does,* what it is *for.* In questioning what constitutes a mind and what does not, this perspective has an extremely liberating effect because it leads you to question what is meant by a mind. Artificial-intelligence (AI) researchers look at the mind in term of outputs, or what the brain does. They therefore investigate whether these outputs can only be produced by *wetware* (that is, the physical composition of the brain) or whether the same results can also be obtained from computer hardware. And once your concept of mind is flexible enough for you to question the commonsense assumption that the physical brain is necessary to the production of a mind, you are then free to wonder whether a mind can also consist of more than one brain.

In his famous "Chinese Room" thought experiment, John Searle (1980) asks us to imagine someone who cannot understand Chinese but who is put into a room containing some Chinese writing together with instructions for handling this writing. The instructions say what writing should be passed out of the room as answers to particular questions. Using these instructions, the person is able to "answer" questions written in Chinese even though he or she does not understand that language. From the outside, the room looks like a thinking mind because when questions are submitted to it, they are correctly answered. (I can cite a similar sort of case from my day job. I am able to produce perfectly adequate minutes of meetings despite having had very little understanding of what was being discussed. I am being serious.) Searle's point is that computers function in the same way as the Chinese room. They appear to work as minds do, but in fact they do not. He wishes to undermine the claim of the "strong AI" argument that computers can have minds. John Searle's Chinese Room experiment is controversial, and people disagree vehemently over its significance. Can you regard the (non-Chinese-speaking) individual-plus-the-writing-plus-the-instructions as a "mind"? Most people would not. But if you are one of those, how do you explain the fact that the brain is also made up of equally blind, unknowing elements? Within the brain, consciousness is distributed across constituent modules that are just as incapable of independent cognition as the various elements that go to make up the Chinese room. Why not just talk of these individual modules pooling their resources to produce better results? Well, we do, except that we have a single word for this process—the mind.

Some of the philosophers and psychologists who subscribe to the notion of socially distributed cognition are also interested in another aspect of the mind that is called *physically distributed cognition:* "our habit of off-loading as much as possible of our cognitive tasks into the environment itself" (Dennett 1996, 134). Andy Clark calls this process *Supersizing the Mind* (2009). It is achieved mainly through tools such as pen and paper and computers. However, in a less obvious sense, we also make use of our whole environment as a cognitive aid. In her seminal study *The Art of Memory*, the historian Frances Yates describes how ancient orators used parts of the auditorium as memorial reference points for sections of their oratory. On a more mundane level, when we are in our own homes, we know where everything is and our cognitive functioning runs smoothly; when we are put into an alien environment, the quality of our thinking can suffer. Dennett convincingly illustrates the importance of physically distributed cognition to old people when he describes how they tend to become disoriented when taken out of their own homes and put into the unfamiliar environment of a nursing home. As Dennett says, "Taking them out of their homes is literally separating them from large parts of their minds" (1996, 128). Examples of physically distributed cognition are mentioned in the following chapters. Within the context of the present discussion, it may be regarded as the argument that a mind can correspond to a brain plus inanimate objects. Yet another opportunity for flexibility in one's conception of the mind is the doctrine of behaviorism, which can be interpreted, in a certain sense, as the argument that when we talk of the mind, we are talking of (the behavior of) the body.

The more you read of philosophical and psychological debates such as these, the more flexible your concept of mind becomes, whether by breaking it down into its constituent elements, or by building it up (that is, distributing it) to include external elements. To summarize, there are at least four different ways in which the cognitive sciences can open up our thinking about the mind and, in particular, loosen the rigid correspondence of one mind to one brain. These are as follows:

- A mind can be realized by machinery: one mind corresponding to no (wetware) brain;

- A mind can be interpreted in terms of behavior: one mind corresponding, in a certain sense, to one body;
- A mind can be physically distributed: one mind corresponding to one brain plus inanimate objects; and
- A mind can be socially distributed: one mind corresponding to more than one brain.

Within this context, I hope that the use of the term *mind* to refer to a group may not seem so surprising. To put the point simply: the mind is a fuzzy concept.

Even so, you may be wondering how intermental units are able to survive Occam's razor, the principle that entities should not be multiplied beyond necessity. Why create a new entity of an intermental unit instead of simply talking of individuals? I would turn the question around and point out that the advocates of socially distributed cognition are postulating one theoretical entity (the intermental unit, made up of two or more different elements) to explain a joint mental operation, whereas the traditional view posits at least two (the sum of the individuals involved). So Occam's razor should apply to the internalist rather than to the externalist position.

Some skeptics argue that cognitivists put old wine into new bottles. I acknowledge that there are points in this book where an analysis in the noncognitive language of mainstream literary theory would produce similar results (for example, the discussions in chapter 4 of the role of the face, nonverbal communication, and the look). However, I would argue that the cognitive orientation displayed in this study links together disparate, previously only partially visible aspects of the novel and combines them into a complete cognitive theory of social fictional minds. Within this theoretical framework, new insights into these various elements, even those that are capable of noncognitive explanations, will, I think, emerge.

CASE STUDY: *MEN AT ARMS*

I will now illustrate some of the concepts discussed so far in this chapter and the previous one by applying them to a short passage of text. I will attempt to reveal what I think are important insights into this passage by approaching it from the following four perspectives: storyworlds, theory of mind, intermental thought, and unconscious thought. My example text is one of the great passages of twentieth-century English literature: the description of Guy Crouchback's departure from Italy at the beginning of Evelyn Waugh's *Men at Arms*. Crouchback is leaving his family home outside the Italian village of Santa Dulcina delle Rocce on the eve of the Second World War in order to go to London to enlist in the army. As he is driven away, he thinks about the Italian word *simpatico* (meaning sympathetic in the sense of congenial, compatible, or of similar mind or temperament):

> He was not loved, Guy knew, either by his household or in the town. He was accepted and respected but he was not *simpatico*. Grafin von Gluck, who spoke no word of Italian and lived in undisguised concubinage with her butler, was *simpatica*. Mrs Garry was *simpatica*, who distributed Protestant tracts, interfered with the fishermen's methods of killing octopuses and filled her house with stray cats.
>
> Guy's uncle, Peregrine, a bore of international repute whose dreaded presence could empty the room in any centre of civilization—Uncle Peregrine was considered *molto simpatico*. The Wilmots were gross vulgarians; they used Santa Dulcina purely as a pleasure resort, subscribed to no local funds, gave rowdy parties and wore indecent clothes, talked of "wops" and often left after the summer with their bills to the tradesmen unpaid; but they had four boisterous and ill-favoured daughters whom the Santa-Dulcinesi had watched grow up. Better than this, they had lost a son bathing from the rocks. The Santa-Dulcinesi participated in these joys and sorrows. They observed with relish their hasty and unobtrusive departures at the end of the holidays. They were *simpatici*. Even Musgrave who had the castelletto before the Wilmots and bequeathed it his name, Musgrave who, it was said, could not go to England or America because of warrants for his arrest, "Musgrave the Monster," as the Crouchbacks used to call him—*he* was *simpatico*. Guy alone, whom they had known from infancy, who spoke their language and conformed to their religion, who was open-handed in all his dealings and scrupulously respectful of all their ways, whose grandfather built their school, whose mother had given a set of vestments embroidered by the Royal School of Needlework for the annual procession of St. Dulcina's bones—Guy alone was a stranger among them. (15–16)

The four issues (storyworlds, theory of mind, intermental thought, and unconscious thought) resolve themselves into the following simple statements:

- The passage constructs a fictional storyworld that readers have to gain access to in order to understand the narrative.
- Readers gain access to this storyworld primarily by trying to follow the workings of the minds of the characters described in it, and, in par-

- ticular, by following how these characters try to follow the workings of each other's minds.
- One of the minds that is active in the passage is the collective or group mind of the inhabitants of the town.
- Some of the thinking that this group mind does is unconscious.

I will now explain the background to each of these statements in turn.

Readers employ the notion of the storyworld when they say of novels, as we all do, that they are "true to life" or "realistic," or that they are "inconsistent" or "farfetched," and so on. When we say things such as these we are positing the existence of a storyworld and then comparing it to our own real world. Let us try the real-world/storyworld comparison on this beautiful piece of writing. I think it is likely that, when we do, the reaction of many readers will be "How true! It's *so* accurate, *so* true-to-life. That *is* how people behave! Life *is* unfair!" But what do we mean when we say these things? After all, we are talking about a semiotic construct: an imaginary town peopled by imaginary characters. Well, we mean that this imaginary world is *like* the real world in certain important ways, but what is the relationship that is conveyed by that single, simple word "like"?

The storyworld described in the passage consists in part of physical spaces containing various objects. Let us have a detailed look at this world. It is set in Italy and the Second World War is about to begin. It contains taxis, households, towns, butlers, fishermen and fishing nets, octopuses, houses, cats, uncles, bores, pleasure resorts, funds, parties, clothes, bills, tradesmen, rocks, holidays, arrest warrants, language, religion, ways of doing things, grandfathers, schools, mothers, vestments, processions, bones, and strangers. I have listed these elements in such exhaustive and slightly surreal detail in order to illustrate how dense even short descriptions of storyworlds can be. The passage that contains these thirty-odd elements is less than three hundred words long. Even the most apparently simple reading process involves a number of complex cognitive operations. An obvious point follows, but it is one that is well worth making explicit: in order to understand the passage, in order to reconstruct this storyworld, the reader has to know what taxis, butlers, and fishing nets are. As the length of the list shows, a good deal of this sort of real-world knowledge is required for narrative comprehension. But, in addition to knowing what these things are, we also have to be capable of the many inferences contained in the language that describes them if we are to achieve full understanding. When the text says that Uncle Peregrine could empty a room, we have to work out what this really means: everybody knows that he is so boring that people leave the room hastily when they see him in it.

Because it is obvious that this storyworld is like the real world in the sense that all of the objects contained in it exist in reality, we are able to apply to it what Marie-Laure Ryan calls the *principle of minimal departure* (1991). That is, we assume that any narrative storyworld is like our own until the text provides evidence of such departures from the real world as magical or supernatural entities or events. Her concept is a description in different terms of the default values contained in the frames that we apply to fictional texts. Our assumption that the storyworld will not depart from the real world unless we are told otherwise is a default position. So, when we study a narrative, we look for the clues that will tell us in what ways, if at all, the storyworld created by that narrative differs from the real world. The default position applies in the case of *Men at Arms,* where there are no magical beings with supernatural powers.

However, a further comparison between the storyworld and the real world is required. In addition to consisting of physical spaces and objects, storyworlds also comprise the minds of the characters who inhabit those spaces: Guy and the other people who live in the town. Although the sense of place and the existence of objects are important, these fictional minds are far more so. If I am right that reader responses to the passage will tend to go along the lines of "Life's just like that!" then these responses would be concerned with fictional minds. Spaces and objects usually have significance only insofar as they affect the mental functioning of the characters in the storyworld. Just as our real minds always operate within a physical and social context, so fictional minds always operate within the specific social and physical context of their storyworld. The fishing nets, the taxis, the cats, and the location of the town are important because they mean something to the fictional minds of the characters who experience those things. Does the principle of minimal departure apply to these fictional minds just as it does to the physical objects? How do the minds described in the text correspond to what we know of our own minds and what we know of the minds of other people? Do the characters behave like real people? These questions bring us to the next issue: theory of mind.

Just as the physical spaces and objects of the storyworld are experienced by characters, so readers also interpret the *events* that take place there as characters' *experiences.* The Wilmots' flight from the town is not simply an event. It is something that is experienced by the Wilmots because it is an action that they take. They arrive at the belief that they have run out of money; they have the desire to escape the consequences of their lack of money; and they come to the decision that it would be in their best interests to take the action of leaving the town. It is also an experience for the town. It watches the departure with relish because it is using its own theory of mind on the Wilmots. It has followed the causal mental network that I have just described, and therefore understands why they are leaving. Finally, and more indirectly, it is an experience for Guy. He, presumably, has also followed the thinking behind the Wilmots' action, and he is also aware of the inexplicably tolerant attitude of the town toward it. The death of the son is another obvious example of an experience for both the family and the town. (By the way, to get back to intermental minds for a moment: please note that I have been talking quite naturally here about both the Wilmot family and the town as joint or group minds. I wonder whether any reader of this book who was having difficulty with the theory presented earlier in this chapter thought to themselves while reading this paragraph: "How can a group of people such as a town or a family have a collective mind?" I doubt it. What may seem bizarre in theory can often seem perfectly natural in practice.)

The *Men at Arms* storyworld is aspectual. Like the real world, it varies depending on the diverse aspects under which it is viewed, and its characters can experience it only from a particular perceptual and cognitive aspect at any one time. The storyworld will therefore appear different to, and be experienced differently by, the various minds of the characters. Guy has a set of knowledge, values, opinions, beliefs, and so on that differs substantially from those of the other people in the passage. The notion of *simpatico* forms an important part of his mind because he so keenly feels its absence, whereas it appears that it does not form part of theirs. Guy obviously knows much more about the town than the Wilmots do as he has taken the trouble to study it. He is respectful and knowledgeable about it; they flaunt the fact that they are not. He therefore views the storyworld as it relates to the town completely differently from them. In fact, the whole *Men at Arms* storyworld is so aspectual in nature that the Guy storyworld is a substantially different one from the Wilmots' storyworld. His town is a different town from theirs. (I pursue this point further when I talk about the "Lydgate storyworld" in chapter 3.) Even this, though, is an oversimplification. The contrast so far has been with the Wilmots, but they are not the only other people in this passage. More generally, the notion of simpatico is one that Guy shares with the whole community. Indeed, it is plausible to speculate that he gets it from that community. In other words, even his intramental thought has an intermental component.

You may be thinking that I have gone too far. "We are only talking here about 298 words on the page. The proper names contained in those words refer only to literary constructs. We should not talk about them as though they're real people." I would fundamentally disagree. In recognizing their status as semiotic constructs, we *do* have to approach fictional characters in similar ways to real people. We have to hypothesize, speculate, and theorize

Introduction to Social Minds | **57**

in precisely the way I have been doing and will be doing in order to make any sense of the 298 words. When we enter a storyworld, we have to try to fill the gaps in it. Guy's relationship with the town is a prelude to the rest of the novel, which is concerned with his relationship with his army regiment. If we do not understand the former, we will not understand the latter. The relationship with the army is explored in much greater depth and over a longer period, but the initial cognitive frame provided by the passage I am discussing here helpfully illuminates the problematical nature of his future army career.

As the passage represents Guy's thoughts and is seen from Guy's point of view, it is focalized through Guy. But look again at this sentence: "Better than this, they had lost a son bathing from the rocks." If the sentence is taken in isolation, the phrase "better than this" is extraordinary. How can it be better for a young boy to die? It cannot be better for the narrator that the Wilmots have lost their son, and it is obviously not better for the Wilmots that they have. The focalization in this case is complex. One approach is to say that it is better for the town, in the sense that his death makes the Wilmots even more simpatico. On this view, the Wilmots are being presented from the town's point of view: the description of the event is focalized through the town. So, although the whole passage is focalized through Guy, this specific intermental focalization is embedded within Guy's focalization. But an alternative and richer interpretation is that the focalization continues to be Guy's: it is he, not the villagers, who is thinking (resentfully) "better than the daughters, there is the dead son" because that loss makes the vulgar Wilmots more simpatico with the villagers than he is. His awareness of the villagers' response to the son's death influences his judgment here, but it is he, not the villagers, who is the focalizer. Saying that it is the villagers who are thinking "better than this" makes them seem awfully callous, and that runs counter to what we learn in the next sentence: "The Santa-Dulcinesi participated in these joys and sorrows." A further complication is that you can also hear in that sentence the ironic timbre of the voice of the cool and dispassionate narrator of the novel.

To put my general point another way, it is revealing to analyze fiction in terms of levels of *intentionality*. (This term is used in the philosophy of mind quite differently from its usual meaning to refer to the "aboutness" of mental states. Such states nearly always have some content, are directed at something, are about something.) In this sentence, I have counted five levels of intentionality:

1. The narrator presents
2. how Guy experiences

3. how the town experiences
4. how the Wilmot family experiences
5. the fact that the son experienced his fatal accident.

So, this apparently simple sentence of only twelve words ("Better than this, they had lost a son bathing from the rocks") contains a complex set of several different levels of thought. Note in particular, though, that the second and fifth levels relate to individual minds while the third and fourth levels relate to group minds. This leads us on to the next point.

An internalist perspective will not by itself tell us much about the mental functioning that is going on in this passage. True, it will show that the text is describing Guy's individual, private feelings, but after that, it is not much use. Only an externalist perspective will reveal, for example, that the town has an intermental mind, that the cognitive functioning of the individual characters is apparent to the town from their action and behavior, and that Guy's feelings make sense only when understood as a reaction to the feelings of the town. The passage is not just about the intramental functioning of one individual, and not just about the intermental functioning of the town: it is about the complex, dialogical relationship between the two. What do I mean by referring to the *mind* of this town? Look again at the passage and at the range of cognitive functioning of which this group mind is capable. It has known Guy since infancy. It does not love him because it does not find him simpatico, but it does accept and respect him. It finds Guy still a stranger. It does find simpatico the other individuals who are listed in the passage. It can forgive those others their faults. It watches the Wilmot daughters grow up. It participates in the joys and sorrows of the Wilmots. It observes "with relish" their departures. It has its language, its religion, and its ways. How can an entity that is capable of such wide-ranging and sophisticated cognitive functioning *not* be called a mind?

I would now like to talk about some of the ideas on unconscious thought that are developed in a fascinating book by the psychologist Timothy Wilson called *Strangers to Ourselves* (2002). The notion of unconscious thought is not central to this book. I am talking about it here simply to illustrate that the social-minds approach is a versatile one that can be taken in many different directions. A good deal of work has been done by a number of psychologists on unconscious thought, but I am using Wilson because he synthesizes this work in a clear and approachable way. Although he discusses only individuals, it will be illuminating, I hope, to apply his ideas on the role of the unconscious to the thinking of groups. I will be arguing that, because the workings of the town's mind have a significant unconscious element, the town judges people in the same way as the intramental unconscious mind, the town's attitudes to individuals are conditioned by *feeling rules,* and, as a result, the town has *dual attitudes* toward Guy and the other individuals. (The two italicized terms are explained below.) And, most importantly, these features account for what is most remarkable and distinctive about the passage—its counterintuitive and apparently paradoxical quality.

The unconscious thought that I will be discussing consists of much more than just the *Freudian* unconscious of psychoanalytical theory. (I referred to this wider concept in *Fictional Minds* as *nonconscious* thought, precisely in order to differentiate it from the Freudian unconscious. However, I will talk about "the unconscious" here because that is what Wilson calls it.) Here are three examples of this much wider category of unconscious thought. First (2002, 164), Wilson quotes an estate agent as saying that she always listens carefully to what her clients tell her about the sort of house they want to buy. She then completely ignores what they have said and simply watches them as they react to the different sorts of houses they visit. Often, a very different picture of their real wants emerges. The estate agent finds the evidence of what customers *do* much more reliable than the evidence of what they *say.* In the second example (2002, 85), students were asked if they would buy a flower as part of a campus charity event and eighty-three percent said they would. In fact, only forty-three percent did. When they were asked whether other people would buy a flower, their prediction (of fifty-six percent) was much more accurate. In a similar sort of study, people predicted that they would donate an average of $2.44 of their earnings to charity and that other people would donate $1.83. The actual figure was $1.53. The final example (2002, 101–2) is an extraordinary one. Young men were approached by an attractive young woman in a park and asked to take part in an experiment. During the discussion, she gave them her phone number. Some of the men were approached while negotiating a flimsy and scary footbridge over a deep gorge and others while sitting on a park bench. Sixty-five percent of the men on the footbridge called her and asked for a date, while only thirty percent of the men on the bench did so. Why the difference? The researchers predicted that the men on the footbridge would mistakenly attribute their beating hearts, shortness of breath, and perspiration to physical attraction rather than just fear of falling off the bridge, and this appears to be exactly what happened.

Psychologists such as Wilson conclude from this evidence that people are often simply mistaken about the nature of their own mental functioning. They think with their conscious mind that they are going to do one thing, but, because the decisions are in fact taken by their unconscious mind, they end up doing another. For this reason, we are often much more accurate in predicting other people's behavior than we are in predicting our own.

According to Wilson, "There is no direct access to the . . . unconscious, no matter how hard we try . . . It can thus be fruitless to try to examine the . . . unconscious by looking inward. It is often better to *deduce* the nature of our hidden minds by looking outward at our behaviour and how others react to us and coming up with a good narrative" (2002, 16). What Wilson is saying is that our private thought is often not immediately accessible and available to us. We have to infer what we ourselves are thinking in much the same way as we infer what other people are thinking. We deduce the nature of the workings of our unconscious mind by looking outward at the behavior that results from it. That is what Guy does in deducing that his behavior has made him non simpatico to the town even though his conscious mind has tried so hard to be simpatico. So, although thought can be private and inaccessible to others (no one else will know *exactly* what thoughts Guy is having in the precise form in which he is having them), thought can also be public and available to others. The workings of the individual minds of Grafin von Gluck, Mrs Garry, and the Wilmots are visible to the town and to Guy, and the workings of the town's intermental mind are visible to Guy as well. In particular, he believes from the behavior of the townspeople that they find others simpatico but not him. This is the externalist perspective in practice.

The notion of unconscious thought can also usefully be linked, not just to specific mental events, but also to the concept of dispositions. According to Wilson, the nineteenth-century psychologist William Hamilton "wrote extensively about the way in which habits acquired early in life become an indispensable part of one's personality. These mental processes are said to constitute a kind of 'automatic self' to which people had no conscious access—an idea that was not to reappear in psychology for more than 100 years" (2002, 11–12). Hamilton argued that our dispositions become part of our unconscious mind. It is in this way that the town has acquired habits of thought that have become an indispensible though unconscious part of its intermental personality.

Am I right in saying that the town has unconscious feelings and does not have any direct access to them? Let us speculate. Imagine an inhabitant of the town being asked to make his or her feelings explicit, and therefore conscious: "How do you feel about Mr Crouchback? Do you like Mr Musgrave more?" I find it quite likely that they would then be conscious of what they are *supposed* to feel and so reply that certainly they like Mr Crouchback as much as Mr Musgrave, if not more. However, that is the sort of insincere reassurance that people feel they have to produce in order to be polite. So let us put the hypothetical question to the inhabitants in a different way and ask them, as Wilson suggests, to analyze their behavior. "Do you *behave* in a less open and more reserved way towards Mr Crouchback than towards Mr Musgrave?" It seems quite plausible to me that they would be genuinely surprised to hear that this was a possibility and that Mr Crouchback had noticed any difference. Their conscious minds would find it difficult to recognize the behavior that has resulted from the workings of their unconscious minds.

The unconscious is "a spin doctor that interprets information outside of awareness [and that] does a reasonably accurate job of interpreting other people's behaviour" (Wilson 2002, 31). "One of the most interesting properties of the . . . unconscious is that it uses stereotypes to categorize and evaluate people" (2002, 11). In doing so, it is fast, unintentional, uncontrollable, and effortless (2002, 49). Specifically, it has a tendency to jump to conclusions, and often fails to change its mind in the face of contrary evidence (2002, 55–56). This sounds to me like a fairly good description of the cognitive functioning of the town. It certainly categorizes and evaluates people. Precisely how it arrives at its views is a gap in the storyworld, but I would suggest that it is likely to be done in a fast, unintentional, uncontrollable, and effortless way. It is difficult to imagine the townspeople agonizing at length about what they should think about Guy, Grafin von Gluck, and the others. It also seems that the town tends to jump to conclusions and fails to change its mind in the face of contrary evidence. Guy has been trying for twenty years to get the town to change its mind about him and has failed. On the other hand, as I will now go on to argue, it has done a reasonably accurate job of interpreting Guy's mind.

Wilson points out that, while forming its views, the unconscious can produce feelings and preferences that are not always "rational." That is to say, the workings of the unconscious have their *own* rationality, which is often different from the alternative rationality of the workings of the conscious mind (2002, chapter 8). He then draws attention to the resulting difficulty in recognizing the feelings generated by the unconscious mind: "The conscious system is quite sensitive to personal and cultural prescriptions about how one is *supposed* to feel . . . People might assume that their feelings conform to these prescriptions and fail to notice instances in which they do not. These '*feeling rules*' can make it difficult to perceive how one's . . . unconscious feels about the matter" (2002, 129; my emphasis). Wilson refers to the resulting "phenomenon in which people have two feelings towards the same topic, one more conscious than the other, as '*dual attitudes*'" (2002, 132; my emphasis). To illustrate, he quotes from a short story in which two adult cousins reminisce about their childhoods. One of them, Blake, says that he was about thirty before he realized that he had always hated their childhood pony, Topper. "It wasn't until Blake said it that Kate realized that she, too, had always hated Topper. For years they had been conned into loving him, because children love their pony, and their dog, and their parents, and picnics, and the ocean, and the lovely chocolate cake" (quoted in 2002, 118). This last sentence is a list of feeling rules: children must have positive feelings about their pony, their dog, and so on. As a result, the cousins had a dual attitude toward the pony: the positive feelings that they knew they were supposed to have according to the feeling rules; and the negative feelings that they subsequently and consciously discovered that they had unconsciously had all along.

The *Men at Arms* passage is a list of feeling rules and also of dual attitudes. It is a list of the reasons why Guy thinks that the conscious mind of the town *ought* to find him simpatico. It is also two other lists: why Guy thinks that the town ought to find the others less so, and why the town nevertheless finds the others more so.

As with individual minds, collective minds can also experience feeling rules and dual attitudes. These feeling rules are implied in all the details that are given about Guy and the others. Every one of the descriptions of the individuals is a reason for disapproval: not bothering to learn Italian, interfering with the fishing, being boring, being gross vulgarians, being a criminal. Every one of the descriptions of Guy is a reason for approval: he speaks their language and follows their religion, and he is open-handed and scrupulously respectful of all their ways. Nevertheless, each of these descriptions is balanced by a conclusion that contradicts it: the others are simpatico; Guy is not. The unconscious mind of the town feels the opposite of what it should feel. It is in this way that every sentence in the passage contains a dual attitude toward Guy or toward the others. This conflict gives the passage its characteristic sense of tension and unease, which arises, as I said earlier, from its apparently paradoxical and counterintuitive nature. The one who seems most likely to be found simpatico is not; all those who seem least likely to be, are. So there are deeper, unspecified reasons at work that must account for the feelings of the town.

I talked just now about the fact that the apparent irrationality of unconscious thought is simply a different rationality from conscious thought. The narrator exploits this difference by making use of readers' assumptions about what they would think the villagers might find simpatico on the conscious level: this is the list of feeling rules. But in the case of the town of Santa Dulcina delle Rocce, these considerations do not seem to rate very highly. Another apparent irrationality is the disregard for the importance of the theory of mind that I discussed earlier. The individuals who are simpatico are not aware of the fact that they are. They do not give the impression that they are particularly self-aware or aware of the feelings of others. Otherwise, they would not behave in such antisocial ways. Guy, on the contrary, tries hard to read the mind of the village and is found to be non simpatico. The moral seems to be that the less you care about being simpatico, the more likely it is that you will be. The reader may then be tempted to conclude that the fictional mind of the town is irrational. But it is clear, I think, that this is not so. It is simply that the town is employing a different rationality. What is this unconscious rationality? In my view, it is simply a love of life. They favor humanity, facing life with gusto, with self-confidence, with self-belief, and, as the passage says, "with relish." They like generosity of spirit. Guy is not simpatico because, for all his timid efforts to be liked, he has a poverty of spirit, a meanness of the soul, a meagerness about him that they recognize. This poverty of spirit is evident in the way that he thinks resentfully of the others and especially in the "better than this" phrase that was discussed above. To use a vulgar British expression, he is "tight-arsed." His life is sterile. In the words of Deuteronomy (30:19), and also of the opening sequence of the film *Trainspotting*, he should "Choose life!" Once this point is realized, the apparent paradoxes dissolve, it is counterintuitive no longer, and the passage makes perfect sense.

CONCLUSION

It may be helpful if I conclude this chapter by specifying how much I want to claim for the significance of the topic of social minds in the novel. I argue that this issue looms large as a technique and as a subject matter in all of the novels that I discuss, but techniques and subject matters are parts of novels, not purposes of them. They are means rather than ends. What matters, ultimately, is the purpose to which a particular sort of consciousness representation is put. So my concern in the chapters that follow is with the *purposes* of presentations of social minds. These chapters are opportunities to expand on the relationship between analyses of collective consciousness and our larger understanding of the whole novel. Put in general terms, I would summarize the purposes of fictional presentations of social minds as follows:

1. Social minds exist in storyworlds because they exist in real life. Our lives consist of a balance between publicly available thought processes and secret and private thoughts. For novels to be worth reading, they have to reflect that balance. Villages and towns tend to behave in reality in the way that Santa Dulcina delle Rocce behaves. An important part of the pleasure that the *Men at Arms* passage gives its readers is the recognition of this fact.
2. The study of social minds sheds a good deal of light on the workings of individual minds. Characters can only be fully understood as elements in complex social networks. Guy's relationships first with the town and then with his regiment have a key role in his situated identity. People

may have many different sorts of relationships with intermental units: fully assimilated into them; within them, but in conflict with other parts of the unit; outside, and in opposition to them; acting as a public mouthpiece for them; and so on. Some of these relationships will be explored in the chapters to come.

3. Narrative progression is regulated by the flow of information that the narrator of a novel makes available to its reader. This information frequently concerns the workings of fictional minds. Characters have different levels of knowledge of, and understanding of, the storyworld they inhabit. The narrative theorist Lubomír Doležel refers to the storyworld knowledge that characters possess as their *encyclopedias* (1998). These encyclopedias are basic plot motors. Storylines tend to revolve around the consequences of some characters knowing more than others. Characters have an interest in keeping secrets in order to keep the balance of knowledge, and therefore power, in their favor. However, the tendency of social minds is toward the sharing of knowledge. As explored in chapter 5, many nineteenth-century novels are concerned with the practical problems that arise when characters attempt to practice secrecy within distributed cognitive networks in which people can see very easily what other people are thinking.

4. As I said at the beginning of this book, a fierce debate took place within the nineteenth-century novel on the nature of social minds. The epistemological aspect related to the extent to which it is possible to have knowledge of the workings of other minds. The ethical aspect questioned the purposes to which our knowledge of other minds should be put. Social minds raise complex and difficult ethical issues. Characters face sharp and painful dilemmas relating to attempts to exercise control over other minds and the motives in trying to doing so. Guy's predicament has just been discussed. Should Dorothea bend to the will of the Middlemarch mind? Should Anne Elliot in *Persuasion* have been so persuadable? What are the moral purposes behind the gaining of information about other characters' thoughts? (For example, in *Little Dorrit*, Henry Gowan uses this knowledge to manipulate others.) What are the moral purposes behind trying to conceal one's own? The reasons for the latter can be immoral (Gowan again) or moral (Anne Elliot concealing her continued feelings for Wentworth). Anne prefers openness except where it would harm herself or others. She knows that Mr Elliot prefers secrecy because he can make use of the resulting control of information and knowledge for his own purposes. Other perplexities will be investigated in the chapters that follow.

CHAPTER 3

Middlemarch

THE CONSTRUCTION OF THE MIDDLEMARCH MIND

ONE OF THE most important characters in *Middlemarch* is the town of Middlemarch itself. I call the intermental functioning of the inhabitants of the town *the Middlemarch mind*. I go much further than simply suggesting that the town provides a social context within which individual characters operate, and argue that, just as in the case of Santa Dulcina delle Rocce in the previous chapter, the town literally and not just metaphorically has a mind of its own. The Middlemarch mind is complex, interesting, clearly visible to a close reader of the text, and vitally important to an understanding of the novel because it explains a good deal of the motivation behind the actions of the other main characters. In discussing the construction of the Middlemarch mind in the opening few pages of the novel, I aim to show that these pages are saturated with this group mind, and that the initial descriptions by the narrator of the three individual minds of Dorothea, Celia, and Mr Brooke are focalized through it.

Here is an edited, unformatted version of the opening section of the novel:

> ... [Dorothea Brooke] was usually spoken of as being remarkably clever, but with the addition that her sister Celia had more common sense. Nevertheless, Celia wore scarcely more trimmings; and it was only to close

observers that her dress differed from her sister's, and had a shade of coquetry in its arrangements; for Miss Brooke's plain dressing was due to mixed conditions, in most of which her sister shared. The pride of being ladies had something to do with it: the Brooke connections, though not exactly aristocratic, were unquestionably "good": if you inquired backward for a generation or two, you would not find any yard-measuring or parcel-tying forefathers—anything lower than an admiral or clergyman . . . Young women of such birth, living in a quiet country-house, and attending a village church hardly larger than a parlour, naturally regarded frippery as the ambition of a huckster's daughter. Then there was well-bred economy, which in those days made show in dress the first item to be deducted from, when any margin was required for expenses more distinctive of rank . . .

[Dorothea's] mind was theoretic, and yearned by its nature after some lofty conception of the world which might frankly include the parish of Tipton and her own rule of conduct there . . . Certainly such elements in the character of a marriageable girl tended to interfere with her lot, and hinder it from being decided according to custom, by good looks, vanity, and merely canine affection . . .

It was hardly a year since [Dorothea and Celia] had come to live at Tipton Grange with their uncle, a man nearly sixty, of acquiescent temper, miscellaneous opinions, and uncertain vote. He had travelled in his younger years, and was held in this part of the county to have contracted a too rambling habit of mind. Mr Brooke's conclusions were as difficult to predict as the weather: it was only safe to say that he would act with benevolent intentions, and that he would spend as little money as possible in carrying them out . . . [Dorothea] was regarded as an heiress, for not only had the sisters seven hundred a year each from their parents, but if Dorothea married and had a son, that son would inherit Mr Brooke's estate, presumably worth about three thousand a year—a rental which seemed wealth to provincial families . . .

And how should Dorothea not marry?—a girl so handsome and with such prospects? Nothing could hinder it but her love of extremes, and her insistence on regulating life according to notions which might cause a wary man to hesitate before he made her an offer, or even might lead her at last to refuse all offers . . . A man would naturally think twice before he risked himself in such fellowship. Women were expected to have weak opinions; but the great safeguard of society and of domestic life was, that opinions were not acted on. Sane people did what their neighbours did, so that if any lunatics were at large, one might know and avoid them.

The rural opinion about the new young ladies, even among the cottagers, was generally in favour of Celia, as being so amiable and innocent-looking, while Miss Brooke's large eyes seemed, like her religion, too unusual and striking . . . Yet those who approached Dorothea, though prejudiced against her by this alarming hearsay, found that she had a charm unaccountably reconcilable with it. Most men thought her bewitching when she was on horseback . . .

These peculiarities of Dorothea's character caused Mr Brooke to be all the more blamed in neighboring families for not securing some middle-aged lady as guide and companion to his nieces. But he himself dreaded so much the sort of superior woman likely to be available for such a position, that he allowed himself to be dissuaded by Dorothea's objections, and was in this case brave enough to defy the world—that is to say, Mrs Cadwallader the Rector's wife, and the small group of gentry with whom he visited in the north-east corner of Loamshire. So Miss Brooke presided in her uncle's household, and did not at all dislike her new authority, with the homage that belonged to it. (1–4)

Let us look at this passage first from an internalist perspective. I would guess that it would strike most casual readers simply as a description of the intramental minds of three characters—Dorothea, her sister Celia, and her uncle Mr Brooke—in a straightforward piece of omniscient characterization. So, within this perspective, is there much here for the classical narrative approaches to sink their teeth into?

I will start with the representation of consciousness in the text. First, there is no intramental free indirect thought. (I put it like this because, as I mention below, the passage contains some *intermental* free indirect thought, but you have to have acquired the concept of intermental thought in order to be able to see it.) Obviously, given the time of writing, there is no stream of consciousness or interior monologue either. In fact, there is no directly quoted thought at all. The passage consists almost entirely of authorial thought report of general descriptions of consciousness. So that does not tell us much. Is characterization theory any more informative? The initial cognitive frames that can be put in place immediately reveal quite a lot about the characters of Dorothea, Celia, and Mr Brooke. As there are two sisters, one studious and the other (relatively) flighty, looked after by a vague, dilettante bachelor uncle, there is certainly potential there for analysis in terms of cultural and literary stereotypes. And we learn a lot about initial instabilities within the storyworld, especially the one resulting from Dorothea's

68 | Chapter 3

yearning for a lofty conception of the world, despite her current condition. Focalization can be revealing too. The internal focalization from Dorothea's perspective highlights the instabilities just referred to. The same is true of Mr. Brooke's mind: "he himself dreaded" et cetera. Finally, will story analysis help? Not so much. We are looking at the first three pages of an eight-hundred-page novel, and so the respective roles of the three actants are as yet unclear. Celia and Mr Brooke may turn out to be helpers or obstacles, for example, but we will not know which for quite a while.

However, here is a reformatted version of the same passage, edited as before:

[Dorothea Brooke] **was usually spoken of (1)** as being remarkably clever, but with the addition that her sister Celia had more common sense. Nevertheless, Celia wore scarcely more trimmings; and **it was only to close observers (2)** that her dress differed from her sister's, and had a shade of coquetry in its arrangements; for Miss Brooke's plain dressing was due to mixed conditions, in most of which her sister shared. The pride of being ladies had something to do with it: the Brooke connections, though not exactly aristocratic, were **unquestionably (3)** "good": if **you (4)** inquired backward for a generation or two, you would not find any yard-measuring or parcel-tying forefathers—anything lower than an admiral or clergyman. . . . Young women of such birth, living in a quiet country-house, and attending a village church hardly larger than a parlour, **naturally (5)** regarded frippery as the ambition of a huckster's daughter. Then there was well-bred economy, which **in those days (6)** made show in dress the first item to be deducted from, when any margin was required for expenses more distinctive of rank . . .

[Dorothea's] mind was theoretic, and yearned by its nature after some lofty conception of the world which might frankly include **the parish of Tipton (7)** and her own rule of conduct there. . . . Certainly such elements in the character of a marriageable girl tended to interfere with her lot, and hinder it from being **decided according to custom (8)**, by good looks, vanity, and merely canine affection. . . .

It was hardly a year since [Dorothea and Celia] had come to live at Tipton Grange with their uncle, a man nearly sixty, of acquiescent temper, miscellaneous opinions, and uncertain vote. He had travelled in his younger years, and **was held in this part of the county (9)** to have contracted a too rambling habit of mind. Mr Brooke's conclusions were **as difficult to predict (10)** as the weather: **it was only safe to say (11)** that he would act with benevolent intentions, and that he would spend as little money as possible in carrying them out.... [Dorothea] **was regarded as (12)** an heiress, for not only had the sisters seven hundred a year each from their parents, but if Dorothea married and had a son, that son would inherit Mr Brooke's estate, presumably worth about three thousand a year—a rental **which seemed wealth to provincial families (13)**...

And how should Dorothea not marry?—a girl so handsome and with such prospects? (14) Nothing could hinder it but her love of extremes, and her insistence on regulating life according to notions which might **cause a wary man (15)** to hesitate before he made her an offer, or even might lead her at last to refuse all offers.... **A man would naturally (16)** think twice before he risked himself in such fellowship. Women **were expected (17)** to have weak opinions; but the great safeguard of society and of domestic life was, that opinions were not acted on. **Sane people did (18)** what **their neighbours did (19)**, so that if **any lunatics (20)** were at large, **one (21)** might know and avoid them.

The rural opinion about the new young ladies, even among the cottagers (22), was generally in favour of Celia, as being so amiable and innocent-looking, while Miss Brooke's large eyes seemed, like her religion, too unusual and striking.... **Yet those who (23)** approached Dorothea, though prejudiced against her by **this alarming hearsay (24),** found that she had a charm unaccountably reconcilable with it. **Most men (25)** thought her bewitching when she was on horseback...

These peculiarities of Dorothea's character caused Mr Brooke to be all the more **blamed in neighbouring families (26)** for not securing some middle-aged lady as guide and companion to his nieces. But he himself dreaded so much the sort of superior woman likely to be available for such a position, that he allowed himself to be dissuaded by Dorothea's objections, and was in this case brave enough to defy **the world—that is to say, Mrs Cadwallader the Rector's wife, and the small group of gentry with whom he visited in the north-east corner of Loamshire (27).** So Miss Brooke presided in her uncle's household, and did not at all dislike her new authority, with the homage that belonged to it. (1–4)

I hope that you found that, seen from the externalist perspective, much of the passage now reads very differently. The formatting in bold type transforms the text into a much more complex and interesting discourse by drawing attention to the intermental functioning of the group of people who form the consensus opinion of the town and surrounding area. In particular, the formatting shows that the descriptions by the narrator of the three individual minds of Dorothea, Celia, and Mr Brooke are presented through the intermental Middlemarch mind by means of the various cues that I will analyze presently. In other words, the point of view is that of the Middlemarch mind, and the passage is primarily focalized through it. The annotated passage shows that there is a good deal of evidence for the existence of the Middlemarch mind: twenty-six references in sixty-one lines (plus the hypothetical lunatics, a separate group, in item 20) is a substantial number. For aesthetic reasons, I have put in bold only the linguistic markers of its presence. If I had included all of the *content* of its views, almost the whole passage would have been in bold. I have used boldface type for the references to the agents responsible for intermental activity where these agents are explicitly mentioned, and, where they are not, I have used boldface for references to the intermental activities themselves. The following paragraphs will make this point clearer. I will now discuss in more detail how the Middlemarch mind has been constructed by asking these questions in turn: Who? How? What? Why?

The first question then is: Who? Who are the individuals who make up the intermental Middlemarch mind? At this stage, in the first few pages of a long novel, the narrator is not able to reflect the complexities of the various intermental minds in the town that are examined later in this chapter (for example, the landed gentry, the middle classes including the professionals, and the working classes). The emphasis in the passage is almost exclusively on the first of these groups, the landed gentry. This group is explicitly named in examples (9) and (22), while the clearest reference to it is in the final example (27): "the world—that is to say, Mrs Cadwallader the Rector's wife, and the small group of gentry with whom [Mr. Brooke] visited in the northeast corner of Loamshire." With a few exceptions, all of the numbered references are to this powerful, norm-establishing core group. Exceptions include some neutral or nonspecific groups ("close observers" [2] and "those who approached Dorothea" [23]). The only transgressive or norm-threatening group, apart from the hypothetical lunatics constructed by the Middlemarch mind (20), is the group of men who find Dorothea attractive on horseback despite being told not to (25). This is an example, indicated early in the novel, of the kind of sexual energy that is traditionally seen as a threat to well-established social norms, and which often results in the sort of norm-disrupting events that are so common in nineteenth-century novels: elopements, secret engagements, unintended pregnancies, and so on.

The second question is: How? How are the views of this group conveyed? In particular, it may not be apparent in all cases precisely how the bold passages indicate the presence of intermental thought. You may be puzzled as to why such items as "unquestionably" (3) and "naturally" (5) have been included as examples of references to the Middlemarch mind. So, a small typology is required. I have identified four types of the means of expression of the views of the Middlemarch mind and I will list them now in order of degree of directness.

The first is explicit reference to the main landed gentry group. This group is referred to either in geographical terms ("the parish of Tipton" [7] and "part of this county" [9]); or in social terms ("provincial families" [13]); or in both geographical and social terms ("neighbouring families" [26], "rural opinion" including the cottagers [22], "the world" et cetera [27]). In fact, the two categories of geographical and social are closely interrelated and difficult to disentangle, and so are best thought of as a spectrum. However, even the areas referred to in simply geographical terms (such as the parish of Tipton [7]) have to be included in this survey because the social implications of naming them, albeit implicit, are potent. The second means of expression is reference to a hypothetical group in order to make a particular rhetorical point. For example, "close observers" (2); "those who approached Dorothea" (23); "men" (15 and 16); and "sane people," "neighbours," "lunatics," and "one" (18–21). Apart from the lunatics, these hypothetical groups tend to be norm-reinforcing: the "close observers" in (2) feel like landed-gentry close observers; the men who might be reluctant to marry Dorothea if she continues to be willful must also belong to the gentry.

The third is the use of the passive voice. There are five examples: "was spoken of" (1); "being decided" (8); "was held" (11); "was regarded" (12); and "were expected" (17). In every case, it is the Middlemarch mind that is doing the speaking, deciding, holding, regarding, and expecting. The fourth and final means of expression is also the most oblique. It is the use of presupposition. Again, there are five examples: "unquestionably" (3); "naturally" (5); "in those days" (6); "And how should Dorothea not marry?" (14); and "hearsay" (24). The use of these phrases by the narrator presupposes some person or group who holds these views, who thinks that the statements are unquestionably or naturally so and who would ask such a loaded question as: "And how should Dorothea not marry?" In Bakhtinian terms, they are examples of double-voiced discourse. More specifically, (3), (5), and (14) feature intermental free indirect thought. The narrator expresses a view that, it soon becomes apparent from the context, is the view of the townspeople. The important point is that, with a few exceptions, the last three means of expression (hypothetical groups, the passive voice, and presupposition) are all different sorts of rhetorical devices for referring, however indirectly, to the controlling social group that expresses the Middlemarch mind. These devices add to the sense that the Middlemarch mind is omnipresent and pervades the whole fabric of the society, and so explicit reference to it is unnecessary.

The following passage from later in the novel neatly illustrates all of the four linguistic techniques:

> (1) Doctor Sprague (a) **was more than suspected** of having no religion, but somehow (b) **Middlemarch** tolerated this deficiency in him... it was perhaps this negation in the doctor which made (c) **his neighbours** call him hard-headed and dry-witted... At all events, it is certain that if any medical man had come to Middlemarch with (d) **the reputation** of having very definite religious views... (e) **there would have been a general presumption** against his medical skill. (125)

(a) is the passive voice: it is the Middlemarch mind that is doing the suspecting; (b) and (c) are explicit references; (d) is presupposition—a Middlemarch mind is presupposed because it is that mind that would create Sprague's reputation. Although (e) is also an example of presupposition (a group would do the presuming), it is there to make a specific rhetorical point about intermental views on medicine and religion.

The next question is: What? What are these examples of intermental functioning about, and what are the different types of judgments that are being made? Only one judgment appears to be factual, the one concerning the extent of Dorothea's wealth (12). Some of the intermental functioning relates to action. There are decisions regarding marriage that are made "according to custom" (8) and behavior such as doing as neighbors do and avoiding lunatics (18–21). Next, there is some mind reading involved in judgments on characters' dispositions. Dorothea has a clever mind although Celia has common sense (1), while Mr Brooke's mind is too rambling and unpredictable (9–11). This mind reading involves predictions regarding intramental minds and actions: What will Mr Brooke think next (10)? Will Dorothea marry (14)? Many of the judgments relate to various aspects of social class. They concern the social standing of individuals and groups, including their connections (3–6); their wealth (12 and 13); etiquette, such as the need for a governess (26 and 27); and manners, such as the need for women to have weak opinions (17). There is also a strong emphasis on aesthetic judgments. There are references to dress sense such as the coquetry in Celia's appearance (2) and frippery (5 and 6); and references to Dorothea's looks and charm (22–25).

Underpinning all of these judgments is a strong moral and ethical impulse. Individuals ought to think predictably, behave in a socially responsible way, marry well, and look aesthetically pleasing because these are all the right thing to do. Common sense is more important than cleverness; weak, predictable, and conforming opinions are desirable; good connections and background are important; young women should ensure that they marry well; and they should have the guidance that is necessary to ensure that they do. The types of judgments made by the Middlemarch mind are closely interconnected and all relate to the moral and political necessity for a closely confined consensus within clearly defined social and aesthetic norms. Class and morality in particular, but also aesthetics and mind reading, are closely linked. It may appear that aesthetic or social or moral elements predominate at any one time, but as soon as you start to pull at a single thread, all of the others unravel with it. The underlying logic is that individuals should behave in certain, well-specified ways and not in other ways, so that social relations will be stable and will continue to benefit those who benefit from them at present.

The last question is: Why? The answer is that the novel consists of an exploration of the pressures that the Middlemarch mind exerts on the individual minds and actions of just about all of the characters in the novel, and especially those who want to do something more than conform to the town's norms and values. In particular, the workings of the Middlemarch mind have a profound effect on the lives of the two main characters, Dorothea and Lydgate, and so on the plot of the novel. The book would be unrecognizable without its presence. For example, the three individuals, Dorothea, Celia, and Mr Brooke, are subject to a continual interrogation by the Middlemarch mind. Are they sufficiently deferential, orthodox in their opinions, and reliable in their social behavior? They, in turn, cast a continual and uneasy "word with a sideways glance" (1984, 32), to use Mikhail Bakhtin's phrase, at the potential approval or disapproval of the town. Dorothea's defiance, Celia's compliance, and Mr. Brooke's unpredictability are, in effect, dialogues with the norms of the large intermental unit. Dorothea's disposition is to defy those norms; Celia's is to comply with them; Mr. Brooke's behavior is unpredictable when measured against them. Even within this opening passage of a long novel, it is obvious that conflicts will arise between Dorothea's intelligence and "lofty conception of the world" on the one hand and, on the other, her sense of duty to her neighbors and her consideration for the feelings of her family. Her mind is a dialogue between her own inclinations and her responses to the various intermental pressures on her.

A number of narrative theorists, in particular Menakhem Perry (1979), have drawn attention to the notion of the *primacy effect*. This suggests that the cognitive frames that are set up by readers at the beginning of a narrative are tenacious and long-lasting, and are abandoned only when there is enough compelling evidence for readers to want to adopt other frames. As I hope to have shown, the primacy effect of the cognitive frame set up by the frequent references to the Middlemarch mind in the opening few pages of the novel is very strong. And, as I will demonstrate later, the rest of the text betrays a fascination with the intermental process: its complexity; how units form, maintain, and modify themselves; their causes and their effects; the dialogical relationships between the units and the individuals they comprise; and, finally, how units fracture and disintegrate.

As stated in the opening paragraph of this chapter, the claim that I am making regarding the role of the town of Middlemarch is a strong one. It should be distinguished from two much weaker arguments. First, I am certainly not simply saying that the town has an important role in providing a social context within which individual characters operate and is thereby a pervasive influence on their intramental thought. Who would disagree with such an anodyne claim? Second, I am not referring to this mind in any metaphorical sense. I am going much further than these two positions in saying that, within the *Middlemarch* storyworld, the town actually and literally does have a mind of its own.

You may still be unconvinced by my arguments so far and so be wondering: What is he talking about? Within a novel, thinking is what individual characters do! It is what happens inside the skull. It is what goes on in free indirect thought, stream of consciousness, and interior monologue. It is this sort of thing, for example—a straightforward piece of thought report about a character's inner thought processes: "Rosamond, in fact, counted on swallowing Lydgate and assimilating him very comfortably." However, there is a simple way to demonstrate that, as readers, we do all know what intermental functioning is and that we unthinkingly accept it as perfectly natural when we are presented with it. The proof is this. I cheated with that quote. The actual words in the text are these: "Middlemarch, in fact, counted on swallowing Lydgate and assimilating him very comfortably" (105). We understand very easily what that sentence means when we encounter it in the context of the surrounding narrative. I doubt whether anybody has ever read it and decided that it has no meaning. So, just as with the town of Santa Dulcina delle Rocce, we know perfectly well what it is to ascribe mental functioning to a whole town. You may now be thinking—well, all right, that was very clever with the made-up quote just then, but any thinking that a town does must surely be different from the thinking that an individual does. But of course! It would be silly to disagree. I am not saying that intermental and intramental minds are the same. I am saying that they are similar in some ways, different in others, but they are both still minds. Just different kinds of minds.

As the Middlemarch mind is not completely monolithic and can be soft or fuzzy round the edges, it follows that some of the minds that go to make up the intermental mind or that would normally acquiesce in its findings can depart from the common view under certain circumstances. Most men, when they come into contact with Dorothea, enjoy the experience, despite the intermental prejudice against her. There is also intramental dissent involved in Dorothea's reluctance to get married. Dorothea and Mr Brooke form a small unit in defiance of the larger one when they agree together that a companion is not necessary. (Celia's views are not mentioned, I notice.) These are small examples of the various intramental and intermental relationships that, as I will now explain, become extremely complex later in the novel. I am therefore using the phrase *the Middlemarch mind* as a convenient shorthand. It is misleading if it suggests that there is only ever one mind that the town possesses. In fact, as the novel progresses, the reader becomes aware that there are several different Middlemarch minds. Disputes frequently occur. There is usually a variety of different opinions on any one subject. Sometimes the town appears to be of one mind, but more often there are references to differences of view between the various social, geographical, and professional groups. So, the town can be in two or more minds at any one time (just as individuals can be, come to think of it).

Studying the Middlemarch mind is like looking at a painting by Turner, Seurat, or Cezanne. Close up, all you see is a mass of apparently incoherent brushstrokes; move away, and you are aware of shapes emerging and the subject of the whole picture materializes. Close up, the individuals that compose this large intermental unit are unique and all have slightly different perspectives on their storyworld. The thought of them collectively swallowing Lydgate makes no sense at all. Move away, however, and the consensus emerges, and it then feels absolutely right to say that Middlemarch intends to swallow Lydgate whole.

MIDDLEMARCH MINDS

I wish now to try to convey the subtlety of the fine shades of intermental thought and the complexity of the relationships between intermental and intramental thought in the rest of the novel. First, I will discuss the various ways in which, over the course of the whole text, readers are able to identify a number of distinct, separate Middlemarch minds within the single unit that is initially constructed. After saying a little about the techniques used for the constructions of these various minds, I suggest that an analysis of the class structure of the town reveals the existence of separate and well-defined upper-class, middle-class, and working-class minds. I then refer to the complexity and fluidity of the myriad other units that occur at various points in the text and introduce a tentative typology for the sorts of intermental focalization to be found in the novel. The rest of this section then turns to the roles played by individuals: not only those inside the large units who act as spokespeople or mouthpieces for their views but also those who, like Lydgate, Dorothea, and Ladislaw, find themselves outside of them and become the object of their judgments.

As with the opening passage, in the longer, indented quotes that follow, I will put all examples of intermental thought in bold. I do this for ease of reference, but also to emphasize in visual form their sheer number. I sometimes continue to refer to *the* Middlemarch mind to denote the large intermental unit of the whole town; I will also refer to *a* Middlemarch mind when a subgroup of the whole town mind is being discussed. This chapter is primarily about large and medium-sized units and much less about small units such as marriages, friendships, and families (with the exception of Lydgate and Rosamond). It is no exaggeration to say that a short book could be written about all of the intermental functioning in *Middlemarch*. The only problem with such a book would be the difficulty, I imagine, in getting it published.

A close study of *Middlemarch* reveals that George Eliot was obviously fascinated by the intermental process: its complexity, its causes and effects, its relationship with individuals. Thought in general and intermental thought in particular are frequently discussed. Many different cognitive terms are used to describe intermental activity in the novel: knowing, thinking, considering, believing, noticing, conjecturing, implying, suspecting, tolerating, hating, opposing, liking, and wanting. These and the many other examples that are to be found throughout the rest of this chapter are verbs of thought and of consciousness. The whole novel is saturated with clear evidence of the variety of communal thought. As with *Little Dorrit* and *Persuasion,* the evidence that is presented in this chapter composes only a small proportion of the total. Much of the language used in *Middlemarch* explicitly invites the sort of cognitive reading that is a feature of this book. It refers several times to "other minds" (401, 504, and 530) and also to "other people's states of mind" (536), "mental action" (546), "social action" (124), "the boundaries of social intercourse" (64), and "consciousness of interdependence" (64). In addition, the language regularly anticipates Bakhtin's already-mentioned notion of the word with a sideways glance: "The vicar's frankness seemed not of the repulsive sort that comes from an uneasy consciousness seeking to forestall the judgment of others" (119); and: "an uneasy consciousness heareth innuendoes" (206).

Other examples of George Eliot's fondness for openly acknowledging the cognitive element in her novel, particularly as it applies to social minds, include "civic mind" (65), "public mind" (99 and 246), "the unreformed provincial mind" (424), and the rather judgmental "many crass minds in Middlemarch" (106). At other times, general terms are used such as "that part of the world" (151), "midland-bred souls" (71), "mortals generally" (105), "the company" (to refer to a party) (107), "vulgar people" (114), "all people young and old" (16), it was "sure to strike others" (17), and "public feeling required" (16). The most obvious names for the intermental groups in the town relate to the town itself. There are a number of variations: "the Middlemarchers" (106 and 114), "good Middlemarch society" (108), "Middlemarch company" (463); "the town" (112), "the respectable townsfolk" (105), et cetera. References to Middlemarch can also be more specific when related to a particular context. During a discussion of the political situation, the text mentions "buyers of the Middlemarch newspapers" (246). During consideration of Bulstrode's possible hypocrisy in example (18) below, there is an ironical reference to "the publicans and sinners in Middlemarch" (83). A description of Rosamond's popularity talks about "all Middlemarch admirers."

Sometimes the descriptions are neutral: "his neighbours" (96) and "the town's talk" (204). At other times they are rather arch constructions that are characteristic of the distinctive voice of the narrator: "the public belief" (527), "all the world round Tipton" (32), "in various quarters" (314), "family party" (240), "in Middlemarch phraseology" (511), and "the laity" (306). Some of the constructions betray the bitterness and frustration of the individual who is on the receiving end of the consensus: "the petty medium of Middlemarch" (129) and "Middlemarch gossip" (240). In addition, as already mentioned, the Middlemarch mind is sometimes presented in intermental free indirect thought: "It was clear that Lydgate . . . intended to cast imputations on his equals" (126), when this thought would be clear only to the Middlemarch mind and no one else. I referred earlier to a particularly striking form of words that identifies Middlemarch as a group mind: "Middlemarch, in fact, counted on swallowing Lydgate and assimilating him very comfortably" (105). This sentence beautifully frames the relationship between Lydgate and Middlemarch for the remainder of the novel. Middlemarch has a double cognitive narrative of Lydgate as the idealistic young doctor who comes to the town and wishes to mould it into conformity with his wishes. However, he will be taught a lesson, and will discover that it is he who has to change.

Some of the general and vague descriptions of the workings of the Middlemarch mind involve oblique references to speech. These include "gossip" (344), "the air seemed to be filled with gossip" (344), "the conversation seemed to imply" (124), "general conversation in Middlemarch" (181), and "It's openly said" (72). The reporting of this speech may be focalized through an individual: Mr Featherstone "had it from most undeniable authority, and not one, but many" (73), Lydgate "heard it discussed" (106), and (an example of what David Herman [1994] calls *hypothetical focalization*) "If Will Ladislaw could have overheard some of the talk at Freshitt that morning..." (433). Later, the reader is told what he would have heard being said:

(2) "Young Ladislaw the grandson of a thieving Jew pawnbroker" was a phrase which had entered emphatically into the dialogues about the Bulstrode business at **Lowick**, **Tipton** and **Freshitt**. (533)

I refer below to the use made of *multiparty talk* to convey this sort of gossip.

The three locations mentioned in example (2) deserve further attention. Although we can only know what happens in a storyworld if we follow the mental functioning of its inhabitants, it is also essential to have a certain amount of knowledge, however rudimentary, of its geography (see Moretti 1998). In this case, we need to have a rough idea in our heads of the fact that Middlemarch is a town surrounded by large country houses with accompanying parishes or villages. These include Tipton (home of Mr. Brooke, and also Dorothea and Celia before they marry), Freshitt (the home of Sir James Chettam and then Celia after they marry), and Lowick (the home of Casaubon and then Dorothea after they marry). However, as this list shows, a knowledge of the geographical storyworld is closely linked to a knowledge of the mental and social storyworld. Tipton, Freshitt, and Lowick are important only because they are the homes of the members of the gentry or upper classes who are leading characters in the story. This is demonstrated by the fact that references to the upper classes are couched in geographical terms, as in example (2), as well as in more obviously social terms. In other words, these place names function as metonymies for the upper classes or the gentry. References to the town of Middlemarch itself sometimes act in the same way for the middle classes, as the Tankard pub does for the working classes.

As this discussion shows, the three social classes are among the most prominent of the subgroups of the Middlemarch mind. The upper classes consist primarily of the Brookes, the Chettams, the Cadwalladers, and the other members of the local landed gentry. The middle classes comprise the professional classes and, in particular, the various medical men. The working classes are much less well represented and are confined mainly to Mrs Dollop's pub, the Tankard. Sometimes the text refers to the upper classes as the "Middlemarch gentry" (186), the "county" (4), or "the county people who looked down on the Middlemarchers" (114). At other times, there are more specific references to the place names: "all Tipton and its neighbourhood" (151), "no persons then living—certainly none in the neighbourhood of Tipton" (17), "the unfriendly mediums of Tipton and Freshitt" (24), "all the world around Tipton" (32), and "opinion in the neighbourhood of Freshitt and Tipton" (58). Occasionally, it is established that these place names describe the middle or working classes who live in them, as in "both the farmers and labourers in the parishes of Freshitt and Tipton" (34). The following single sentence illustrates the class structure behind the intermental functioning in the town by containing references to the whole social spectrum:

> (3) The heads of this discussion at **"Dollop's"** had been the common theme among **all classes in the town,** had been carried to **Lowick Parsonage** on one side and to **Tipton Grange** on the other, had come fully to the ears of **the Vincy family,** and had been discussed with sad reference to "poor Harriet" by **all Mrs Bulstrode's friends,** before Lydgate knew distinctly why **people** were looking strangely at him, and before Bulstrode himself suspected the betrayal of his secrets. (500)

"All classes" can be subdivided into upper (Lowick Parsonage and Tipton Grange), middle (the Vincy family and Mrs Bulstrode's friends), and lower (Dollop's pub).

At several points in the discourse Middlemarch gossip is conveyed through what the narrative theorist Bronwen Thomas (2002) calls *multiparty talk* (that is, conversations between more than two people). A surprisingly large number of conversations in the novel, at least twenty I would say, feature three or more people. Scenes of this sort in which Middlemarch minds are at work include the following:

- A The dinner party at which Lydgate is introduced to Middlemarch society (60–63)
- B The public meeting at which the vote on the chaplaincy takes place (126–29)
- C Sir James Chettam, the Cadwalladers, and Mr Brooke talk about politics (261–67)
- D Hackbutt, Toller, and Hawley discuss Lydgate (308–9)
- E The Chettams, the Cadwalladers, Dorothea, and Celia have a discussion about widowhood (378–79)
- F The Bulstrode scandal breaks and comes to a climax at the public meeting (494–505)
- G The Chettams, the Cadwalladers, and Mr Brooke exchange views on Dorothea's second marriage (560–65)

There are two sorts of multiparty talk here. C, E, and G are conversations between members of the gentry that establish a set of characteristically upper-class views on Dorothea's marriages and on politics. By contrast, B, D, and F are the town or middle-class views on Lydgate and Bulstrode (together with the addition of a working-class view in F). A is, as the text states, an uneasy mixture of both the upper and middle classes. In most cases, but particularly in F, there is a mixture of direct speech in the form of dialogue and multiparty talk, and intermental thought report. The hypothetical book devoted to social minds in *Middlemarch* alone that I referred to earlier would allow space for a detailed analysis of the endlessly fascinating ways in which the intricately shifting dynamics of the various group minds are traced in passages such as these.

In addition to these big set-piece occasions there are many short passages, often only a paragraph in length, in which intermental views are presented. These paragraphs act as a kind of low-level, continuous communal commentary on events. Several of these paragraphs are used for illustrative purposes during the rest of this chapter. In addition, there are dialogues in which intermental norms have been internalized to such an extent that they have a subtle and indirect, though still profound and pervasive, influence on intramental thought processes. This point is particularly true of concerns about reputation or honor. To take just one example, there is an important discussion between Sir James Chettam and Mr Brooke on the codicil to Casaubon's will in which Mr Brooke says:

> (4) As to **gossip**, you know, sending [Ladislaw] away won't hinder **gossip**. **People** say what they like to say, not what they have chapter and verse for [. . .] In fact, if it were possible to pack him off . . . **it would look** all the worse for Dorothea. (336–37)

Every word spoken by Mr Brooke is informed by the need for intermental approval. It is apparent that all of the thoughts of both men are dominated by what must be the four most dreaded words in the English language: What will people think?

Subgroups and the Discursive Rhythm

Although the most common of the intermental minds at work in the town are divided along class lines, such a distinction comes nowhere near reflecting the complexity of intermental thought in the novel. A large number of other ephemeral, localized, contextually specific groups can be identified. In a number of the examples given in this section, there is a bewilderingly complex variety of perspectives, usually composing the whole Middlemarch mind together with some of its subgroups. Sometimes the subgroups appear to be in agreement and therefore form *the* Middlemarch mind. They may be separate from each other but have an overlap in membership; they may be distinct from and even opposed to each other; sometimes sub-subgroups of a particular subgroup are featured. With the exception of the social classes, it is rare for subgroups to be referred to more than once. In the discussions that follow, it will be apparent that many of these groups are mentioned in a particular context in order to provide a specific perspective on a particular issue. They then vanish. I was originally tempted to try to create a kind of taxonomy or map of intermental thought in the novel by listing all the groups mentioned and analyzing their relations with each other. However, it took only a quick look at the large amount of evidence of intermental thought in *Middlemarch* to see that such a task would be impossible. The complexity would simply be overwhelming. In any event, little would be achieved because of the contextual nature of many of the references to subgroups.

As was apparent in the reference in the opening passage to "the world— that is to say, Mrs Cadwallader the Rector's wife" et cetera, the narrator can sometimes be self-knowingly ironic about the imprecision that is required when discussing intermental thought:

> (5) At Middlemarch in those times a large sale was **regarded** as a kind of festival . . . The second day, when the best furniture was to be sold, **"everybody"** was there . . . **"Everybody"** that day did not include Mr Bulstrode. (415)

The reader is alerted to the fact that locutions such as "the world," "everybody," and "all Middlemarch" must not be taken literally. It is difficult to be precise about the membership of large intermental units. Generalizations are required even though they may not be strictly accurate. To pursue this line of thought, the narrator sometimes uses a particular example of intermental thought, as in the discussion on prejudice in (6), to muse on the nature of intermentality generally and the imprecision of descriptions of it in particular:

> (6) **Prejudices** about rank and status were easy enough to defy in the form of a tyrannical letter from Mr Casaubon; but **prejudices**, like odorous bodies, have a double existence both solid and subtle. (300)

Intermental units have a double existence that is both solid and subtle. On the one hand, the Middlemarch minds are collections of completely different individuals, all with slightly different perspectives on the social issues affecting the town: they are subtle. On the other hand, and at the same time, these groups come together with a collective force, particularly as it appears to an individual, that is far greater than the sums of their parts: they become solid.

It follows that it is too simplistic to suggest that intermental units are so fixed and clearly bounded that individuals are either inside or outside of them. The situation is much more complex than that. Some people occupy ill-defined positions with regard to any consensus. The vicar, Farebrother, is one who is on the fringes of the town mind. He regrets the common view on the Bulstrode/Lydgate affair because he likes Lydgate and, although he dislikes Bulstrode, he does not wish to see him hounded. His case is made apparent because he is a major character and his views on the matter add to the complexity of the whole situation. However, the reader will know that other characters have their own, individual views even if the precise nature of these views is not articulated. When intermental thinking takes place, significant intramental variations will always occur within it.

One example of this complex combination of intramental and intermental functioning takes place at a dinner party at the Vincy household. The various members of the middle classes who are present discuss the chaplaincy. Individual views are expressed and they are often in disagreement with each other. People are thinking intramentally. Then: "Lydgate's remark, however, did not meet the sense of the company" (107). What happens here is that the individuals who were previously expressing conflicting views coalesce and close ranks in the presence of an outsider, as families tend to do. The presence of a "company" with a common view is explicitly acknowledged. The party is no longer a random collection of intramental perspectives; it becomes an intermental unit. From a literary studies standpoint, Elizabeth Deeds Ermarth (1998) has shown how the dominant authorial perspective in classical realism subsumes divergent voices and intramental dissent, as in this case, into a consensus narrative that constructs a social, embodied, engaged, and specific mind.

The attention paid in the text of the novel to the bewildering variety of the intricately interlocking subgroups results in the presence of a characteristic discursive rhythm. This highly distinctive rhythm is sometimes present in single sentences, sometimes in a group of two or three sentences, sometimes in a whole paragraph. Once it has been noticed, it is difficult to understand how it could have been overlooked. Its tone is often ironic and even playful. The narrator regularly seems to backtrack on earlier statements and to qualify generalizations. The language meditates on the difficulty of pinning down precisely how these fluid and protean minds are initially and temporarily constituted, dissolve, reform and dissolve again, and so on. Example (1) gives a flavor of this rhythm. Other examples include (18), (19), and (20).

Note this discursive rhythm as illustrated in the following two passages—in particular, the careful balancing of different intermental perspectives, all trained on a single intramental mind:

> (7) However, Lydgate was installed as medical attendant on the Vincys, and the event was a subject of **general conversation in Middlemarch. Some** said, that the Vincys had behaved scandalously . . . **Others** were of the opinion that Mr Lydgate's passing by was providential . . . **Many people** believed that Lydgate's coming to the town at all was really due to Bulstrode; and Mrs Taft . . . had got it into her head that Mr Lydgate was a natural son of Mr Bulstrode's. . . . (181–82)

> (8) **Patients who had chronic diseases** . . . had been at once inclined to try him; also, **many who did not like paying their doctor's bills,** thought agreeably of opening an account with a new doctor . . . and **all persons thus inclined to employ Lydgate** held it likely that he was clever. **Some** considered that he might do more than others "where there was liver" . . . But these were **people of minor importance. Good Middlemarch families** were of course not going to change their doctor without reason shown. (305–6)

In both (7) and (8), a large group is split into subgroups in what might be called a "many people thought . . . some said . . . others considered . . ." rhythm. (7) is an excellent example because it starts with the whole Middlemarch mind, "general conversation in Middlemarch," and then refers to three subgroups: some, others, and many people. The relationship between these three groups is unclear. Are they mutually exclusive, or is there an overlap in membership? We cannot be sure. Example (8) concerns an implicit subgroup, patients, instead of the whole Middlemarch mind, but is otherwise similar in shape. Again, it would be difficult indeed to establish the precise relationship between the various sub-subgroups of patients: those willing to change to Lydgate for different reasons and those who are not. It would be tempting to try to express the relationships between these groups as Venn diagrams, but, as in many cases in this particular novel, I do not think it would be possible.

The intermental rhythm is characteristic of descriptions of collective thinking in *Middlemarch* because it reflects George Eliot's interest in the messiness or complexity of this kind of mental functioning. It is invariably inaccurate to claim that everybody in an intermental unit thinks in exactly the same way for exactly the same reasons. Within the Middlemarch minds, the strength of view on the Bulstrode/Lydgate case will vary. Some people will be convinced of their guilt; others will be less so; some will care very much; others will not; some will be pleased at the general view because they dislike Bulstrode and/or Lydgate or because a loss of their status will benefit them; others, such as Farebrother, will regret it because they like one or both of them or have moral objections. (Note that I too have just unthinkingly slipped into the intermental rhythm.) The narrator is invariably scrupulous in reflecting these fine shades of opinion. The delicate balance between intramental and intermental thought is always maintained.

Intermental Focalization

The point about the narrator being scrupulous in reflecting shades of opinion can be restated in terms of the concept of focalization. In what follows, I wish to propose the following three binary distinctions within the umbrella term *focalization* that, I think, go some way toward reflecting the complexity of the passages quoted in this chapter:

- intramental and intermental;
- single and multiple; and
- homogeneous and heterogeneous.

The difference between *intramental* and *intermental* focalization refers to the distinction between mental activity by one (intramental) and by more than one (intermental) consciousness. *Single* focalization occurs when there is one focalizer. The term *multiple* focalization refers to the presence of two or more focalizers of the same object. These multiple focalizers may be intramental individuals, or intermental groups, or a combination of the two. However, a further distinction is required. In the case of *homogeneous* focalization, the two focalizers have the same perspective, views, beliefs, and so on relating to the object. By contrast, *heterogeneous* focalization reflects the fact that the focalizers' views differ, and their perspectives conflict with one another. For more on this issue of multiperspectivalism, see Nünning (2000).

If focalization is single, then it can be either intramental (one individual) or intermental (one single group), but it will be homogeneous and not heterogeneous unless an individual or group has conflicting views on an issue. One example of single focalization is (1) where all of the italicized phrases look superficially as though they are references to different groups, but are simply different ways of naming the Middlemarch mind. Other examples are (5) and (14). However, two points should be made. First, single focalization is comparatively rare in this novel, and the majority of the examples quoted in this chapter are multiple points of view that display a balance of distinct and distinctive collective views and fine shades of subtly differing judgments. Second, a succession of single focalizations will become multiple in a Bakhtinian effect on the reader when aggregated over the course of a novel.

If focalization is multiple, then it can involve different individuals, or different groups, or a combination of both; and, completely independently, it can be either homogeneous or heterogeneous. Obviously, a fairly large number of potential combinations can be derived from these variables. I have not conducted an exhaustive analysis of the *Middlemarch* text to find out, but my guess is that most combinations are contained in it. Of the various examples of multiple intermental focalizations used in this chapter, some are homogeneous and some are heterogeneous. Multiple intermental *heterogeneous* focalization is featured in examples (7), (8), (11), (13), and (18). In all these cases, the various intermental units mentioned have different views on the object of their cognitive functioning. To be strictly accurate, examples (7) and (11) have an intramental element as well and so are examples of multiple intermental *and intramental* heterogeneous focalization. Multiple intermental *homogeneous* focalization is present in examples (2), (3), (10), (12), (16), (19), and (22). Again, examples (12) and (22) also have an intramental element. Apologies for the highly technical nature of this analysis, but it is a complex subject.

Individuals Inside Intermental Units

I will now focus on the relationships between groups and individuals. First I will say a little about how the leaders or spokespeople of each of the three social groups are used to present the results of their class-based mental functioning. I will then discuss those individuals who are outside of the social groups in the sense that they are the objects of their intermental cognitive activity.

Both Mrs Cadwallader and Sir James Chettam act as powerful mouthpieces for the upper-class mind. Here is a dramatic illustration of this function:

> (9) But Sir James was a power in a way unguessed by himself. Entering at that moment [as Ladislaw is saying goodbye to Dorothea], he was **an incorporation of the strongest reasons** through which Will's pride became a repellent force, keeping him asunder from Dorothea. (377)

86 | Chapter 3

Chettam embodies, or represents or, to use the word chosen in the passage, "incorporates" the upper-class Middlemarch mind. It is stressed that he, thinking of himself as an individual, is not aware of this power and this may make his role even more influential. His mouthpiece role is also evident in example (22) below. Mrs Cadwallader has a similar role. Two whole pages are devoted to an explanation of it (39–40): "She was the diplomatist of Tipton and Freshitt, and for anything to happen in spite of her was an offensive irregularity" (40). When something *does* happen in spite of her (the reference is to Dorothea's engagement to Casaubon instead of to Chettam), "It followed that Mrs Cadwallader must decide on another match for Sir James" (40). This is intramental thought and action in the sense that it relates to a single individual, but her power to take this action results from her ability to represent the local consensus. Her intentionality is much more clearly foregrounded than with the Sir James quote. "It followed" to Mrs. Cadwallader in her capacity as a mouthpiece for the Middlemarch mind and, in addition, to her as an individual agent. Example (9) is different in that Sir James does not actually do, say, or even think anything. He simply has a representative role in Ladislaw's uneasy consciousness. At that moment, for Ladislaw, Sir James is less an individual and more the "incorporation" of Bakhtin's word with a sideways glance.

The middle-class mind has several mouthpieces: they include at various times Sprague, Minchin, Toller, Chicheley, and Standish. They regard "themselves as Middlemarch institutions" (126). The following quote gives a useful insight into the dynamics of this particular group mind:

> (10) What **they** [Sprague and Minchin] disliked was [Lydgate's] arrogance, which **nobody** felt to be altogether deniable. **They** implied that he was insolent, pretentious, and given to that reckless innovation for the sake of noise and show which was the essence of the charlatan. The word charlatan once thrown on the air **could not be let drop**. (313)

Here we have a balance between a small unit (the pair formed by Sprague and Minchin) and the much larger middle-class mind. The wider group acquiesces in the views of the pair. The final sentence makes use of the passive voice and presupposition to give an accurate indication of how views spread. People seize on an idea or a word and hang on to it. It is in this way that the use of the term *charlatan* becomes attached to Lydgate. However, the thought also has individual characteristics. Fred's illness "had given to Mr Wrench's enmity towards Lydgate more definite personal ground" (312). Despite the fact that Mr Wrench is a mouthpiece for a medium-sized intermental unit, his thinking here has a consciously intramental shading.

Mrs Dollop is the acknowledged leader of the working-class mind.

This is a group that is based in the Tankard pub (the middle-class pub is the Green Dragon). As the passages describing the working classes are easily the weakest in the book and, to be honest, make quite painful reading, I will refer only briefly to this topic. Here are two passages that illustrate the workings of the working-class mind and the leadership role of Mrs Dollop:

> (11) This was **the tone of thought chiefly sanctioned by Mrs Dollop,** the spirited landlady of the Tankard in Slaughter Lane, who had often to resist the shallow pragmatism of **customers** disposed to think that their reports from the outer world were of equal force with what had "come up" in her mind. (498)

> (12) If that was not reason, Mrs Dollop wishes to know what was; but there was **a prevalent feeling** in her audience that her opinion was a bulwark, and that if it were overthrown there would be no limits to the cutting-up of bodies, as had well been seen in Burke and Hare with their pitch-plaisters—such a hanging business as that **was not wanted in Middlemarch.** (305)

The use of a representative voice and a supporting chorus is a notable characteristic of both passages. Regarding (11), the term *sanctioned* is revealing of Mrs Dollop's power. The group-defining force of the phrase *outer world* is also worth noting. There is an occurrence toward the end of (12) of intermental free indirect discourse. It is obvious from some of the phrases in this sentence ("Mrs Dollop wishes to know what was"; "as had well been seen in Burke and Hare with their pitch-plaisters"; and "such a hanging business as that was not wanted in Middlemarch") that the narrator is making use of the distinctive speech and thought patterns of Mrs Dollop and her customers.

Individuals Outside Intermental Units

Having examined the role of the mouthpieces of the three class-based units, I will now scrutinize the ways in which the text presents the judgments of those units on individuals who are outside of them. Both Dorothea's and also Lydgate's character and behavior are, at various times, focalized through a variety of Middlemarch minds. The relentlessly judgmental quality of intermental thought in the novel remains fairly constant in relation to them both. However, focalization can work in the opposite direction, and intermental units can be focalized through intramental cognitive functioning, too. Within Lydgate's free indirect discourse, there are references to "Middlemarch gossip" (240) and to "the circles of Middlemarchers" (299). Dorothea is critical of the "society around her" (23). Sometimes the two directions are at work simultaneously. In a good example of a reciprocal intermental/intramental relationship, Lydgate comments that "I have made up my mind to take Middlemarch as it comes, and shall be much obliged if the town will take me in the same way" (112). Lydgate talks here of Middlemarch in the way that the narrator does in the final sentence of (19), as a sentient being that is capable of independent thought. In (13), the presentation of power relations in the town is focalized through Lydgate:

> (13) The question whether Mr Tyke should be appointed as salaried chaplain to the hospital was an exciting topic to **the Middlemarchers;** and Lydgate **heard it discussed** in a way that threw much light on the power exercised in the town by Mr Bulstrode. The banker was evidently a **ruler,** but there was **an opposition party,** and even among **his supporters,** there were **some** who allowed it to be seen that their support was a compromise . . . (106)

Lydgate is aware that, on this question, the whole intermental mind ("Middlemarchers") is subdivided into support for Bulstrode and opposition to him (and perhaps those who have no strong opinion?). The support is then further subdivided into strong and weak or "compromise" support.

The term *cognitive narrative,* you will remember, designates a character's whole perceptual, cognitive, ethical, and ideological viewpoint on the storyworld of the novel and is intended to be an inclusive term that conveys the fact that each character's mental functioning is a narrative that is embedded within the whole narrative of the novel. Double cognitive narratives are versions of characters' minds that exist within the minds of other characters. So, one way to describe the relationships that I am discussing is to say that Middlemarch minds regularly form double cognitive narratives of individuals, especially Dorothea and Lydgate. Equally, these narratives can work in the reverse direction. As Lydgate's wish that the town take him as it finds him shows, some individuals form their own double cognitive narratives for the Middlemarch mind.

Theory of mind is usually thought to work in novels on the intramental level. In *Persuasion,* when Wentworth is snubbed by Anne Elliot's father and sister, Anne knows that he feels contempt and anger, Wentworth knows that Anne knows what he feels, Anne knows that Wentworth knows that she knows, and so on. Theory of mind is operating here solely in relation to individuals. However, as we saw in the case of Santa Dulcina delle Rocce, groups use theory of mind too and, in addition, can be the subject of individuals' theory of mind. Various sorts of different attributions can be made by intermental minds regarding the supposed workings of intramental minds. Throughout the novel, Middlemarch groups judge individuals and place them accordingly. "Most of those who saw Fred... thought that young Vincy was pleasure-seeking as usual" (163). So Fred is constructed as a pleasure seeker. In example (1), Sprague is defined as "hard-headed and dry-witted." Attributions by large units also have a profound effect on smaller units such as marriages: "In Middlemarch a wife could not long remain ignorant that the town held a bad opinion of her husband" (511).

When Lydgate takes Bulstrode out of the public meeting in which he, Bulstrode, has been humiliated,

> (14) [i]t seemed to him [Lydgate] as if he were putting his sign-manual to that **association** of himself with Bulstrode, of which he now saw the full meaning as it must have presented itself to **other minds**. [And then, within Lydgate's free indirect discourse.] The **inferences** were closely linked enough: the **town** knew of the loan, believed it to be a bribe, and believed that he took it as a bribe. (504)

In theory of mind terms, the passage can be decoded as follows:

A   Lydgate believes
B   that the Middlemarch mind believes
C   that Bulstrode believed
D   that Lydgate was bribable
E   and that Bulstrode intended to bribe him
F   and that Lydgate knew of Bulstrode's intention
G   and that Lydgate did accept Bulstrode's bribe.

Note that, as with the *Men at Arms* passage, this cognitive chain involves intermental (item B) as well as intramental reasoning.

All this inter- and intramental complexity has a powerful teleological role in the development of the various plots in the novel. The two most important examples are the Lydgate and Bulstrode crisis and the Dorothea and Ladislaw relationship. Example (9) demonstrated that it is the upper-class mind that keeps Dorothea and Ladislaw apart through her and especially his uneasy awareness of its workings.

> (15) Will was in a defiant mood, his consciousness being deeply stung with the thought that the **people** who looked at him probably knew a fact tantamount to an accusation against him as a fellow with low designs which were to be frustrated by a disposal of property. (417)

It is striking how many examples can be found in this novel of Bakhtin's word with a sideways glance, the nervous and uneasy anticipation of the view of another. It was also apparent in example (4). The end result for Dorothea and Ladislaw is that they are kept apart for some time:

> (16) His position [in Middlemarch] was threatening to divide him from her with those **barriers of habitual sentiment** which are more fatal to the persistence of mutual interest than all the distance between Rome and Britain. (300)

Intermental units construct socially situated identities for individual characters:

> (17) There was **a general impression,** however, that Lydgate was not altogether a common country doctor, and in Middlemarch at that time such an impression was significant of great things being expected from him. (96–97)

Lydgate is considered to be a gentleman doctor. His intramental identity emerges from the intermental consensus. In particular, group minds make use of the past lives of individuals. While cognitive narratives are being constructed for individuals, their origins are carefully examined for any clues relating to their identities. Here, Bulstrode's lack of known social origins is held to be deeply suspicious:

> (18) Hence Mr Bulstrode's close attention was not agreeable to **the publicans and sinners in Middlemarch;** it was attributed by **some** to his being a Pharisee, and by **others** to his being Evangelical. **Less superficial reasoners among them** wished to know who his father and grandfather were, observing that five-and-twenty years ago nobody had ever heard of a Bulstrode in Middlemarch. (83)

The establishment of a single, stable, assured social identity for poor Bulstrode is not going to be possible. All of these groups (loud men, those persons who thought themselves worth hearing, others, the publicans and sinners in Middlemarch, some, others, the less superficial reasoners among them) have their own conflicting, colliding, contradictory perspectives on him.

This interest in the past is even more obvious in the next example, which is revealing about the ways in which intermental constructions of intramental cognitive narratives require individuals' pasts to be filled out:

(19) **No one in Middlemarch** was likely to have such a notion of Lydgate's past as has here been faintly shadowed, and indeed **the respectable townsfolk** there were not more given than **mortals generally** to any eager attempt at exactness in the representation to themselves of what did not come under their own senses. **Not only young virgins of that town, but grey-bearded men also,** were often in haste to conjecture how a new acquaintance might be wrought into their purposes, contented with very vague knowledge as to the way in which life has been shaping him for that instrumentality. **Middlemarch,** in fact, counted on swallowing Lydgate and assimilating him very comfortably. (105)

The passage starts by saying, reasonably enough, that the Middlemarch mind does not know what happened to Lydgate before he arrived in the town. But it then goes on to say that the hypothetical construction of his cognitive narrative (in the absence of real evidence) will owe more to the Middlemarch mind's own needs ("wrought into their purposes") than any disinterested pursuit of the actual truth of his real history. The previously discussed final sentence emphasizes the point. It will make use of Lydgate as it wishes. The need is to create a "Middlemarch Lydgate" who can be comfortably swallowed and easily assimilated. That "Lydgate" need only have a tenuous relationship with the "real" Lydgate (whatever and whoever that is). This line of thinking regarding the creation of different Lydgates is pursued further in the next section on the Lydgate storyworld.

In example (19) above, and also in examples (20) and (22) below, there is a strong emphasis on the almost mythic power of intermental, and also intramental, minds to modify reality to their own requirements. This is especially true, as can be seen above, of the construction of Lydgate's cognitive narrative. The intricate and messy detail of a life as it is actually lived by a particular individual is smoothed and flattened out into a simple story, a narrative that is molded according to the collective desire for a simple moral to the tale. In (20) the narrator again uses the opportunity of some complex shared views of an individual, this time Bulstrode, for some general musings on how group minds create intramental cognitive narratives:

(20) But **this vague conviction** of interminable guilt, which was enough to keep up much head-shaking and biting innuendo even among **substantial professional seniors,** had **for the general mind** all the superior power of mystery over fact. **Everybody** liked better to conjecture how the thing was, than simply to know it; for **conjecture** soon became more confident than knowledge, and had a more liberal allowance for the incompatible. Even the more definite **scandal** concerning Bulstrode's earlier life

was, **for some minds,** melted into the mass of mystery, as so much lively metal to be poured out in dialogue, and to take such fantastic shapes as heaven pleased. (498)

This is a general assessment by the narrator of a certain type of intermental thought. Although it is related to the workings of the Middlemarch mind, it appears to have a wider application. The narrator seems to be suggesting that this is how intermental systems in general work. It is heavily ironic and rather jaundiced. It makes the obvious point that the investigations of the Middlemarch mind are not aimed at a pure disinterested pursuit of the objective truth. The driving force in this case is not the discovery of fact but, rather, the enjoyment of mystery. The facts might result in an uninteresting narrative for Bulstrode and Lydgate. Also, the result might not suit the purposes or interests of those people who are hostile to the two men. Even the "more definite" facts are warped to fit into a more satisfying story. A cognitive narrative that fits the needs of the group is created. As I said, this modification of reality is almost mythic in direction.

In the next passage, the narrator warns the reader against the distortions in the construction of individual identity that are inherent in the mythmaking process:

> (21) For surely **all** must admit that a man may be puffed and belauded, envied, ridiculed, counted upon as a tool and fallen in love with, or at least selected as a future husband, and yet remain virtually unknown—**known** merely as a cluster of signs for **his neighbours'** false suppositions. (96)

The mythmaking process continues even after death. The following passage occurs at the end of the book:

> (22) Sir James never ceased to regard Dorothea's second marriage as a mistake; and indeed this remained **the tradition concerning it in Middlemarch,** where she was spoken of to a younger generation as a fine girl who married a sickly clergyman, old enough to be her father, and in little more than a year after his death gave up her estate to marry his cousin—young enough to have been his son, with no property, and not well-born. **Those who had not seen anything of Dorothea** usually observed that she could not have been "a nice woman," else she would not have married either the one or the other. (577)

It is Dorothea's fate to be focalized though the Middlemarch mind for ever. Her life exists now only as a Middlemarch double cognitive narrative. In its reductive simplicity and naivety, this story is completely different from the warm, sympathetic, complex one that is presented by the narrator over the course of the novel. It is a long way indeed from the woman described in the final paragraph of the novel, the one whose "finely-touched spirit had still its fine issues," "who lived faithfully a hidden life," and who rests in an unvisited tomb (578).

THE LYDGATE STORYWORLD

The Lydgate storyworld is the whole of Lydgate's mind in action. When we attempt to follow his mental functioning, we experience the whole *Middlemarch* storyworld from his perceptual, cognitive, and ethical viewpoint. In analyzing the presentation of his consciousness, we need to study not just the passages of text that present his inner speech in the speech modes of direct thought, free indirect thought, and thought report; not just whether he is a flat or round character or which of the various intertextual stereotypes readers will apply to him; not just his position as an actant or function within the structure of the story; and not just his role as a focalizer. All of those things are important and will contribute to an understanding of how Lydgate's mind works. But, as Lydgate's identity is, in part, socially distributed or situated among the minds of the other inhabitants of the town, much more is needed.

Reading Lydgate's narrative within the context of the whole text is an extremely "gappy" experience: he is referred to in a number of passages that, added together, amount to less than a third of the total novel. (I am talking here about the gaps in the narrative's attention to the character, and not gaps in reader understanding.) To demonstrate how gappiness can be measured, I have set out below a schedule of all the passages in the text that relate to Lydgate. It includes not only the occasions when he is physically "on stage," but also, and most importantly, those occasions when he is being talked about by other characters. Although the schedule is a little impressionistic and could be presented in slightly different ways, it nevertheless gives a fairly accurate picture of Lydgate's presence in the novel. (The passage totals may not correspond exactly with the page references—in the first example, an eight-page passage within the nine pages 61 to 69—either because the passage begins toward the end of the first page or ends toward the beginning of the last page, or because I have rounded the totals up or down to whole numbers.)

Passage 1 (61–69):   8 pages (then a 9-page gap)
Passage 2 (78–86):   8 pages (10-page gap)
Passage 3 (96–130):   34 pages (49-page gap)

Passage 4 (179–88):	9 pages (8-page gap)
Passage 5 (196–209):	13 pages (27-page gap)
Passage 6 (236–45):	9 pages (46-page gap)
Passage 7 (291–93):	2 pages (27-page gap)
Passage 8 (299–316):	17 pages (4-page gap)
Passage 9 (320–23):	3 pages (17-page gap)
Passage 10 (340–44):	4 pages (57-page gap)
Passage 11 (401–15):	14 pages (26-page gap)
Passage 12 (441–73):	32 pages (9-page gap)
Passage 13 (482–531):	49 pages (8-page gap)
Passage 14 (539–40):	2 pages (5-page gap)
Passage 15 (545–52):	7 pages (23-page gap)
Passage 16 (575):	1 page
Total: 212 out of 578 pages	(a little over a third of the total)

It is worth making a number of points about this schedule. First, the passages featuring Lydgate tend to be shorter in length than the gaps between those passages. Only three of the sixteen passages are above seventeen pages in length. (These three compose half of Lydgate's total narrative.) Ten of the other passages are under ten pages in length. By contrast, seven of the gaps are over twenty pages long and three are over forty-five pages long. As I say, reading Lydgate's narrative within the context of the whole text is an extremely gappy experience. During these gaps, the reader has to continue to apply the continuing-consciousness frame. That is, we have to be aware that Lydgate continues to exist within the reality of the storyworld and will have on his mind such important issues as the hospital chaplaincy affair, his relationship with Rosamond, his money troubles, and the receding prospects of further medical research. Following Clennam's cognitive narrative in *Little Dorrit* is an equally gappy experience; Anne Elliot's is less so because she is the main character-focalizer in *Persuasion,* but the rarely focalized Wentworth's is more so. Lydgate's gappiness is especially notable when one considers that, with Dorothea, he is the main character in the novel. Less important characters will obviously be even gappier in nature. I am not contrasting him with other important characters in similar texts of the same sort of size: for example, Rogozhin in *The Idiot* or Rhett Butler in *Gone with the Wind*. In fact, it seems to me quite likely that similarly significant characters are equally gappy. To find out whether this is the case would be an interesting exercise to undertake, but is beyond the scope of this study.

Second, because the Lydgate storyworld is aspectual in that it views the whole *Middlemarch* storyworld only from Lydgate's subjective point of view, a good deal of the whole storyworld is missing from his own. It is plausible to speculate that Lydgate has no or limited knowledge of the following important areas of the novel: Dorothea's relationships with Casaubon, Ladislaw, her sister Celia, and Sir James Chettam; the relationships between Mary Garth, the Garth family, Fred Vincy, and Farebrother; Mr Featherstone; Raffles and the precise nature of Bulstrode's secret; and the extent of the relationship between Rosamond and Ladislaw, and Dorothea's discovery of them in a compromising situation. This general point emerges powerfully from the film of *Little Dorrit* that was made by Christine Edzard in 1987. Part one of the film presents the storyworld from Clennam's limited point of view; part two from Little Dorrit's. The effects can be surprising. For example, the financial crash occurs with no warning, without the buildup related to Merdle's fragile state of mind and eventual suicide that is featured in the novel, because, of course, Clennam would have been unaware of all of that.

Third, it is an artificial exercise to try to examine Lydgate's mind in isolation from the other minds in the storyworld. Lydgate's narrative is deeply embedded within the whole novel. To say that it composes a third of the whole novel is misleading. This third consists not only of his narrative, but also of large portions of the narratives of Rosamond (obviously), Farebrother, Bulstrode, Dorothea, Casaubon, and Ladislaw. All of these characters have versions of his mind, or double cognitive narratives, contained within their own minds. A consequence of this exercise is that their narratives have been aspectually adjusted, and these characters are now seen mainly from his cognitive and ethical viewpoint.

Fourth, notwithstanding the third point, these passages, embedded though they are within the larger *Middlemarch* narrative, add up to a coherent and continuous narrative in their own right. They would require the addition of only a little explanatory material to make an excellent short novel (rather, I imagine, like the one that was originally planned by George Eliot).

Finally, it is striking how Lydgate's narrative is dominated both by conversations with others in which he takes part and also by discussions about him by others when he is not present. His mind is actively engaged with its social context. Within his narrative, there are only five passages of private thought, totaling fourteen pages. However, this label, "private," is rather misleading because these passages are also profoundly social and are informed by his mind's dialogic relationships with other minds. Also, they frequently refer to his engagement with the social world in the form of action, both past ("He had quitted the party early" [63]) and future ("He had come to Middlemarch bent on doing many things" [64]). Many of these actions and plans for action relate to his assumptions about the workings of other minds. In the first and second passages of private thought (64) and (112–15), he is deciding not to marry and is planning his future research. In the third (122–24), he is wondering how to vote on the chaplaincy question. In the fourth (404–8), he is trying to work out what to do about his growing money troubles and his inability to get Rosamond to understand them. In the final passage (509–11), he is thinking over past actions such as his marriage and his acceptance of a loan from Bulstrode, the joint actions of others ("The general black-balling had begun" [511]), and his own actions in response ("And yet how was he to set about vindicating himself?" [509]).

The presentation of Lydgate's mind in the discourse is dominated in these and other ways by the concept of action. His mind is generally described in terms of what he does. As Gilbert Ryle says, when we talk about the mind, we talk about the doing and undergoing of things in the ordinary world. The presentation of his actions is dominated by the narrative's purpose of creating a cognitive character frame for the reader that highlights the contrast between Lydgate's lofty aims and his rather less elevated maneuverings. His actions and also his reasons for them can be interpreted within this framework. The story of his slide into mediocrity then has even greater impact.

The reader is able to see Lydgate's mind in action, among other ways, in his medical work and specifically in his diagnoses of illness. It is also visible during the various conversations in which he takes part. In our first encounter with him he is "listening gravely" (60) while nonsense is being talked to him. This is *dramaturgical* action: evoking in a public audience a certain image or impression. A good deal of thought report is what I refer to as *contextual*: the short unobtrusive clauses, phrases, or even single words describing a character's thought processes that are often combined with descriptions of actions. Much of the contextual thought report that refers to Lydgate's mind is used to explain the purpose of his actions. These actions are often the speech acts that occur during conversations. This combination of a description of an action and the reason for it in the form of contextual thought report is common: "Lydgate, not willing to let slip an opportunity of furthering a favourite purpose, ventured to say . . ." (302). Also: "Lydgate's ear had caught eagerly her mention of the living, and as soon as he could, he reopened the subject, seeing here a possibility of making amends for the casting-vote he had once given with an ill-satisfied conscience" (342). Here is a more complex example: "He sat looking at her, and did not rise to pay her any compliments, leaving that to others, now that his admiration was deepened" (110). Here, an action (looking), a nonaction (not complimenting her), the decision that is the specific reason for the nonaction (leaving it to others), and the general state of mind that is the basic reason for all three of these (admiration) are combined in a sentence that causally links action and consciousness together. I say more about action in the next chapter.

As I said in chapter 1, the concept of fictional minds is intended to encompass the issue of characterization as well as that of the representation of consciousness. Consider this example: Rosamond's refinement is "beyond what Lydgate had expected" (109). It would be reasonable to infer from this statement a single mental event: say, Lydgate realizes in a self-conscious flash of intuition that this is how he feels about Rosamond. It is also his settled belief that this is so, and his belief is a state of mind that will exist over time, and will be true of his mind whether or not he is thinking about Rosamond at any given moment. It is also a reflection of the dispositions that are characteristic of his character or personality: his tendency to be arrogant, to be class-conscious, and to be attracted to women. These short-, medium-, and long-term elements of his mind relate to both consciousness and characterization and cannot be separated. Here is another, among countless examples in the novel: "Lydgate had often been satirical on this gratuitous prediction, and he meant now to be guarded" (199). Again, there is a complex balance here between characterization and dispositions (the past), current mental events and states (the present), and the kind of functional, purposive, problem-solving mental functioning that is oriented toward the future.

Lydgate's Relationship with Middlemarch

Lydgate's relationship with Middlemarch is negotiated in terms of the double cognitive narratives they have of each other. His relationship with Rosamond fails to become an intermental unit because the double cognitive narratives they have of each other differ so widely from their own internal narratives. These are the most important relationships in his life, and I will now analyze them in turn. (Some of the quotes that have been used already will be repeated during this discussion because they will now be interpreted from Lydgate's, rather than the town's, perspective. There will also be a similarly small amount of repetition in the next chapter for the same sort of reason.)

Lydgate is introduced within an intermental frame. His identity is socially situated before we meet him, and there are a number of discussions of him throughout the novel that continue the town's exploration of his identity. It is striking that the early part of the novel contains far more information on the "Lydgates" that exist in the minds of other characters than it does on the "Lydgate" that emerges from direct access to his own mind. It is worth examining the beginning of this process in a little detail. The reader begins the initial, tentative, and hypothetical construction of Lydgate's cognitive narrative by making use of the double cognitive narratives of other characters. We first hear of him indirectly, while Lady Chettam and Mrs Cadwallader are discussing him. "Tell me about this new young surgeon, Mr Lydgate. I am told he is wonderfully clever: he certainly looks it—a fine brow indeed" (61). Mrs Cadwallader replies that "He is a gentleman . . . He talks well" (61). Lady Chettam agrees that he is "really well connected . . . One does not expect it in a practitioner of that kind" (62). Mrs Cadwallader then notices that Dorothea Brooke "is talking cottages and hospitals with him . . . I believe he is a sort of philanthropist" (62). So, we find out before we actually meet him that he is apparently young, clever, good-looking, a well-connected gentleman, someone who talks well, a sort of philanthropist, and innovative and successful. These few words on the page are now transformed by the reader into an already pre-existing imaginary individual with a past that is part of the *Middlemarch* storyworld. His cognitive narrative started twenty-five-odd years ago, and the reader is now engaged in reconstructing it.

The conversation between Mrs Cadwallader and Lady Chettam is largely a consideration of Lydgate's mind. Some features are obviously related to his mental life: being clever, philanthropic, and successfully innovative. Others are slightly more indirect: "talking well" is a description of behavior that implies a series of mental attributes such as cleverness, confidence, awareness of others, and so on. Being a gentleman is yet more indirect, but presumably has implications for the way the mind works. In addition, it is also part of the competence of the reader to construct, this time by indirect means, some aspects of Lydgate's mental life that are implicit in what we have been told. Let us say, for example: having the above qualities makes it likely that he is not only self-confident and ambitious, but also altruistic, imaginative, and idealistic. The reader is using material on Lydgate's social and publicly available mind that has been refracted through the conflicting worldviews of Mrs Cadwallader and Lady Chettam. A version of his mind exists within their minds. Their minds are interacting with, conflicting with, and interrogating the constructions that others have formed of his mind. They disapprove of his being both a gentleman and a doctor and also of the fact that he is a doctor with ideas about the advancement of medicine. Although the characters do not openly speculate about the causal network behind Lydgate's behavior, there is an implicit puzzlement over the motives that a gentleman would have for wanting to become a doctor. Lydgate's own motivation becomes more explicit during the direct access to his mind later in the passage. Future events appear to show that the views of the two characters on his mind were fairly accurate. To use a familiar but revealing phrase, there are some respects in which he may not "know his own mind." In the next chapter of the novel Lydgate is scornful about the possibility of losing his balance through thinking himself to be falling in love, and we find out later that this is precisely what he does do.

Scenes recur throughout the novel in which various groups of townspeople discuss Lydgate's mind. An intermental consensus emerges from a variety of intramental perspectives and a joint double cognitive narrative is constructed. These scenes result in an interesting dual perspective on the town mind. Seen from one perspective, although these conversations create a consensus, they also contain intramental dissent. People disagree over the precise extent of Lydgate's guilt in the matter of the bribe. But seen from the point of view of Lydgate's mind, the Middlemarch mind is fully shared, uniform, and monolithic. And in a sense he is not necessarily wrong. Once the consensus has emerged it becomes extremely powerful, and the reservations of some individuals around the edges do not count for much.

The town's views are sometimes related simply to the facts of the case and, interestingly, the speculation that Lydgate's windfall is a loan from Bulstrode turns out to be factually correct. More often, though, Middlemarch is concerned with the attribution of motives. "The inferences were closely linked enough: the town knew of the loan, believed it to be a bribe, and believed that he took it as a bribe" (504). The Middlemarch mind is always inclined to attribute unworthy reasons to Lydgate's actions: "After this, it came to be held in various quarters that Lydgate played even with respectable constitutions for his own purposes" (314). The cognitive operations involved in the attribution of motives can become quite complex: "Thus it happened that on this occasion, Bulstrode became identified with Lydgate and Lydgate with Tyke; and owing to this variety of interchangeable names for the chaplaincy question, diverse minds were enabled to form the same judgment concerning it" (126). A fully fledged narrative for Lydgate emerges from the network of attribution: "There was hardly ever so much unanimity among them as in the opinion that Lydgate was an arrogant young fellow and yet ready for the sake of ultimately predominating to show a crawling subservience to Bulstrode" (312). At other times the consensus consists simply of abuse: "they agreed that Lydgate was a jackanapes" (126).

Throughout the novel, a dialogical relationship exists between the intramental Lydgate and the intermental Middlemarch. He is concerned with anticipating, reconstructing, arguing against the common view of the workings of his mind. His mind is in a conflicted dialogue with the minds of the various groups and individuals concerned with the question of the chaplaincy of the hospital. Sometimes this relationship is expressed in general terms: "For the first time Lydgate was feeling the hampering threadlike pressure of small social conditions, and their frustrating complexity" (124). This specific issue brings home to Lydgate the power of the intermental mind: "The affair of the chaplaincy remained a sore point in his memory as a case in which the petty medium of Middlemarch had been too strong for him" (129). Much of the conflict occurs within the context of his medical work: "He was impatient of the foolish expectations amidst which all work must be carried on" (181). This "feud between him and the other medical men" (188) is regularly explained in terms of mind-reading difficulties. On occasions, Lydgate is unable to develop a double cognitive narrative that is sufficiently sophisticated to make his social relations easier. This can sometimes relate to the group mind: "Lydgate's remark did not meet the sense of the company" (107); and: "But Lydgate had not been experienced enough to foresee that his new course would be even more offensive to the laity" (306). At other times, it is focused on an individual: "Lydgate had really lost sight of the fact that Mr Chichely was his Majesty's coroner" (108).

The novel contains a balanced picture of Lydgate's double cognitive narrative of Middlemarch. In some ways, he performs quite well. There is plenty of evidence to show that, despite his undoubted arrogance, he does at least make some effort to reconstruct other minds and is quite successful in doing so. For example: "But would the end really be his own convenience? Other people would say so, and would allege that he was currying favour with Bulstrode" (124). Later, he hopes that Dorothea's actions can "clear [him] in a few other minds" (530). He can also be quite sensitive in his constructions of individual double cognitive narratives: "For Lydgate was acute enough to indulge him with a little technical talk" (311); "That there might be an awkward affair with Wrench, Lydgate saw at once" (180); and, "Lydgate was conscious of having shown himself something better than an everyday doctor, though here too it was an equivocal advantage" (311). He is being quite flexible here and not overtly confrontational. When things become more serious during the Bulstrode loan crisis, he becomes extremely sensitive. He notices "a peculiar interchange of glances when he and Bulstrode took their seats" (502); and, while he helps Bulstrode out of the room after he is accused, "It seemed as if he were putting his sign-manual to that association of himself with Bulstrode, of which he now saw the full meaning as it must have presented itself to other minds" (504).

On the other hand, he feels "some zest for the growing though half-suppressed feud" (188). When he makes a successful diagnosis and another doctor does not, "Lydgate did not make the affair a ground for valuing himself or (very particularly) despising Minchin" (311). The parenthetical phrase reveals that he *does* despise Minchin to some degree. "We see that he was bearing enmity and silly misconception with much spirit, aware that they were partly created by his good share of success" (314). "Enmity and silly misconception," on a free indirect discourse reading, are his terms, and he is obviously rather self-satisfied with his ability to bear them with "much spirit" in light of his success. The undertones in these quotes reveal that he underestimates the Middlemarch mind. His tendency to arrogance will have an important role in the narrative progression as a contributory factor in his eventual downfall.

Before going on to discuss Lydgate's relationship with Rosamond it may be useful, as a contrast, to describe briefly Lydgate's friendship with Farebrother, an inhabitant of the town who is not part of the Middlemarch mind. Lydgate has a fairly full and accurate double cognitive narrative of Farebrother. As their friendship develops, difficulties arise when Farebrother tries to help Lydgate. Initially, "Lydgate took Mr Farebrother's hints very cordially, though he would hardly have borne them from another man" (315). (This sentence, by the way, is a good example of the inseparability of consciousness and characterization that I referred to earlier: it consists of mental events [cordial taking of hints], states of mind [feelings for Farebrother], and character [general unwillingness to take hints].) Later, Farebrother offers more specific help. First, this is how it appears to Lydgate: "He knew as distinctly as possible that this was an offer of help to himself from Mr Farebrother, and he could not bear it" (446). Next, this is how it appears to Farebrother: "Could this too be a proud rejection of sympathy and help? Never mind; the sympathy and help should be offered" (492). What is significant here is that the empathy or mind reading between the two men is accurate. Lydgate knows that Farebrother knows that Lydgate knows et cetera that the offer of help is embarrassing but must be made. The mutual attribution of motives and states of mind is far more successful in this case than, as shown now, between Lydgate and his wife.

Lydgate's Relationship with Rosamond

Both Lydgate and Rosamond have deeply developed double cognitive narratives of each other that are very different indeed from their actual narratives, and so, as a result, there is no evidence at all of any genuinely intermental thinking. In contrast, in Evelyn Waugh's *Vile Bodies,* the precise opposite is the case. Within a social group called the "Bright Young Things" who are active in London in the 1920s, there is a good deal of intermental thought, but no double cognitive narratives. They act together, but have no interest in each other's inner lives. Lydgate and Rosamond are interested: it is just that they are completely wrong about each other.

The narrator remarks that Lydgate and Rosamond "lived in a world of which the other knew nothing, it had not occurred to Lydgate that he had been a subject of eager meditation to Rosamond . . . In Rosamond's romance, it was not necessary to imagine much about the inward life of the hero, or of his serious business in the world" (114). Reading the engagement scene (208) carefully, it is apparent that it comes about through a series of misunderstandings about what the other is thinking. Rosamond was "keenly hurt by Lydgate's manner," which was simply the result of embarrassment. The long-term result is predictable: "Between him and her indeed there was that total missing of each other's mental track, which is too evidently possible even between persons who are continually thinking of each other" (405). As his money troubles grow, Lydgate decides to try to make their relationship intermental, to bring about a meeting of minds, and he fails. "Perhaps Lydgate and she had never felt so far off each other before" (409). He refers to the possibility of making the marriage an intermental unit, when he suggests that "there are things which husband and wife must think of together" (410). But this never happens. During the crisis, "He did not speak to her on the subject, and of course she could not speak to him" (522). The narrator concludes, "The beginning of mutual understanding and resolve seemed as far off as ever; nay it seemed blocked out by the sense of unsuccessful effort" (524).

It does not help the accuracy of Lydgate's double cognitive narrative of Rosamond that she is so adept at dramaturgical action. Even at an early stage in their relationship she calculates well what kind of behavior will attract him. "In two minutes he was in the room, and Rosamond went out, after waiting just long enough to show a pretty anxiety conflicting with her sense of what was becoming" (180). Later, she is still careful to control Lydgate's image of her: "Rosamond, however, was on her side much occupied with conjectures, though her quick, imitative perception warned her against betraying them too crudely" (244). During the crisis, her *private* impression management becomes rather more perfunctory: "She received his kiss and returned it faintly, and in this way an appearance of accord was recovered for the time" (413). However, her *public* impression management is studied and elaborate. During a party, "Rosamond was perfectly graceful and calm, and only a subtle observation . . . would have perceived the total absence of that interest in her husband's presence which a loving wife is sure to betray, even if etiquette keeps her aloof from him . . . In reality, however, she was intensely aware of Lydgate's voice and movements; and her pretty good-tempered air of unconsciousness was a studied negation by which she satisfied her inward opposition to him without compromise of propriety" (443).

Rosamond constructs a double cognitive narrative of Lydgate that owes far more to the emotional needs of *her* mind than to the actual workings of *his*. They meet and she is attracted: "Yet this result, which she took to be a mutual impression, called falling in love, was just what Rosamond had contemplated beforehand" (80). "Rosamond, in fact, was entirely occupied not exactly with Tertius Lydgate as he was in himself, but with his relation to her" (115). Later, looking back, and making explicit the existence of different Lydgates, the narrator comments that "the Lydgate with whom she had been in love had been a group of airy conditions for her" (457). When the problems arise, her reaction is predictable: "The thought in her mind was that if she had known how Lydgate would behave, she would never have married him" (412). "In her secret soul she was utterly aloof from him" (448). "Open-minded as she was [about the bribe allegation], she nevertheless shrank from the words which would have expressed their mutual consciousness, as she would have shrunk from flakes of fire" (518). "Even this trouble, like the rest, she seemed to regard as if it were hers alone. He was always to her a being apart, doing what she objected to" (523). Her solipsism even extends to the class implications of having Lydgate as a husband: "She was so intensely conscious of having a cousin who was a baronet's son staying in the house, that she imagined the knowledge of what was implied by his presence to be diffused through all other minds" (401). To summarize, the narrator comments that "she had been little used to imagining other people's states of mind except as a material cut into shape by her own wishes" (536). "It seemed that she had no more identified herself with him than if they had been creatures of different species and opposing interests" (412).

The narrator is kinder to Lydgate and acknowledges that he makes an effort to understand Rosamond's mind. But there are difficulties: "Perhaps it was not possible for Lydgate, under the double stress of outward material difficulty and of his own proud resistance to humiliating consequences, to imagine fully what this sudden trial was to a young creature who had known nothing but indulgence" (411). Nevertheless, "he had made many efforts to draw her into sympathy with him about possible measures for narrowing their expenses" (448). He suggests that "We two can do with only one servant" (448). Lydgate then acknowledges the distance between their narratives: "To many women the look Lydgate cast at her would have been more terrible than one of anger: it had in it a despairing acceptance of the distance she was placing between them" (412). Regarding the relationship between Dorothea and Ladislaw, "It was significant of the separateness between Lydgate's mind and Rosamond's that he had no impulse to speak to her on the subject; indeed, he did not quite trust her reticence toward Will. And he was right there; though he had no vision of the way in which her mind would act in urging her to speak" (414). The attribution is interesting here. He correctly assumes that she will speak to Ladislaw, but does not know about the thought processes that will lead her to do so.

In the end, he renounces thoughts of an "ideal wife" and begins to plan the adjustments necessary for living with his real one. He has to ensure that his double cognitive narrative will correspond more closely in the future to her actual narrative. As if to compensate, he fantasizes about a virtual intermental unit: "he was beginning now to imagine how two creatures who loved each other, and had a stock of thoughts in common, might laugh over their shabby furniture, and their calculations how far they could afford butter and eggs" (484). It is a poignant and rather moving fact about the novel that the only references that I can find to Lydgate's and Rosamond's joint actions are these hypothetical or imaginary situations regarding making do with one servant, laughing over their furniture, and calculating what they could afford. This married couple shares no *actual* joint actions within the reality of their storyworld.

CONCLUSION

I would like to end with a reminder that I am not saying that the minds that compose a particular intermental unit necessarily fuse completely and become totally available to each other. Toward the end of the novel, Dorothea realizes that she and Rosamond "could never be together again with the same thrilling consciousness of yesterday within them both. She felt the relation between them to be peculiar enough to give her a peculiar influence, though she had no conception that the way in which her own feelings were involved was fully known to Mrs Lydgate" (549). There was an intermental moment between them, but it was not a complete fusion. They now have different understandings of the event. The three statesmen mentioned in the example from *Vile Bodies* that was used in the previous chapter are hiding together, but they may be doing so for different reasons, and may even have misunderstood the reasons of the others for wanting to hide. Intermental units are fuzzy.

CHAPTER 4

Little Dorrit

SOCIAL MINDS IN *LITTLE DORRIT*

*I*T IS COMMON, when reading discussions of the sustained inside views of characters' private minds in the novels of, say, Henry James, to be told that, by contrast, characters in novels by Charles Dickens are really only ever seen from the outside. We only see their surface. They are flat when they should be round. The effect is often to sound rather patronizing about Dickens's achievement: "Brilliant novelist in his way, of course, but without the *depth* of James!" I would like to reverse that perspective. In cognitive terms, nearly all of your life is spent on the surface, on the outside, in the sense that all of the minds with which you are involved (with the admittedly rather important exception of your own!) are only ever experienced on the surface, and from the outside. From this point of view, it is not surprising that Oscar Wilde said, as quoted at the beginning of this book, that it is only shallow people who do not judge by appearances, and that the true mystery of the world is the visible, not the invisible. Dickens is the novelist of appearances, and of the visible, and his achievement can only be fully appreciated from the externalist perspective.

Intramental Thought

There are few extended passages of inside views of private thought in *Little Dorrit*. One such is a long passage of Clennam's inner speech regarding his love for Minnie Gowin (more usually referred to as "Pet") and his concern about growing old: "And he had plenty of unsettled subjects to meditate upon . . . First, there was the subject seldom absent from his mind, the question, what he was to do henceforth in life" (231). However, in addition to these passages, there is a good deal of contextual thought report scattered around the rest of the text relating to private thinking. This intramental thought benefits from an externalist perspective just as much as intermental thought does. To illustrate, I will draw attention to three of the features of intramental thought that are undervalued by the internalist perspective.

First, it is worth questioning for a moment the apparent inaccessibility of private thought to others. How much mental functioning is there in the novel that at least one other character is not aware of, albeit in general terms? The answer that I would suggest is: not much. Regarding the passage quoted from just now, Little Dorrit for one is aware of Clennam's feelings. She knows immediately that something is wrong with Clennam after he gives up thoughts of Pet, and she knows about his anxieties about growing old. "He never thought that she saw in him what no one else could see" (432). When asking this question of each character in turn ("Does another character know about how their mind works?"), I am struck by the public nature of the thought in the novel. Characters may have their secrets, such as Little Dorrit's love for Clennam, but in most cases their thought is generally public. Miss Wade is obviously secretive by nature, but she reveals her mind to Clennam by showing him her life story. The minds of Frederick Dorrit and Mr F.'s Aunt are pretty inaccessible (and perhaps Casby's and Flintwinch's to some extent?), but there are few others, it seems to me.

Second, intramental thought is intensely dialogic. In a splendidly Bakhtinian phrase that is used of Mrs Clennam, "It was curious how she seized the occasion to argue with some invisible opponent" (407). In a form of words that brings to mind Daniel Dennett's notion of mind-ruts, Mrs General is described as having "a little circular set of mental grooves or rails on which she started little trains of other people's opinions" (503). The point is that it is *other people's* opinions that are running along her mind-grooves. The private thoughts of Mrs Clennam and Mrs General, in common with all of the other characters in the novel, are filled with the thoughts of others.

Finally, the presence of intermental thought is often concealed within descriptions of intramental functioning. "From the days of their honeymoon, Minnie Gowan felt sensible of being usually regarded as the wife of a man who had made a descent in marrying her" (541). At first reading, this sounds like a simple example of intramental contextual thought report. However, her dialogic anticipation of the feelings of others contains an intermental component which, using the technique that was noted in the discussion of the opening passage of *Middlemarch,* is disguised within a passive construction ("regarded as"). It may be decoded as follows: the group of people who know her regard her (Pet thinks) as that sort of wife. When Miss Wade is part of the quarantine party at the beginning of the novel, the narrator says of her: "And yet it would have been as difficult as ever to say, positively, whether she avoided the rest, or was avoided" (62). Although this is a statement about Miss Wade's disposition to be unsociable, it is also about the shared functioning of "the rest": their awareness of her disposition and their resulting behavior in avoiding her. Similarly, it is said of Little Dorrit that "She passed to and fro in it [the Marshalsea] shrinkingly now, with a womanly consciousness that she was pointed out to every one" (118). This is a description of her state of mind, but it also refers to the joint state of mind of the prison population in considering her the Child of the Marshalsea that results in the communal pointing behavior. The externalist perspective is required in order to tease out the intermental element in sentences that appear to be simply presentations of private thought. And, as in *Middlemarch,* these examples show that much of the purpose of the narrative is to question the accuracy and authority of the collective judgments on the individuals who are experiencing the intermental gaze. The issue of accuracy in particular brings us to unreadability, or, at the very least, the possibility of incomplete, inaccurate, or otherwise defective reading of other minds.

As I have said, some characters tend to be difficult to read. Much is made of Flintwinch's impassivity and impenetrability. Despite being physically pushed about by Blandois, he "bought himself up with a face completely unchanged in its stolidity" (602). When Mr Casby is questioned by Clennam about Miss Wade, being determined to tell him nothing of what he knows about her, he "knew his strength lay in silence" (594). When Miss Wade herself is similarly intent on revealing nothing of her mind, she "stood by the table so perfectly composed and still after this acknowledgement of his remark that Mr Meagles stared at her under a sort of fascination, and could not even look to Clennam to make another move" (376). This is a vivid illustration of the importance of publicly available cues when reading other minds. When those cues are missing, as when Miss Wade deliberately eliminates them to order to keep her thoughts hidden and makes use of "her distant, proud, and self-secluded manner" (719), then Meagles is at a loss to know how to deal with it. Miss Wade herself thinks that she is able to read other minds accurately: "From a very early age I have detected what those about me thought they hid from me" (725). However, it is apparent from the context that she was frequently wrong, and was simply misinterpreting genuine kindness. On a more amusing level, the workings of Mr F.'s Aunt's mind are, mercifully perhaps, completely opaque: "Mr F.'s Aunt may have thrown in these observations on some system of her own, and it may have been ingenious, or even subtle: but the key to it was wanted" (199).

Visible Thought

More typical of the novel, though, are the copious examples of thought that is easily available to others. Even a solipsistic character such as Mr Dorrit is able to notice when Merdle is out of sorts (674). The fairly unobservant Young John Chivery knows that Little Dorrit is in love with Clennam, and can make a remark to Clennam such as "I *see* you recollect the room, Mr Clennam?" (791; my emphasis). Even reserved characters such as Miss Wade are not always able to conceal their thoughts. During a discussion with Clennam, "She heard him with evident surprise, and with more marks of suppressed interest than he had *seen* in her" (719; my emphasis). This is a novel in which the visibility of thought is frequently and pointedly emphasized. When Pancks gives a glass of wine to Blandois, it is "not without a *visible* conflict of feeling on the question of throwing it at his head" (814; my emphasis). The narrator mocks the efforts made by Merdle and Lord Decimus to keep their thoughts secret. They move about at their dinner party, "each with an absurd pretence of not having the other on his mind, which could not have been more transparently ridiculous though his real mind had been chalked on his back" (624).

This visibility is a characteristic not only of the specific mental events that occur in the minds of characters but also of the dispositions that persist over time and that form part of their personality. Blandois' selfishness is made visible by the way in which he moves around a room soiling the furniture (402). In a particularly vivid image, when Clennam watches Gowan while he is unawares, "There was something in his way of spurning [stones] out of their places with his heel, and getting them into the required position, that Clennam thought had an air of cruelty in it" (245). The externalist Dickens is particularly adept at observing the surface of the storyworld in order to create telling descriptions of small, inconsequential examples of behavior that appear to other characters and also to the reader to sum up the personality of the character performing the action.

Characters pass judgments, often spiteful but accurate, that are based on their ability to see other characters' personalities in action. Fanny says of her loved one, Sparkler, "If it's possible—and it generally is—to do a foolish thing, he is sure to do it" (664). Fanny is again perceptive, this time in judging Mrs General's mind by her mannerisms: "*I know her sly manner of feeling her way with those gloves of hers*" (666). Flintwinch is another character whose disposition is to be unsparing about the failings of others. He says of Clennam's father, "He was an undecided, irresolute chap, who had everything but his orphan life scared out of him when he was young" (224). At the end of the novel, he shouts to Mrs Clennam, "But that's the way you cheat yourself" (851). In each case, dispositions link specific mental events and actions (doing foolish, sly, irresolute, or dishonest things) to those characters' stable, long-lasting personalities (being a foolish, sly, irresolute, or dishonest person). Occasionally, the insight that one character has into another extends beyond their dispositions and encompasses their whole mind. Miss Wade feels that Gowan knows her completely, all about how her mind works. "He understood the state of things at a glance, and he understood me. He was the first person I had ever seen in my life who had understood me . . . He accompanied every movement of my mind" (732).

The Face

One of the obvious ways in which thought is made public is by means of the face. As we do in real life, characters pick up cues about the mental functioning of others by reading facial expressions. Of course, this is only one means among many. At one point, Blandois does not need to see Clennam's face; he knows what he is thinking simply by watching the back of his head: "Though Clennam's back was turned while [Blandois] spoke . . . he kept those glittering eyes of his . . . upon him, and evidently saw in the very carriage of the head . . . that he was saying nothing which Clennam did not already know" (819). Nevertheless, the face is a particularly important source of knowledge about the minds of others, and there is a continual stream of references in the novel to this fact. Some relate to individual mental events. Mrs Clennam says to Little Dorrit,"You love Arthur. (I can see the blush upon your face.)" (859). Clennam "saw a shade of disappointment on [Mrs Plornish's] face, as she checked a sigh, and looked at the low fire" (178). "There was an expression in his face [Blandois] as he released his grip of his friend's [Cavalletto's] jaw, from which his friend inferred that . . . [et cetera]" (174). "'My God!' said Bar, starting back, and clapping his hand upon the other's breast. '. . . I see it in your face'" (773). On other occasions, the face is seen as an indicator of long-term dispositions. When Clennam was a child, Mrs

Clennam could see him looking at her "with his mother's face" (859) and therefore knows that he will, as she thinks, take after her. Little Dorrit is able to see that "there was neither happiness nor health in the face that turned to her" (857). The narrator comments of Mr Chivery that, "As to any key to his inner knowledge being to be found in his face, the Marshalsea key was as legible as an index to the individual characters and histories upon which it was turned" (346). Changes in the flow of events can be signaled by changes in characters' faces. In the climax of the novel, Mrs Clennam's face is, at first, as inscrutable as ever: "Her face neither acquiesced or demurred" (837), and "Her face was ever frowning, attentive, and settled" (839). However, as events unravel and get beyond her control, "Mrs Clennam's face had changed. There was a remarkable darkness of colour on it, and the brow was more contracted" (841).

Many of the most powerful moments in the novel involve descriptions of facial expressions. In the scene in which Little Dorrit is meditating on London Bridge and is caught unawares by Young John Chivery, "She started and fell back from him, with an expression in her face of fright and something like dislike that caused him unutterable dismay . . . It was but a momentary look, inasmuch as she checked it . . . But she felt what it had been, as he felt what it had been; and they stood looking at one another equally confused" (260). Here, her facial expression inadvertently reveals her true feelings and both she and Young John are shocked by the result. In marked contrast, facial expressions can also serve a dramaturgical function. Characters self-consciously use them to present to the world the sort of self that they want the world to see. "With these words, and with a face expressive of many uneasy doubts and much anxious guardianship, he [Mr Dorrit] turned his regards upon the assembled company in the Lodge; so plainly indicating that his brother was to be pitied for not being under lock and key" (269). However, these efforts can be unsuccessful: "Do what he could to compose his face, he could not convey so much of an ordinary expression into it, but that the moment she saw it, she dropped her work and cried, 'Mr Clennam! What's the matter?'" (465). Characters are continually attempting to read faces as cues to action. Clennam "suffered a few people to pass him in whose face there was no encouragement to make the inquiry" (118). This face-reading may be only partially successful. A character may find out something of what another is thinking, but not the whole story. "As she [Little Dorrit] looked at him [Clennam] silently, there was something in her affectionate face that he did not quite comprehend: something that could have broken into tears in a moment, and yet that was happy and proud" (885). This example brings out the differences between characters and readers as interpreters of facial expressions. Here, Dickens's implied reader comprehends more than Clennam does. This balance between the implied reader and other characters is always present: sometimes characters and readers are equal, at times characters comprehend more than readers (at least initially), and at other times, as here, they comprehend less.

In addition, a facial expression can serve almost as the kind of nonverbal communication that is the subject of the next section. Clennam has difficulty following Mrs Plornish's train of thought because she is rather inarticulate: "He was at a loss to understand what she meant; and by expressing as much in his looks, elicited her explanation" (178).

Nonverbal Communication

Another way in which social minds are made publicly available to each other is through nonverbal communication. This may be defined as the intentional use of the body to communicate information. There is a surprisingly large amount of it in the novel. It generally occurs between characters who know each other well and who therefore form an intermental unit. An example is the Dorrit family. Little Dorrit "looked in amazement at her sister and would have asked a question, but that Fanny with a warning frown pointed to a curtained doorway of communication with another room" (284). Tip "asked her the question with a sly glance of observation at Miss Fanny, and at his father too" (505). He also gives Fanny "a slight nod and a slight wink; in acknowledgement of which, Miss Fanny looked surprised, and laughed and reddened" (536). Within such a unit, nonverbal communication is an efficient supplement to speech. "In answer to Cavalletto's look of inquiry, Clennam made him a sign to go; but he added aloud, 'unless you are afraid of him.' Cavalletto replied with a very emphatic finger-negative, 'No, master'" (821). This is a cooperative, beneficial unit. Fanny and Mrs General form a conflicted, competitive unit but the signing is just as efficacious. When "Miss Fanny coughed, as much as to say, 'You are right'" (661), Mrs General knows exactly what she means.

The choreography of the nonverbal communication in this novel is beautifully judged and often extremely subtle. So much so that the absence of any sign can sometimes be sign enough. Within people of the same social class, who understand each other well, the significance of doing nothing can be well understood. "Ferdinand Barnacle looked knowingly at Bar as he strolled upstairs and gave him no answer at all. 'Just so, just so,' said Bar, nodding his head" (614). In addition, a refusal to admit to an understanding of nonverbal signs can be as significant. Plornish, "having intimated that he wished to speak to her [Little Dorrit] privately, in a series of coughs so very noticeable" (326) that Mr Dorrit must be aware of their meaning, Mr Dorrit nevertheless refuses to admit that he understands Plornish. To do so would be an admission that he knows that Little Dorrit works to support him. At the end of the novel, Mrs Clennam is reduced to a cruel parody of communication. "Except that she could move her eyes and faintly express a negative and affirmative with her head, she lived and died a statue" (863).

One example of the absence of a sign is worth dwelling on because it raises interesting issues relating to the concept of action. Meagles tactlessly praises Gowan's connections with the Barnacles in Doyce's presence. "Clennam looked at Doyce, but Doyce knew all about it beforehand, and looked at his plate, and made no sign, and said no word" (248). It is clear from the rhythm of the prose, the emphasis of each clause, that Doyce makes a conscious decision to do nothing. But this decision differs little, in cognitive terms, from a decision to perform an actual physical action. In addition, it must be remembered that this is a social situation in which certain actions are expected, such as showing interest by nodding, smiling, and agreeing. Doyce's refusal to do any of these things is a nonaction that has a dramaturgical function. He is demonstrating that he is unhappy with Meagles's remarks. But who is he demonstrating this disapproval for? I would suggest that it is primarily for Clennam, who may well be expecting disapproval-action, but will also pick up on the significance of nonaction. To an extent, also, it is for Meagles too, who will perhaps insensitively be expecting approval-action, but may, perhaps Doyce is hoping, interpret the nonaction as approval. In effect, Doyce is doing nothing in order to manage these conflicting expectations. Again, characters' interpretations and readers' interpretations will differ. The reader will know immediately what Doyce means; Clennam will pick up on it pretty quickly; Meagles is, Doyce will anticipate, likely to misunderstand the silence.

The pair formed by Clennam and Pancks may, at first sight, appear to be a distinctly unpromising illustration of the use of signs within an intermental unit. I referred above to characters with inscrutable faces, and Pancks is one. "With his former doubt whether this dry hard personage were quite in earnest, Clennam again turned his eyes attentively upon his face. It was as scrubby and dingy as ever, and as eager and quick as ever, and he could see nothing lurking in it that was at all expressive of a latent mockery that had seemed to strike upon his ear in the voice" (322). When Pancks speaks highly of Casby, "Arthur for his life could not have said with confidence whether Pancks really thought so or not" (462). The difficulty that Clennam has in reading Pancks's mind becomes particularly important when Clennam does not know whether Pancks's interest in the history of the Dorrit family is well meant or not. His activities "caused Arthur Clennam much uneasiness at this period" (367), and "awakened many wondering speculations in his mind" (323).

However, over time, Clennam comes to know Pancks's mind better. "Between this eccentric personage and Clennam, a tacit understanding and accord had been always improving . . . Though he had never before made any profession or protestation to Clennam, and though what he had just said was little enough as to the words in which it was expressed, Clennam had long had a growing belief that Mr Pancks, in his own odd way, was becoming attached to him" (637). Note the emphasis on the fact that their relationship does not rely on words. During the conversation in which Pancks tempts Clennam to speculate (638–43), much is understood, or partly understood, between the two men, but little is actually said. It is not even explicitly stated that Pancks has been successful in persuading Clennam to invest in Merdle. Later, the understanding between Clennam and Pancks becomes sufficiently intermental for them to be able to communicate by signs. "Mr Pancks in shaking hands merely scratched his eyebrow with his left forefinger and snorted once, but Clennam, who understood him better now than of old, comprehended that he had almost done for the evening and wished to say a word to him outside" (594). When outside, "Arthur thought he received his cue to speak to him as one who knew pretty well what had just now passed" (595). However, the resulting conversation demonstrates that the efficiency of intermental thought should not be overestimated. Misreadings can occur. When Pancks says that he wants to take a razor to Casby (in fact, to cut his hair), Clennam thinks that he wants to cut his throat!

The Look

A subcategory of the emphasis on the importance of the face is the significance of the look. For minds to be public and available, it is necessary for characters to look attentively at each other in order to pick up the sorts of cues that I have been describing. This may even require staring at the other person. In fact, there is a noticeable preponderance in the text of those three words, *attentive*, *look*, and *stare*. Table 4.1 sets out some comparative usages for these words and their variants in four novels: *Persuasion*, *Little Dorrit*, *Middlemarch*, and Henry James's *The Ambassadors*. The numbers in parentheses are adjusted to take account of the total length of the text: that is, the figures for *The Ambassadors* are doubled because it is approximately half the length of *Little Dorrit* and *Middlemarch*; and the figures for *Persuasion* are quadrupled because it is approximately a quarter of their length. The information is taken from the invaluable *Victorian Literary Studies Archive*

TABLE 4.1

	PERSUASION	LITTLE DORRIT	MIDDLEMARCH	AMBASSADORS
Total word length	84,000	345,000	324,000	170,000
Attention	27 (108)	60	42	19 (38)
Attentive	6 (24)	21	4	4 (8)
Attentively	1 (4)	11	0	1 (2)
TOTALS	34 (136)	92	46	24 (48)
Look	56 (224)	331	242	105 (206)
Looks	14 (56)	35	31	7 (14)
Looked	42 (168)	367	230	137 (274)
Looking	45 (180)	281	265	42 (84)
TOTALS	157 (628)	1014	768	291 (578)
Stare	0 (0)	16	6	8 (16)
Stares	1 (4)	0	1	1 (2)
Stared	0 (0)	16	7	16 (32)
Staring	2 (8)	32	8	2 (4)
TOTALS	3 (12)	64	22	27 (54)

Web site (http://victorian.lang.nagoya-u.ac.jp/concordance.html). The differences in usage are significant. *Little Dorrit* scores higher than the other three novels in every case but one, and usually by a substantial margin. (The only exception is the number of attention words in *Persuasion*.)

In *Little Dorrit,* the act of looking fulfills a number of different functions. The list that follows is a selection. Some of the quotations from the text that are used elsewhere in this chapter reveal other uses of the look. Some of the following examples could equally well have been used to illustrate other functions.

- *Information-seeking:* "Monsieur Rigaud's eyes . . . were so drawn in that direction that [Cavalletto] more than once followed them to and back from the pavement in some surprise" (46).
- *Information-giving:* When Mrs Clennam talks to Clennam, "Her emphasis had been derived from her eyes quite as much as from the stress she laid on her words" (747). "Their looks met. Something thoughtfully apprehensive in [Pet's] large, soft eyes, had checked Little

Dorrit in an instant" (544).
- *Warning:* "To Arthur's increased surprise, Mistress Affery, stretching her eyes wide at himself, as if in warning that this [Blandois] was not a gentleman for him to interfere with" (599).
- *Thanking:* "Mother, with a look which thanked Clennam in a manner agreeable to him" (581).
- *Expressing curiosity:* Blandois and Mrs Clennam "looked very closely at one another. That was but natural curiosity" (403).
- *Bonding:* "There was a silent understanding between them [Little Dorrit and Pet] . . . She looked at Mrs Gowan with keen and unabated interest" (544).
- *Intimidating:* Flintwinch says to Mrs Clennam, "Now, I know what you mean by opening your eyes so wide at me" (850).
- *Controlling:* "As Mrs Clennam never removed her eyes from Blandois . . . so Jeremiah never removed his from Arthur" (602).

The use of the look can be an important element in a character's whole personality. Little Dorrit looks at Clennam "with all the earnestness of her soul looking steadily out of her eyes" (214). The look is often expressive of the attitude of the looker toward the "lookee." "The visitor [Miss Wade] stood looking at her [Tattycoram] with a strange *attentive* smile. It was wonderful to see the fury of the contest in the girl, and the bodily struggle she made as if she were rent by the Demons of old" (65; my emphasis). "Mrs Clennam and Jeremiah had exchanged a look; and had then looked, and looked still, at Affery" (834). However, it can sometimes be that the accusation of staring is more informative about the uneasy state of mind of the "staree" than it is about the alleged starer. Miss Wade refers to someone in her past who "had a serious way with her eyes of watching me" (727). Fanny unfairly reproaches Little Dorrit for staring at her (665), and Mr Dorrit thinks that the Chief Butler looks at him "in a manner that Mr Dorrit considered questionable" (678). When Mr Dorrit's mind is collapsing and "his daughter had been observant of him with something more than her usual interest," he demands peevishly, "Amy, what are you looking at?" (701).

The mechanics are interesting to observe. A look may be combined with the nonverbal communication discussed above: Clennam, "more with his eyes than by the slight impulsive motion of his hand, entreated her [Little Dorrit] to be reassured and to trust him" (121). Characters sometimes see significance in an exchange of looks by others. When Pancks comes to break the news of the Dorrit wealth, "The excitement of this strange creature was fast communicating itself to Clennam. Little Dorrit with amazement, saw this, and observed that they exchanged quick looks" (437). Characters are frequently uncomfortably aware of being the subject of a stare. When Mr

Dorrit goes to see Mrs Clennam, "he felt that the eyes of Mr Flintwinch and of Mrs Clennam were on him. He found, when he looked up, that this sensation was not a fanciful one" (686). Mrs Clennam (perhaps the major starer in the novel) "sat looking at her until she attracted her attention. Little Dorrit coloured under such a gaze, and looked down" (390). Flintwinch comments drily to Clennam, "You'll be able to take my likeness, the next time you call, Arthur, I should think" (744). Clennam is comically uncomfortable with a look from Flora: "In his ridiculous distress, Clennam received another of the old glances without in the least knowing what to do with it" (194). Occasionally, a look can be so compelling that the lookee has to return it. "Throughout he [Blandois] looked at her [Little Dorrit]. Once attracted by his peculiar eyes, she could not remove her own, and they had looked at each other all the time" (546). Mr F.'s Aunt "looked at Clennam with an expression of such intense severity that he felt obliged to look at her in return, against his personal inclinations." "None of your eyes at me," she scolds him (590).

Physically Distributed Cognition

I explained in chapter 2 that the term *physically distributed cognition* refers, as Daniel Dennett says, to our habit of off-loading as much as possible of our cognitive tasks into our environment. Dickens, in keeping with his absorption in the surface, and therefore physical, nature of thought, was acutely aware of this phenomenon. Consider again the passage quoted in my opening chapter in which Meagles comes close to saying that the information that Miss Wade lives in Park Lane is literally contained in the Meagles's family house. Mrs Clennam's house is another example of this sort of cognition. Take this description of her room, which she has not left for many years: "Yet there was a nameless air of preparation in the room, as if it were strung up for an occasion. From what the room derived it . . . no one could have said without looking *attentively* at its mistress, and that, too, with a previous knowledge of her face" (832; my emphasis).

Characters can suffer when taken out of their physically distributed network or when their environment is disrupted. Affery is "sensible of the danger in which her identity stood" (405) partly because of the menacing noises that she hears in Mrs Clennam's house (which are eventually explained by its collapse). At the climax of the novel, when Mrs Clennam leaves her room, she is "made giddy by the turbulent irruption of this multitude of staring faces into her cell of years, by the confusing sensation of being in the air, and the yet more confusing sensation of being afoot, by the unexpected changes in half-remembered objects" (856). Disoriented by the sudden absence of her physically distributed cognitive network, Mrs Clennam behaves so strangely while she is stumbling to the Marshalsea to see Little Dorrit that people in the streets think she is mad. The most extreme example is Mr Dorrit, who, after his release from the Marshalsea prison, never loses the feelings of discomfort and unease that he experiences while trying to cope with the absence of that familiar environment. His mind eventually gives way under the pressure. During his breakdown, Mr Dorrit "looked about him, as if the association were so strong that he needed reassurance from his sense of sight that they were not in the old prison-room" (702). Afterwards, "from that hour his poor maimed spirit, only remembering the place where it had broken its wings, cancelled the dream through which it had since groped, and knew of nothing beyond the Marshalsea" (710). Interestingly, Little Dorrit also suffers from the same syndrome, albeit, of course, in a much milder form. She is described as "quite displaced even from the last point of the old standing ground in life on which her feet had lingered" (517). Life in Rome for her "greatly resembled a superior sort of Marshalsea" (565). She has the insight to be aware of what is happening to her and writes to Clennam that "These new countries and wonderful sights . . . are very beautiful, and they astonish me, but I am not collected enough—not familiar enough with myself, if you can quite understand what I mean—to have all the pleasure in them that I might have" (522).

In addition, I cannot resist adding (at the suggestion of Porter Abbott) an extraordinary example of physically distributed cognition from a different Dickens novel, *Hard Times* (1854): "'I think there's a pain somewhere in the room,' said Mrs Gradgrind [on her deathbed], 'but I couldn't positively say that I have got it'" (193).

Large Intermental Units

The large units in *Little Dorrit* include the speculators, the Marshalsea, and "Society." The speculators who invest in Merdle and are subsequently ruined by him are always referred to as an intermental unit, even though, like most large units, it is necessarily an ill-defined set composed of individuals who have bought into Merdle to varying extents. "All people knew (or thought they knew) that he had made himself immensely rich" (611). "Nobody . . . knew what he had done; but everybody knew him to be the greatest that had appeared" (627). When explanations for Merdle's death are sought, the entirely spurious physical condition of "pressure" is decided upon, and, in an interesting echo of the language that is used in *Middlemarch,* the narrator remarks that this is "entirely satisfactory to the public mind" (775). In a chilling analysis of the working of this type of intermental thought, one that lies behind the exploitative functioning of the medium-sized units of the Barnacle family and the Circumlocution Office, Ferdinand Barnacle remarks to Clennam when he visits him in the Marshalsea, "Pardon me, but I think you really have no idea how the human bees will swarm to the beating of any old tin kettle; in that fact lies the complete manual of governing them" (807).

The intermental unit of the Marshalsea prison is referred to by the narrator as *the collegians,* as in "the Collegians were not envious" of the Dorrit family's newfound wealth (475). It has a common view on Mr Dorrit in particular: "It was generally understood that you must deduct a few [years] from his account [of how long he has been in the prison]; he was vain, the fleeting generations of debtors said" (105). Clennam is able to read this shared mind. He notices that "It was evident from the general tone of the whole party, that they had come to regard insolvency as the normal state of mankind, and the payment of debts as a disease that occasionally broke out" (128). Distinctions can be made within units, and, when appropriate, subgroups may be delineated: "All the ladies in the prison had got hold of the news, and were in the yard . . . the gentleman prisoners, feeling themselves at a disadvantage, had for the most part retired" (101). Generally, the vision of intermental identity in *Little Dorrit* is rather different from that in *Middlemarch,* where the inhabitants of that town manage to retain their subjective individuality while being at the same time part of its group mind. But in the Dickens novel many of the descriptions of joint thought are relentlessly negative and despairing. This is a world in which individuals have a tendency to become "human bees" who lose their identity and gain nothing in return: "There was a string of people already straggling in, whom it was not difficult to identify as the nondescript messengers, go-betweens and errand bearers of the place . . . All of them wore the cast off clothes of other men and women, were made up of patches and pieces of other people's individuality, and had no sartorial existence of their own proper" (131).

Turning to the other end of the social scale, it is a noteworthy feature of Mrs Merdle's conversational style that she constantly refers to the demands of "Society." This is the shorthand used for a network of different, overlapping subgroups such as the "Hampton Court Bohemians" (440) that Mrs Gowan belongs to, and "the Circumlocution Barnacles, who were the largest job-masters in the universe" (441). Gowan is well aware that he belongs to this network, remarking to Clennam that "I belong to a clan, or a clique, or a family, or a connection, or whatever you like to call it" (451). Mrs Merdle uses the mention of Society in order to enforce and reinforce ideological norms on others. However, it can be difficult for individuals to know how to put these norms into practice in particular circumstances. When Mr Merdle complains that he does not enjoy Society events, she points out that he has to pretend: "Seeming would be quite enough" (448). Similarly intermental difficulties tend to arise during crises. "On the first crash of the eminent Mr Merdle's decease, many important persons had been unable to determine whether they should cut Mrs Merdle, or comfort her" (873). Luckily for her, they choose the latter.

I mentioned above, in the sections on the expressiveness of the face, the use of nonverbal communication, and the importance of the attentive look, that much can be left unsaid when a character knows fairly well what another is thinking. This is true of cooperative and constructive intermental units such as Clennam's relationships with Pancks and Doyce, as well as more dysfunctional examples such as the relationship between Little Dorrit and her father. Here too, a good deal is often left unspoken. However, the unexpressed nature of much of the intermental functioning in the novel is even more apparent in the conflicted and destructive small units that exist within the norms established by the large unit of Society. These units are characterized by shared thought that is based on pretence and, in particular, on the pretence that intermental understanding is absent. On the contrary, though, these units rest on a network of shared assumptions that make their vicious verbal jousting possible.

Two of an entertaining bunch of examples are the relationships between Fanny and Mrs Merdle and between Fanny and Mrs General. In the former case, Fanny and Mrs Merdle understand each other so perfectly that the real subjects of their conversations need never be made explicit. It is in this way that the two of them spend the second half of the novel ("Riches") pretending that they never met in the first ("Rags"). Indeed, "The skilful manner in which [Mrs Merdle] and Fanny fenced with one another on the occasion almost made her quiet sister [Little Dorrit] wink" (566). In a good example of the competitive nature of encounters fought under the rules of Society, the discussion between Mr Dorrit and Mrs Merdle over the engagement between their offspring becomes a zero-sum game, a "skilful seesaw . . . so that each of them sent the other up, and each of them sent the other down, and neither had the advantage" (657). The conversation between Mrs Merdle and Mrs Gowan over the engagement between Gowan and Pet is a more cooperative affair, but is still governed by the same rules: "Knowing, however, what was expected of her, and perceiving the exact nature of the fiction to be nursed, she [Mrs Merdle] took it delicately in her arms, and put her required contribution of gloss upon it . . . And Mrs Gowan, who of course saw through her own threadbare blind perfectly, and who knew that Mrs Merdle saw through it perfectly, came out of this form, notwithstanding, as she had gone into it, with immense complacency and gravity" (444). What is happening here is that there is one apparent or surface intermental understanding that is based on a lie (the marriage is regrettable), while the real understanding (the marriage is to be welcomed) must never be explicitly acknowledged.

The Dorrit Family

One of the ways in which a group of people can be identified as an intermental unit is a strong sense among those people of being part of that group. Such a group often has a clearly defined self-image in the sense that it is important to its constituent individuals that they identify themselves as belonging to it. Some families are like this; others are not. The Dorrit family definitely has a strong self-image. During Frederick's unforgettable outburst to William in which he complains about the family's treatment of Little Dorrit, he refers to the "family credit" (538). Earlier, Mr Dorrit had "felt that the family dignity was struck at by an assassin's hand" (511). The same words, "family dignity," are used again several pages later (551). These phrases refer to the shared consciousness within the family of their alleged importance and social standing. They contain a strong sense of them and us, insiders and outsiders. The outsiders have to be made aware of the importance of the family name, and the insiders are uneasily aware of outsiders' skepticism on this point.

The following passage is a remarkable one. The word "family" is repeated four times in such quick succession that the phrases containing the word, and referring thereby to different aspects of the workings of the Dorrit intermental mind, comprise eleven words out of a total of forty-four. The passage attempts to convey by means of this repetition a sense of the creation of what may be termed the *family ideology:* "It was *the family custom* to lay it down as *family law,* that she was a plain domestic little creature, without the great and sage experience of the rest. *This family fiction* was *the family assertion* of itself against her services" (280; my emphasis). The background to the phrase quoted earlier about Mr Dorrit feeling that the family dignity had been struck at by an assassin's hand is that he is excessively self-conscious about the recent family history. Fanny knows well that it is "often running in his mind that other people are thinking about [the Marshalsea], while he is talking to them" (647). As with many intermental units, though, generalizations should be employed with care. This sort of cognitive functioning is complex. To repeat, most groups have a core membership but are looser around the edges. Significantly, Wittgenstein used the notion of family resemblances in the *Philosophical Investigations* to illustrate the fuzziness of concepts (1958, 32). The consciousness of the Dorrit family credit is shared by the core family of William, Fanny, and Tip. It is not characteristic of the other members who, for different reasons, are much more peripheral: Frederick and Little Dorrit.

The workings of the Dorrit mind in action are evident in characteristic shared patterns of behavior. These behavioral patterns can relate to individuals who are either inside or outside of the unit. The passage quoted above that referred to the family four times in three lines is a good illustration of the former. From an intramental point of view, Little Dorrit is referred to as "retiring," "unnoticed," "overlooked and forgotten" (all in one paragraph on page 337), and is regarded in Venice as "the little figure of the English girl who was always alone" (520) and who always "asked leave to be left alone" (519). However, much of this intramental shyness arises from her treatment by William, Fanny, and Tip. Its origins are intermental. It is laid down as family law that Little Dorrit is to be treated in a certain way, and should have a certain function within the unit as a plain domestic creature who does not possess their wisdom. It is a central element in the shared consciousness of the core family. Little Dorrit is intramentally aware of the place allotted her. It is stated that she "submitted herself to the family want in its greatness as she had submitted herself to the family want in its littleness" (556–57). Intermental cognitive functioning is often revealed in the joint actions that arise from these family dispositions to behave in certain ways. In the John Chivery affair, "Little Dorrit herself was the last person considered" (257). Of the triumphant leaving of the Marshalsea, the narrator states that "This going away was perhaps the very first action of their joint lives that they had got though without her" (480). And they fail spectacularly by completely forgetting her and leaving her behind.

Family customs can often reveal a lot about a family to outsiders. When Clennam hears Little Dorrit being praised by her uncle, Frederick Dorrit, he resents the family tone of voice: "Arthur fancied that he heard in these praises a certain tone of custom, which he had heard from the father last night with an inward protest and feeling of antagonism . . . He fancied that they viewed her, not as having risen away from the prison atmosphere, but as appertaining to it; as being vaguely what they had a right to expect, and nothing more" (134). It is quite common, I think, for outsiders being introduced to a family to see at a glance what is revealed by joint patterns of behavior: say, which members of it are excessively over- or undervalued. The narrator comments of the family treatment of Little Dorrit that "She took the place of eldest of the three, in all things but precedence; was the head of the fallen family; and bore, in her own heart, its anxieties and shames" (112). The narrator also describes Little Dorrit in the act of sighing by referring to "the whole family history in that sigh" (648). Both are moving descriptions of the ways in which individuals may acquire and internalize some of the characteristics of the intermental unit to which they belong, and how painful this internalization process can be.

Intermental units can also function in similarly characteristic ways toward individuals who are outside of the unit. Such mechanisms as scapegoating are powerful tools for defining group consciousness. William, Tip, and Fanny develop a common antagonism toward Clennam, based mainly on his skepticism toward their core value, the family credit. Fanny says of him that "He obtruded himself upon us in the first instance. We never wanted him" (507). Clennam is well aware of their shared hostility because of their unsubtle joint behavior and comes "to a clearer and keener perception of the place assigned him by the family" (573). Again, though, it should be stressed that the peripheral members do not share these communal attitudes. Little Dorrit is in love with him and it is doubtful whether Frederick has any view at all on the matter.

It is often rewarding to investigate the subunits that develop within an intermental unit because they tend both to illuminate and be illuminated by the social dynamics of the larger group. Within the relationship between Little Dorrit and her father, much is often left unspoken. They understand each other but do not make this knowledge of the other apparent: he because he is emotionally dishonest; she for reasons of delicacy and a reluctance to confront that dishonesty. "For a little while there was a dead silence and stillness" (271) between them, "They did not, as yet, look at one another" (272). In that silence, it is apparent that she knows that he has encouraged young John Chivery to court her for his own selfish purposes, he knows that she knows, she knows that he knows that she knows, and so on. Much of the relationship between father and daughter is expressed in terms of gesture: "To see her hand upon his arm in mute entreaty half-repressed, and her timid little shrinking figure turning away, was to see a sad, sad sight" (123). Like Fanny, Little Dorrit knows about how her father's mind works, in particular on the question of the family credit: "She felt that, in what he had just now said to her and in his whole bearing towards her, there was the well-known shadow of the Marshalsea wall" (530). As is to be expected over the course of a long narrative, their relationship changes: "From that time the protection that her wondering eyes had expressed towards him, became embodied in action, and the Child of the Marshalsea took upon herself a new relation towards the Father" (111). The shared cognitive functioning within this intermental pair is flawed, however, by his dishonesty. He pretends that there has been no change.

Fanny and Little Dorrit also form an intermental pair within the larger unit of the whole family. The latter is quick to pick up on behavioral cues from her sister: she "became aware that Fanny was more showy in manner than the occasion appeared to require" (549). As a consequence of their intimacy, Fanny shares secrets with her. She tells Little Dorrit how she always knows when a man is interested in her (558). She also explains in great detail the reasons why she and Mrs Merdle will pretend that they have not met before (551). When Fanny cries after telling her that she is engaged, "It was the last time Fanny ever showed that there was any hidden, suppressed, or conquered feeling in her on the matter" (654). From that time onward, her feelings will be hidden from others, but Amy will know of them, having been shown them once.

As shown in the discussion of large cognitive units, Fanny and Mrs Merdle understand each other so perfectly that the real subjects of their conversations need never be openly referred to. The relationship between Fanny and Mrs Merdle's son, Sparkler, is much less well balanced. Fanny toys with Sparkler, and her knowledge of his mind, such as it is, enables her to calibrate the torture perfectly. Her control over him, while enjoyable in itself, causes problems in terms of Fanny's acute awareness of the perceptions of others. "Miss Fanny was now in the difficult situation of being universally known [to be the object of Mr Sparkler's affections], and of not having dismissed Mr Sparkler . . . Hence she was sufficiently identified with the gentleman to feel compromised by his being more than usually ridiculous" (645). She is aware of the intermental consensus, presented in the passive voice, that identifies her relationship with Sparkler as a serious one. She knows that such a consensus can solidify quickly and cannot thereafter be easily changed. Fanny therefore jumps quickly to Sparkler's defense whenever Gowan ridicules him. The enslavement has consequences for Little Dorrit too, as she realizes how their two minds are working: "Thenceforward, Little Dorrit observed Mr Sparkler's treatment by his enslaver, with new reasons for attaching importance to all that passed between them" (651). "Little Dorrit began to think she detected some new understanding between Mr Sparkler and Fanny" (651). She notices that "Mr Sparkler's demeanor towards herself changed. It became fraternal" (652).

The bulk of this section has analyzed intermental units that are characterized by conflict, competition, exploitation, dishonesty, solipsism, and selfishness. The ideology of the Dorrit family credit, despite the complete absence of evidence for it, is imposed on others in order to devalue them. Their joint exploitation of, and dishonesty toward, Little Dorrit is morally reprehensible, as is their attempted scapegoating of Clennam. In addition, Fanny in particular forms conflicted and competitive pairings with others such as Mrs Merdle and Mrs General. This bleak picture is in stark contrast to the nature of the intermental unit formed by the relationship between Little Dorrit and Clennam, which is examined now.

Clennam and Little Dorrit

Intermental units can be approached in a number of different ways. One is simply to trace the development of the relationship as a whole over time. Another is to examine it in terms of the variation in focalization: in this case, the relationship is mostly focalized through Clennam. A third is to examine the degree of intermental thought: individuals may understand each other perfectly, imperfectly, or even (as with non-units such as Lydgate and Rosamond) not at all. It may be that different units will be illuminated by different sorts of approaches. In the case of Clennam and Little Dorrit, I will evaluate a few general aspects of their relationship before concentrating first on Clennam's knowledge of Little Dorrit's mind and then on her knowledge of his.

As the reader would expect of the central romance of the novel, Clennam and Little Dorrit share a good deal of their thinking: not all, but a good deal. The following excerpt from her letter to him gives a flavor of the complexity of the self-conscious theory of mind that is involved in their relationship: "It looked at first as if I was taking on myself to understand and explain so much . . . But . . . I felt more hopeful for your knowing at once that I had only been watchful for you, and had only noticed what I think I have noticed, because I was quickened by your interest in it" (608). This is written by someone who is well aware of the workings of her own mind and the mind of the one she loves, and how the two minds can function together. As is often the case, though, their mind reading is not perfect. A common characteristic of theory of mind involving two people who know each other well is that one will often know that something is wrong with the other, but not know precisely what: "She feared that he was blaming her in his mind for so devising to contrive for them, think for them, and watch over them, without their knowledge or gratitude; perhaps even with their reproaches for supposed neglect. But what was really in his mind, was the weak figure with its strong purpose" (211–12). In this case she knows that something is on his mind, but she is wrong about what it is. (As we will see, something similar happens with Anne Elliot and Wentworth.) Near the end of the novel, after they have been apart for some time, he sees something in her face although he does not know exactly what it is: "As she looked at him silently, there was something in her affectionate face that he did not quite comprehend: something that could have broken into tears in a moment, and yet that was happy and proud" (885).

There is a paradox that commonly arises in narratives with a comic structure. On the one hand, the central couple in a comedy often exhibits a high degree of intermentality. This is what one would expect when people are attracted to each other and are on the same wavelength. On the other hand, there is often a huge gap or blind spot in their joint mind reading that relates to the most important matter of all—their feelings for each other. In the case of this novel, Clennam does not know that Little Dorrit is in love with him; she does not know that Clennam is in love with her. "She was quicker to perceive the slightest matter here, than in any other case—but one" (544). There are interesting parallels here with the development of the relationships between Anne and Wentworth and Dorothea and Ladislaw. There is a certain logic to such intermental breakdowns in the relationships of lovers. It may be that they will have a tendency to put the other on a pedestal and think something along the lines of "he/she is so wonderful that he/she will not be interested in me."

Mind reading involves reading one's own mind as well as reading the minds of others, and both can be unreliable. Little Dorrit's first-person attribution is accurate because she knows that she is in love with Clennam. However, for the majority of the novel, Clennam is not aware of the most important fact about the working of his own mind: that he is in love with Little Dorrit. Efficient first-person attribution is as necessary as the third-person sort for successful participation in an intermental unit. For any unit of this sort to function properly, with a fair degree of accuracy and concern for the feelings of the other, the individuals within it have to try to come to a reasonable working knowledge of their own feelings as well as the feelings of the other in order to make informed and sensitive ethical judgments about how to behave. Clennam becomes aware that his feelings for Little Dorrit are complex, and this awareness leads him to exercise the sort of care in dealing with her feelings that I will be describing. Nevertheless, he sometimes hurts her because he does not yet know that he is in love with her or that she is in love with him. Toward the end of the novel, Clennam finds his private thoughts "remarkable" to him (787), suggesting that he is aware of the fallibility of introspection.

The issue of control often arises even within beneficial intermental units. There is evidence from the beginning of the novel that Clennam attempts to influence Little Dorrit's mind: "He wished to leave her with a reliance upon him, and to have something like a promise from her that she would cherish it" (140). He is concerned, though, that the Little Dorrit who exists in his mind may not be the one who exists in her own. "To make a domesticated fairy of her . . . would be but a weakness of his own fancy" (305). The feeling will not go away. "Something had made her keenly and additionally sensitive just now. Now, was there someone in the hopeless unattainable distance? Or had the suspicion been brought into his mind, by his own associations?" (309). Clennam is showing a sensitive awareness of his and her aspectuality. He is acutely conscious of the possibility that *his* Little Dorrit could become a "domesticated fairy" and thereby lose contact with what he thinks might be her own conception of herself. He knows that he is using her for his own emotional needs by creating an image of her in his mind that may not fit her own self-image. Importantly, he does not wish to do so. Unfortunately, though, he then overcompensates by talking about himself as much older than he is, and thus inadvertently hurts Little Dorrit's feelings. The narrator comments that he would not talk of himself as though he was old "If he had known the sharpness of the pain he caused the patient heart, in speaking thus!" (432). To make matters worse, Clennam does not realize that reinforcing the age gap by calling her a child is equally hurtful. "A slight shade of distress fell upon her, at his so often calling her a child. She was surprised that he should see it, or think such a slight thing" (208). Again, this may be a familiar sensation. Many of us have inadvertently hurt someone close to us by unsuccessfully trying to second-guess their feelings. As is said of Oedipa and Mucho, the married couple in Thomas Pynchon's *The Crying of Lot 49* (1966), "Like all their inabilities to communicate, this too had a virtuous motive" (30).

In any event, despite these difficulties, Clennam's theory of mind is, in ethical terms, far superior to that of the Dorrit family. In a number of passages early in the novel, we see Clennam fully understanding Little Dorrit's love for her father. "Evidently in observance of their nightly custom, she put some bread before herself, and touched his glass with her lips; but Arthur saw she was troubled and took nothing" (122). "He understood the emotion with which she said it, to arise in her father's behalf; and he respected it, and was silent" (126). "He gathered from a tremor on her lip, and a passing shadow of great agitation on her face, that her mind was with her father" (306). He is considerate about her poverty. "He was going to say so lightly clad, but stopped himself in what would have been a reference to her poverty" (208). Little Dorrit becomes aware that he knows her mind well. "'Can you guess,' said Little Dorrit . . . looking at him with all the earnestness of her soul looking steadily out of her eyes, 'what I am going to ask you not to do?'" (214). He guesses correctly that her request is to stop giving money to her father and brother. She tells him that "I know you will understand me if anybody can" (523). And she is right. "He saw the bright delight of her face, and the flush that kindled in it, with a feeling of shame . . . The same deep, timid earnestness that he had always seen in her, and never without emotion, he saw still" (826). Their nonverbal communication is noticeably efficient. "She started, coloured deeply, and turned white. The visitor, more with his eyes than by the slight impulsive motion of his hand, entreated her to be reassured and to trust him" (121). He can read her emotional behavior (starting and turning white); she can read the intention behind his gesture.

The following small detail beautifully encapsulates the closeness of their mind reading: "'Little Dorrit,' said Clennam; and the phrase had already begun, between these two, to stand for a hundred gentle phrases, according to the varying tone and connection in which it was used" (213). I think many readers of this book will have had personal experience of the use of a private language within a close relationship.

However, in a troubling and difficult scene, there is a breakdown in the communication between them. Little Dorrit confides that she does not understand why, after spending so long in the debtors prison, her father still has to pay off his debt before he is released. Clennam cannot understand why she does not understand that it is the honorable thing to do. The narrator remarks that "It was the first speck Clennam had ever seen, it was the last speck Clennam ever saw, of the prison atmosphere upon her" (472). I refer to this passage as troubling and difficult because it is possible that the ethical judgments made by most readers today would not necessarily be in line with Clennam's or the implied author's on this issue. My interpretation of this sentence, guided by its beautiful cadence, is that the implied reader is being invited by the implied author to identify with Clennam's disapproval. It may well be that the actual readers of Dickens's period would have been readier to accept that invitation than the actual readers of today, who may, I think, be more likely to regard Little Dorrit's question as, at the least, a reasonable one to ask. How is it, they might ask themselves, that people who *steal* money are penalized only once by the prison sentence and do not have to pay back the money, while people who *owe* money have to suffer both penalties? Because the actual reader may be at some distance from the implied reader in this case, the effect could be to make Clennam look heavy-handed and judgmental. In terms of readers' responses to *Little Dorrit,* the effect is rather paradoxical. A familiar criticism of Dickens is that he makes his heroines into saints. These days, we would like more imperfections. However, the "flaw" that he gives Little Dorrit in an attempt to humanize her is unlikely to be seen as such by modern readers.

As the bulk of the text is focalized through Clennam, there is less evidence of Little Dorrit's mind reading. Nevertheless, for large stretches of the novel, she is obviously well aware of Clennam's feelings. In addition to some of the examples given above, she knows immediately that something is wrong with Clennam after he gives up thoughts of Pet. She asks if he has been ill (431), and she knows about his anxieties about growing old. "He never thought that she saw in him what no one else could see" (432). There is a noticeable emphasis on the face in her mind-reading of Clennam. She can read his facial expressions with ease. "As she made the confession, timidly hesitating, she raised her eyes to the face, and read its expression so plainly that she answered it" (211). "Do what he could to compose his face, he could not convey so much of an ordinary expression into it, but that the moment she saw it, she dropped her work and cried, 'Mr Clennam! What's the matter?'" (465). Intermental units are not sealed off from the rest of the storyworld, and Little Dorrit is perceptive when she sees Clennam interacting with others. When Pancks comes to break the news of the Dorrit wealth, "The excitement of this strange creature was fast communicating itself to Clennam. Little Dorrit with amazement, saw this, and observed that they exchanged quick looks" (437). Knowledge of others can be contextual as well as relying on external indicators such as facial clues and signs. She understands his awareness of her feelings about her father because she knows the sort of person that he is. "Little Dorrit had a misgiving that he might blame her father" (208). I said earlier that William Dorrit is too frightened to recognize and acknowledge change in his relationship with Little Dorrit. This one is different. At the end of the novel, she realizes immediately that Clennam knows that it has altered. As a consequence, "He hesitated what to call her. She perceived it in an instant" (825), and reassures him that she still wishes to be known as "Little Dorrit."

Clennam and Mrs Clennam

This is a dysfunctional relationship in which there is evidence only of the most basic kind of intermental thinking. What they know about each other is the sort of person that the other is, their character or personality, their dispositions to behave in certain ways. He knows her to be cold, arrogant, and unbending. She knows him well enough to identify what she regards as weakness in him. But it is precisely this knowledge that fuels her hostility toward him and drives them further apart. Clennam knows that his mother has a secretive disposition and he guesses that she has a secret that might be connected in some way to Little Dorrit. But these are circumstantial or contextual guesses based on his knowledge of her character. They do not arise from any knowledge of her detailed thought processes as they occur in everyday contexts. Clennam is well aware that Mrs Clennam does not have any sort of intermental bond with him. "He touched the worsted muffling of her hand—that was nothing; if his mother had been sheathed in brass there would have been no new barrier between them" (76). As a sensitive man, he feels the lack of any connection deeply. In consequence he has little desire for her company: "He had no intention of presenting himself in his mother's dismal room that night, and could not have felt more depressed and cast away if he had been in a wilderness" (203). Clennam is watchful in her presence, forever unsuccessfully seeking clues to her state of mind. "Mrs Clennam glanced at her son, leaning against one of the windows. He observed the look" (92).

Clennam is a character who believes in social minds. For him, it is an ethical decision to be as open as possible in his cognitive functioning. He thinks that people should be capable of empathy and he tries to empathize with his mother: "A swift thought shot into his mind. In that long imprisonment here, and in her own long confinement to her room, did his mother find a balance to be struck" (129). What little knowledge he has of his mother's thought processes leads him to try to achieve a reconciliation with her. She rejects the offer. Indeed, the conflicted conversations that result reveal fresh complexities. "'You knew I would. You knew *me*' she interrupted. Her son paused for a moment. He had struck fire out of her, and was surprised" (87). Although she is acknowledging that he knows what sort of person she is, the key point is that he is surprised. He still does not know her well enough to be able to predict her emotional reactions. There is a lack of balance in that Clennam is trying to find a meeting of minds and his mother is not. His mother's rejection of an open relationship is echoed in the behavior of Gowan, which I will examine later. However, to put this relationship in context, it is worth noting that Mrs Clennam can be surprisingly sensitive to the thought processes of others. This seems particularly true of Little Dorrit. She tells her, "You love Arthur. (I can see the blush upon your face.)" (859). When Little Dorrit later recoils from her, she seems to care, responding, "Even now, I see *you* shrink from me, as if I had been cruel" (860).

Clennam and Flora

Clennam usually displays a sensitive awareness of the aspectuality of individuals and of the fact that identities are situated. I have mentioned that he is aware that he may be using Little Dorrit by creating an image of her in his mind that might not fit her own self-image in order to supply his own emotional needs. However, he is noticeably less aware of a similar sort of problem that arises in his relationship with Flora. For about twenty years, the image of Flora that is present in Clennam's mind is of the young Flora. This image takes no account of the passing of time. He neglects to make any adjustments to anticipate what an older Flora might be like. The inevitable happens. Clennam's previous, young Flora dies instantly as soon as he meets the older one. "Clennam's eyes no sooner fell upon the subject of his old passion than it shivered and broke to pieces" (191). Interestingly, Flora realizes what has happened. "'I know I am not what you expected, I know that very well." In the midst of her rapidity, she had found that out with the quick perception of a cleverer woman" (195). However, what is so amusing about Flora's character is that she keeps forgetting what she has so perceptively noticed. She keeps morphing into young Flora, thereby attempting to transform Clennam correspondingly into young Clennam. This, of course, causes the older Clennam great discomfort. "In his ridiculous distress, Clennam received another of the old glances without in the least knowing what to do with it" (194). However, Flora's sympathy for Little Dorrit and her wholehearted interest in Clennam's happiness eventually press her to stay in older-Flora character.

Flora's mental functioning is locked into a dialogical relationship with Clennam's. To use Gregory Bateson's formula as described in chapter 2, for increased explanatory power, the way to delineate Flora's cognitive system is to draw the limiting line so that you do not cut out anything that leaves things inexplicable. That means not leaving out of account either young Flora or older Flora, either Clennam's Flora or her own Flora. Together, these different Floras comprise her situated identity.

Mrs Clennam, Flintwinch, and Affery

The business partnership of Flintwinch and Mrs Clennam, frequently referred to by Affery as "the clever ones," is a fiercely conflicted and competitive relationship. Their conversations are games of chess that anyone overhearing would find difficult to follow (a sure sign of a high-functioning intermental unit). The closeness of their joint thinking is frequently emphasized by Flintwinch's recriminations during their regular arguments: "It doesn't matter whether you answer or not, because I know you are, and you know you are" (224). Flintwinch knows what she is thinking, she knows that he knows, he knows that she knows, and so on. Their minds are transparent to each other. He remarks to her, "Now, I know what you mean by opening your eyes so wide at me" (850). He even shouts at Mrs Clennam, "But that's the way you cheat yourself" (851). He is saying that his third-person attributions of her states of mind are more accurate and reliable than her own first-person ones. Nevertheless, despite these very real tensions, they form an alliance, knowing that they are stronger together than they are alone. "Perhaps this had originally been the mainspring of the understanding between them. Descrying thus much force of character in Mr Flintwinch, perhaps Mrs Clennam had deemed alliance with him worth her while" (225). Each uses his or her knowledge of the other's mind to further his or her own interests.

Both try to exercise control over others by their watchfulness, their use of the look. When Mr Dorrit goes to see Mrs Clennam, "he felt that the eyes of Mr Flintwinch and of Mrs Clennam were on him. He found, when he looked up, that this sensation was not a fanciful one" (686). "As Mrs Clennam never removed her eyes from Blandois . . . so Jeremiah never removed his from Arthur" (602). The power of the look is an outward manifestation of their control. This look is employed with regularity on Affery in order to subjugate her to their joint will: "Mrs Clennam and Jeremiah had exchanged a look; and had then looked, and looked still, at Affery" (834).

Both recognize that the other is a strong character. In a telling phrase, strongly reminiscent of Middlemarch's desire to swallow Lydgate whole, Flintwinch tells Mrs Clennam that "The peculiarity of my temper is, ma'am, that I won't be swallowed up alive" (224). When two people are in such a close relationship, to the point where it can be said that an intermental mind has been formed (even in the case of a conflicted unit such as this), the fear of being swallowed up, of losing one's individuality, can be a pressing one. This is, in fact, what happens to Affery. At a conference that I attended once, I noticed that one of my hosts was becoming uncomfortable with my talk of social minds and intermental units. When I pressed her she admitted as much, explaining that she found repugnant the idea of having her freedom as an independent individual curtailed by being in such a unit. By contrast, others will welcome the intimacy and love that can arise within them.

Intermental units are fluid. This one is sometimes a pair but, at other times, it becomes a trio, when "the clever ones" exercise their large degree of control over Affery's mind. Despite her sluggish intramental functioning, Affery, by her repeated use of this phrase, recognizes the strength of the intermental pair formed by Flintwinch and Mrs Clennam. She asks herself, "What's the use of considering? If them two clever ones have made up their minds to it, what's left for *me* to do? Nothing" (78). "But as 'them two clever ones'—Mrs Affery's perpetual reference, in whom her personality was swallowed up—were agreed to accept Little Dorrit as a matter of course, she had nothing for it but to follow suit" (94). Note the recurrence of the phrase "swallowed up" that was used by Flintwinch earlier. The difference is that Affery really is being swallowed up. The unit is so strongly defined that the narrator often drops the quotation marks: Affery is "held in very low account by the two clever ones, as a person, never of strong intellect, who was becoming foolish" (389). She is an example of a character who loses her intramental identity by being subsumed into an intermental unit that contains much stronger characters than her. She becomes as mysterious to herself as she is to others. "In the vagueness and indistinctness of all her new experiences and perceptions, as everything about her was mysterious to herself she began to be mysterious to others: and became as difficult to be made out to anyone's satisfaction as she found the house and everything in it difficult to make out to her own" (229). Because her personality really is being swallowed up, it is no surprise to be told that Affery is "sensible of the danger in which her identity stood" (405).

Clennam and Gowan

The relationship between Clennam and Gowan is a particularly interesting one. Although the two men form a conflicted unit, it differs from the equally conflicted "clever ones" because it is also unbalanced and asymmetrical. That is to say, it is Gowan who wishes it to be conflicted; Clennam does not and he tries hard to understand the workings of Gowan's mind in order to make it cooperative. Clennam can see, while watching the unaware Gowan, that "There was something in his way of spurning [stones] out of their places with his heel, and getting them into the required position, that Clennam thought had an air of cruelty in it" (245). At other times, though, despite Clennam's best attempts, his theory of mind lets him down. He cannot understand Gowan's dilettante attitude toward the arts and his casual attitudes toward Pet and others. Gowan enjoys Clennam's struggles to understand him and his resulting discomfiture: "Mr Henry Gowan seemed to have a malicious pleasure in playing off the three talkers against each other, and in seeing Clennam startled by what they said . . . His healthy state of mind appeared even to derive a gratification from Clennam's position of embarrassment and isolation among the good company" (362). Clennam keeps trying and "tried to convey by all quiet and unpretending means, that he was frankly and disinterestedly desirous of tendering him any friendship he would accept. Mr Gowan treated him in return with his usual ease, and with his usual show of confidence, which was no confidence at all" (451).

To use Anne Elliot's damning condemnation of Mr Elliot that I discuss in the following chapter, Gowan, despite appearances to the contrary, is not "open." To adapt the words of the narrator of this novel, it is the usual show of openness, which is no openness at all. Gowan is using his theory of mind dishonestly: he knows that Clennam wants openness; he pretends to be open; he knows that he is not really being open; he enjoys Clennam's disappointment that he is not. Gowan uses his knowledge of Clennam's mind precisely to repel the possibility of mutual thought, making this an asymmetrical relationship. Clennam's disappointment in Gowan leads him into a familiar phenomenon related to first-person attribution: "It would have been so cruel if he had meant it, that Clennam firmly resolved to believe he did not mean it" (453). In the modern phrase, Clennam is in denial. However, it does him no good because Gowan knows well how minds of this sort work and is ruthless in exploiting such weakness. During a later encounter, Clennam is described as "smarting under these cool-handed thrusts, of which he deeply felt the force already" (721). Such cruelty requires a refined theory of mind.

Gowan uses this refined mind reading on his wife for equally cruel purposes. In encouraging Blandois to become a friend, Gowan does so for the sole reason that he knows that Pet would much rather that he did not. He "opposed the first separate wish he observed in his wife" (541). The Jamesian tone of that sentence is a reminder that the relationship between Gowan and Pet, set as it is in Italy, has marked similarities to the marriage between Osmond and Isobel Archer in *The Portrait of a Lady*. To use the term employed as the title of a book by the philosopher Colin McGinn, Gowan, like Osmond, likes *Mindfucking* (2008).

Little Dorrit and Pet

During Pet's growing realization that her marriage will not be the genuinely intermental unit that she had hoped for, she has a consolation in the strong relationship that she forms with Little Dorrit. The narrator points out that "There was a sympathetic understanding already established between the two" (563); and also that "There was a silent understanding between them . . . She [Little Dorrit] looked at Mrs Gowan with keen and unabated interest; the sound of her voice was thrilling to her; nothing that was near her, or about her, escaped Little Dorrit" (544). Little Dorrit tells Clennam that "I loved her almost as soon as I spoke to her" (521). Her love for Pet enables her to read her mind well. During their first meeting, "There was a sorrowfully affectionate and regretful sound in [Pet's] voice, which made [Little Dorrit] refrain from looking at her for the moment" (496). In addition to such vocal cues, Little Dorrit's face-reading works well too. "Little Dorrit stopped. For there was neither happiness nor health in the face that turned to her" (857). Little Dorrit is aware of the consensus, referred to above, that Pet and her family had set out to catch Gowan as a good social connection. However, "Little Dorrit's interest in the fair subject of this easily accepted belief was too earnest and watchful to fail in accurate observation . . . She even had an instinctive knowledge that there was not the least truth in it" (563).

Part of the reason for Little Dorrit's skepticism is her perceptive awareness of the dynamics within the Gowan marriage. Although, oddly, she becomes a favorite of Gowan (544), this does not prevent her from being unsparing in her judgments of his mental functioning: "Little Dorrit fancied it was revealed to her that Mr Gowan treated his wife, even in his very fondness, too much like a beautiful child. He seemed so unsuspicious of the depths of feeling which she knew must lie below that surface, that she doubted if there could be any such depths in himself" (548). She is also penetrating in her judgments of Gowan's behavior generally. When the Dorrit family is being insufferably munificent in its patronage of Gowan as a painter, "Little Dorrit was not without doubts how Mr Henry Gowan might take their patronage" (554). And her doubts are justified when he takes it badly. Little Dorrit is also aware of the fact that Pet (like Clennam) is in denial about the quality of Gowan's mind: she writes, "I believe she conceals [all his faults], and always will conceal them, even from herself" (607).

A rather surprising intermental unit that develops in the second half of the novel is that formed by Little Dorrit, Pet, and Blandois. To both Little Dorrit and Pet, "Blandois behaved in exactly the same manner; and to both of them his manner had uniformly something in it, which they both knew to be different from his bearing towards others" (563). Little Dorrit's aversion to Blandois is visible and therefore public: "She went down, not easily hiding how much she was inclined to shrink and tremble; for the appearance of this traveller was particularly disagreeable to her" (497). She becomes fascinated by his stare: "Throughout he [Blandois] looked at her [Little Dorrit]. Once attracted by his peculiar eyes, she could not remove her own, and they had looked at each other all the time" (546). Pet is equally repelled by him and knows that he killed her dog. The two women are reduced to a conspiracy and they use secrecy and silence in their communications whenever he is near. "Their looks met. Something thoughtfully apprehensive in [Pet's] large, soft eyes, had checked Little Dorrit in an instant" (544).

ACTION IN *LITTLE DORRIT*

When the firm Doyce and Clennam is ruined by the collapse of Merdle's financial empire, Clennam knows that it is his fault because, under the influence of Pancks, he speculated in Merdle's schemes without Doyce's knowledge. He decides to do all he can to spare Doyce. He tells his solicitor, Mr Rugg, that he will publicly accept all the responsibility for the bankruptcy.

> (1) Clennam then proceeded to state to Mr Rugg his fixed resolution. (2) He told Mr Rugg that his partner was a man of great simplicity and integrity, and that in all he meant to do, he was guided above all things by a knowledge of his partner's character, and a respect for his feelings. (3) He explained that his partner was then absent on an enterprise of importance, and that it particularly behoved himself publicly to accept the blame of what he had rashly done, and publicly to exonerate his partner from all participation in the responsibility of it . . .

(4) The disclosure was made, and the storm raged fearfully. (5) Thousands of people were wildly staring about for somebody alive to heap reproaches on; and this notable case, courting publicity, set the living somebody so much wanted, on a scaffold. (6) When people who had nothing to do with the case were so sensible of its flagrancy, people who lost money by it could scarcely be expected to deal mildly with it. (7) Letters of reproach and invective showered in from the creditors; and Mr Rugg, who sat upon the high stool every day and read them all, informed his client within a week that he feared that there were writs out.

(8) "I must take the consequences of what I have done," said Clennam. (9) "The writs will find me here." (781–83)

For the remainder of this chapter I aim to show how the presentations of actions contained in this passage are extremely informative about mental functioning. In particular, I will evaluate the discursive purposes that are served by these presentations. The concept of *action* is an important one in structuralist narratology. Propp's morphology is basically a classification of different types of actions. The French structuralists of the 1960s onwards based their whole conception of narrative on actions, events, moves, and so on. In this way, the notion of action became the cornerstone of narrative theory, and a good deal of illuminating and insightful work was done on this concept. However, it seems to me that this work was undertaken within the *story* side of the story/discourse distinction and that there is much more to say about how action is presented or described in the *discourse*. The question then becomes not so much "*What* actions are *performed*?" as "*How* are those actions *described*?" I will investigate the latter question in relation to the above passage within the following four conceptual frameworks:

- philosophy of action;
- sociocultural action;
- intermental action; and
- discursive action.

Philosophy of Action

The theoretical study of narrative fiction is based on the assumption that there is a distinction between those parts of the discourse that present characters' actions and those that present their consciousnesses. The former are regarded as statements that describe the surface events of the storyworld such as physical movements; it is thought, by contrast, that the latter convey interiority, subjectivity, and private flows of thought. This discussion will dispute that dichotomy and will argue that what appear to be simple action descriptions in novels frequently contain a good deal of explicit information about characters' minds. In fact, it can often be difficult to establish whether a statement refers to an action or to a state of consciousness. In the *Philosophical Investigations,* Wittgenstein quotes the sentence "I noticed that he was out of humour," and asks, "Is this a report about his behaviour or his state of mind?" (1958, 179). (I refer to this in *Fictional Minds* as *Wittgenstein's question* [2004, 120–21]). He is drawing attention to the fact that the mental and physical sides of action and behavior coexist and interpenetrate to the point where they are difficult to disentangle. The mental network that lies behind all actions contains intentions, reasons, motives, purposes, and causes, and elements of this network are often present in the discourse that is used to describe an action.

For that reason, there is a continuum rather than a simple dichotomy between action descriptions and descriptions of consciousness. I call it *the thought–action continuum* (2004, 212–14). Here again is the simple example from *Vile Bodies* that was used in chapter 2 in the context of intermental thought: "The three statesmen hid themselves." A statement such as "they *hid* behind the curtain" looks at first glance like an action description, pure and simple. This sentence would certainly not be considered as a presentation of consciousness within traditional narratological approaches. But compare it with another, similar-sounding sentence: "They *stood* behind the curtain." In the context of the second sentence, the first description, *hiding,* starts to look rather different. Although it may appear to be merely a description of an action, it contains important information about the mental functioning of the people standing behind the curtain because it explains the *reason* why they are doing so, their *motive* for doing so, their *intention* in doing so. Saying that they are *standing* there leaves open any number of reasons why they would be standing there. It leaves more work for the reader to do. From this angle, the more you look at the word *hid,* the more like a consciousness verb it becomes. The sentence can be decoded in consciousness terms as follows: the three agreed that it was in their interest to conceal themselves from someone, realized that it was possible for them to do so, and decided together to take the action of hiding. Put another way, the word *stood* is at the action end of the thought–action continuum while the word *hid* is nearer the middle; it describes the action but also contains a reference to the mental functioning behind the action. Applying Wittgenstein's question to "stood," the answer is that it is a report of their behavior. Applying it to "hid," the answer is that it is a report both of their behavior and their state of mind. Of course, although the word "hide" explains the reason for the action in a way that "stand" does not, it still leaves open the *reason* for wanting to hide. Other, fuller descriptions could reveal yet more detail on the motivation.

The phrase "wildly staring about for somebody alive to heap reproaches on" (sentence 5) is a description of two actions: wildly staring and heaping reproaches. However, both phrases are also descriptions of states of mind: feeling wild and feeling reproachful. They can therefore be placed in the middle of the continuum. "Wildly staring" may also be termed *indicative description* (2004, 172): it is an action description that, through the use of the adverb "wildly," indicates the frame of mind behind the action. In making these attributions, readers also rely on what I call *cue-reason words* (2004, 216–17). These are words that signal that the causal network behind an action is about to be made explicit. "Because," "so that," "in order to," and "for" are common cue-reason words, the last of which occurred twice in the discussion of disposition statements in *The Portrait of a Lady* in chapter 1. In sentence (5), the description of the action of wildly staring is followed, after the cue-reason word "for," by the reason why people were doing so. Or take this statement: "Clennam watched her face for some explanation of what she did mean" (365). The first four words describe the action; the words following the cue-reason word "for" explain the reason for the action. As with Clennam's action of watching, the accompanying mental event is often made part of the description, rather than left implicit. Novels tend to contain few action descriptions that simply describe only the surface of physical behavior.

Part of the work of decoding action statements involves readers following the attempts of characters to read other characters' minds. The characters in this passage are doing a good deal of mind reading. In order to convey the complexity of this cognitive work, I have set out below a summary of it:

(1) Clennam explains his view of the workings of Doyce's mind: he is simple and has integrity.
(2) Clennam also explains his view of the workings of his own mind: he has been rash.
(3) Clennam wants to make sure that the public mind will understand his intention to accept responsibility.
(4) Clennam knows that Rugg, as a lawyer, is unhappy about his intention.
(5) So, to achieve his purpose, Clennam has to make sure that Rugg understands his "fixed resolution" to make the disclosure.
(6) Rugg conveys to Clennam that he understands his intention (because he arranges for the disclosure).
(7) Rugg deduces from the letters of reproach and invective that writs will follow.

(8) The public forms a view on Clennam's intentions: that he is wantonly seeking publicity.
(9) Rugg and Clennam become aware of the public's view.

In fact, though, this list, detailed as it is, is an oversimplification. For example, item 1 can be broken down into much more detail as follows:

- Clennam thinks that
- Doyce will think that
- the public will think that
- Doyce will think that
- the public will acquiesce in
- Doyce trying to get away with not paying his debts.

As with previous lists of this sort, the thinking here is both intermental and intramental.

The reader of this passage has to undertake this complex theory of mind processing without being able to rely on any *explicit* representations of consciousness by the narrator because the passage does not contain any, as traditionally defined; instead, it is a presentation of several actions, some of which are speech acts. In the first paragraph, Clennam tells Rugg about the action that he intends to take in the future. The second paragraph is a description of the actions of other people. The third paragraph contains another speech act. However, these descriptions allow the reader to attribute various states of mind to Clennam. He feels the emotions of guilt, remorse, shame, and embarrassment. He knows that the bankruptcy is his fault. Further, he has decided that the right thing to do is to accept the blame. Any analysis of action in the discourse has to take account of the questions of personal responsibility that are at the heart of readers' responses to novels. (This is the issue that was raised so thought-provokingly by Paris Hilton in chapter 1: "In the future, I plan on taking more of an active role in the decisions I make.") In the case of a death by shooting, do you describe the action of the killer as the twitching of the finger, the pulling of the trigger, the firing of the gun, the killing of a person, or the murdering of a person? These descriptions differ to the extent to which they ascribe consciousness to the agent, take account of the consequences of the physical movement, and assign responsibility to the agent for those consequences. Clennam is right to accept responsibility for the outcome of his action (bankrupting Doyce), even though that was an unintended consequence of his intended action of investing the money. This question of responsibility is pursued further in the discussion below on the discursive approach to action descriptions.

Sociocultural Action

The following typology of sociocultural action (following James Wertsch, but in part derived from Jürgen Habermas) was first introduced in *Fictional Minds* (2004, 166–67). There, I illustrated it with examples from Aphra Behn's *Orinokoo* (1688). Here, I relate it to the passage under discussion. Wertsch refers to the five categories as alternative types of action, but they can also be regarded as different perspectives on, or descriptions of, the same action. The choice of which perspective or description to use depends on the context and the point being made about that action. Again, this issue is pursued further in the discussion on discursive action.

(a) *Teleological action.* A person attains a goal or brings about the occurrence of a desired state by choosing the means that have the promise of being successful in a given situation and applying them in a suitable manner. The central concept is that of a decision among alternative courses of action, based on an interpretation of the situation, in order to realize an end (Wertsch 1991, 9–10). Clennam wishes to bring about the desired state of minimizing the effect of the catastrophe on Doyce. The means that he chooses involve making a public disclosure of his responsibility. He has made a decision that this course of action is the best means of achieving his end. The concept of teleological action dovetails neatly with the emphasis within the philosophy of action on the concepts of intentions, reasons, motives, and purposes.

(b) *Dramaturgical action.* People evoke in their public audience a certain image or impression of themselves by purposefully disclosing their own subjectivity. Each agent can monitor public access to the system of his own intentions, thoughts, attitudes, desires, and feelings. Thus, the presentation of the self does not signify spontaneous, expressive behavior: it stylizes the expression of experience with a view to the audience. A person typically carries out this impression management with strategic goals, type (a), in mind (Wertsch 1991, 10). I have already referred to this type of action in this chapter and the previous one. You may recall that Rosamond Vincy is adept at dramaturgical action. This perspective on action as impression management fits the first and third paragraphs of the passage extremely well. In Clennam's presentation of his proposed action there is a stylized feel to the language that he uses (sentence 3 in particular). His directly quoted language in (8) also has the air of a public declaration. His course of action is referred to pejoratively by the public in (5) as "courting publicity."

(c) *Normatively regulated action.* This refers, not as (a) and (b) do, to the behavior of solitary individuals, but to members of a social group who orient their action to common values, or the norms that obtain within a social group. The individual may comply with, or may violate, a particular norm or generalized expectation of behavior (Wertsch 1991, 11). This is a reference to the social situatedness of action, and it is also a precise statement of the plots of a large number of novels in which protagonists initially comply with, and then violate, the social norms of their storyworld. Clennam's motives as explained in sentences (2) and (3) are social norms that regulate his action. The use of a word such as "behoved" (3) is also an indication of how deeply Clennam has internalized these norms.

(d) *Communicative action.* This is the interaction of at least two persons. The actors seek to reach an understanding about the present situation and future plans in order to coordinate their actions by way of agreement (Wertsch 1991, 11, following Habermas 1984, 86). This is a restatement, within a different context, of the notion of intermentality. Given the close links between thought and action, it follows that action as well as thinking can be joint, group, shared, or collective. It is significant that there is often little difference, in practice, between the two terms *intermental action* and *intermental thought.* I say more on this in the following section on intermental action.

(e) *Mediated action.* This type can be seen as a more sophisticated restatement of type (a). Like type (a), it is goal-directed, but it does not assume that the appropriate focus of analysis is the solitary individual, or that there is a neat separation between means and ends. It takes account of the fact that human action typically employs mediational means such as tools and language that shape the action in essential ways (Wertsch 1991, 12). The passage is obviously about Clennam's choice of the best means or tools for achieving his ends.

Intermental Action

Intermental or communicative action is described by the discourse analyst Teun van Dijk as interactions between several agents that include all forms of cooperative social behavior such as the use of language (1976, 296). The simplest examples are those cases where two agents together accomplish the same action, while having the same intention. More complex are the cases where the intended actions are the same, but where the purpose is different, and so the joint action is done for different reasons. Alternatively, the purposes may coincide, but the actions may be different (for example, preparing dinner with each agent fulfilling different tasks within the overall action). Some actions can be carried out by either one or more agents, while others, such as marrying or fighting, must have at least two agents (van Dijk 1976, 298). Although, with regard to the example of fighting, possible exceptions might include such British football club managers as Sir Alex Ferguson and Roy Keane who, as the cliché has it, could start a fight in an empty room.

In my view, it is possible to make use of a looser notion of intermental or communicative action than is employed by van Dijk. You may have noticed that I have been using the term *the public* when discussing the reaction to Clennam's declaration. This term designates the intermental unit responsible for the communicative actions that are described in the second half of sentence (4), all of (5) and (6), and the first half of (7). This passage makes no sense if the existence of the public as an intermental agent is not recognized. Sentence (5) in particular is an example of the group focalization that is such a noticeable feature of the intermental activity in *Middlemarch*. Clennam is being judged by a large group in much the same way as Lydgate is by the town of Middlemarch. Much of the public's intermental construction of Clennam's actions, first in investing the money in Merdle's empire and then in accepting responsibility for the loss of the money, is left implicit. If the reader does not try to reconstruct this group cognitive functioning, the public's behavior will be inexplicable. So, although (4) is quite oblique, the phrase "the storm raged fearfully" can only be understood as a metaphorical presentation of intermental action. This is the case despite the fact that, as many people are involved, there is not the explicit joint understanding and coordination that Wertsch, Habermas, and van Dijk have in mind (although van Dijk concedes the possibility that people may take part in a communicative action for different reasons and purposes).

The group behavior being described in this passage is different from individual action. We recognize this difference in phrases such as "mob rule," "mass hysteria," and "groupthink." As Nietzsche put it in *Beyond Good and Evil* (part four, aphorism 156), "madness is something rare in individuals—but in groups, parties, peoples, ages it is the rule" (1990, 103). In a sense, these are individual actions—it is individuals who are heaping reproaches and sending letters—but in another sense they are also collective. The individual actions make more sense, in this case, when they are regarded as part of a joint action because people have become caught up in a group mind made up of wildness, reproach, and invective. They are behaving differently from the way in which they would behave as individuals because they have become part of this shared mind.

Discursive Action

The subdiscipline within psychology known as *discursive psychology* provides an important perspective on action theory. Discursive psychologists such as Derek Edwards, Grant Gillett, Rom Harré, and Jonathan Potter argue that attributions of mental states to individuals are discursive in the sense that the descriptions arising from these attributions are performative speech acts that occur within complex language games and are always embedded in specific social contexts. Attributions tend to be discursively constructed as apparently factual and objective, but often contain self-interested attributions of motives. "Pure" mental descriptions are rare. A mental state or an action will be described in a certain way and not in other ways for particular purposes, and these alternatives can vary greatly as to how they ascribe agency, impose responsibility, justify behavior, explain motivations, assign praise, deflect criticism and blame, and so on. This approach has obvious relevance to the novel, where mental functioning can only exist within the words of a fictional discourse. Readers have to undertake a continual stream of attribution of mental functioning to characters in order to understand novels, but the descriptions of actions, dispositions, and emotions on which readers rely for these attributive purposes are not neutral. Many different choices can be made by narrators and characters regarding the wording of such descriptions and by readers regarding their interpretations of such wording. These choices have a profound effect, not only on the cognitive attribution of a wide range of mental states, but also on the ethical attribution of responsibility, criticism, praise, or blame.

These psychologists see the mind "as dynamic and essentially embedded in historical, political, cultural, social, and interpersonal contexts" (Harré and Gillett 1994, 25). The fundamental premise of discursive psychology is that "no description of anything is the only one that is reasonable or possible" (Edwards 1997, 8). It is difficult to disentangle pure action description from attribution because descriptions will usually contain hidden attributional cues. Specifically, "descriptions *constitute* events as understandable sorts of human actions" (Edwards 1997, 6). "Accounts *of* actions are invariably, and at the same time, accounts *for* actions" (Edwards 1997, 8). "Versions of mind, of thought and error, inference and reason, are constructed and implied in order to bolster or undermine versions of events, to accuse or criticize, blame or excuse and so on" (Edwards and Potter 1992, 16). These "causal inferences and implications are often handled indirectly via ostensibly descriptive or factual accounts" (Edwards and Potter 1992, 78). Put simply, "attributional work is *accomplished by* descriptions" (Edwards and Potter 1992, 91).

A similar perspective may be derived from the philosophy of action. The philosopher Donald Davidson states that "*Explaining* an action by giving an intention with which it was done provides new descriptions of the action" (1980, 110). Davidson lists various descriptions of the action of writing a check to clear a gambling debt. "I am writing my name. I am writing my name on a piece of paper. I am writing my name on a piece of paper with the intention of writing a check. I am writing a check. I am paying my gambling debts" (1980, 110). He also states that "Redescription may supply the motive ('I was getting my revenge'), place the action in the context of a rule ('I am castling'), give the outcome ('I killed him'), or provide evaluation ('I did the right thing')" (1980, 110). Different discursive purposes, often relating to issues of personal responsibility, may be served by the different contexts within which actions can be placed.

So, what discursive purposes are served by the attributions that have been described so far? The passage is marked by a deliberate and self-conscious use of discourse in order to achieve certain goals. Clennam's actions are revealed to be situated, public, and social. The narrator shows him to be choosing his words carefully in order to give credit to Doyce's character ("simplicity" and "integrity"), to emphasize his need to be guided by "respect" for his feelings, to acknowledge the pressure of social and moral norms (feeling "behoved"), and "to accept the blame for what he had *rashly* done." In the language of discursive psychologists, he is *positioning* himself (Bamberg 2005) as the person responsible for the calamity. Also, Clennam's language in the third paragraph is principled and direct in that he does not portray himself as a passive, hapless, or reluctant recipient of the writs. It is easy to imagine the different ways in which Clennam could have talked to Rugg if, say, his purpose had been to avoid responsibility. Much of the theory on discursive psychology assumes that people generally try to avoid responsibility for bad things, acquire responsibility for good things, avoid blame, and acquire praise. However, while this may be true in general terms, characters in novels tend to be more complex than that. In this case, the whole purpose of Clennam's discursive construction of his actions is to accept responsibility for a bad thing and to acquire blame.

That the same action can be described in different ways is vividly demonstrated in the second paragraph, where Clennam's action of disclosure is pejoratively referred to as "courting publicity." This presentation by the narrator of the viewpoint of the public is completely different from Clennam's own positioning. It is also worth noting how cleverly the narrator frames the discourse in the second paragraph in order to encourage the reader to come to a negative judgment on the behavior of the public. There is a deliberately exaggerated style to the descriptions of the public's actions: "storm raged fearfully," "wildly staring," "scaffold," and "reproach and invective." This exaggeration makes it clear that the apparent justification in sentence (6) (the "flagrancy" of Clennam's actions, the appeal to disinterested parties, people who had lost money "could scarcely be expected to deal mildly with it") is ironic. The reader is made aware that the narrator is indicating that the supposed justifications for the collective actions are insufficient to excuse them. This appeal to an apparently objective moral standard is typical of the kind of positioning that is analyzed by discursive psychologists. An important element in this process is the construction of consensus: "everybody knows that . . ."; "it is understood that . . ."; "we always do that," and so on. Many other descriptions were available to the narrator to describe the actions of the public. The one chosen leaves little doubt as to how the implied reader is being asked to judge them.

CONCLUSION

Both perspectives on fictional minds, the internalist and the externalist, are required. *Little Dorrit* recognizes this truth. Employing the internalist perspective on those aspects of the mind that are inner, introspective, solitary, private, individual, psychological, mysterious, and detached, it is said of Mr Dorrit that "Only the wisdom that holds the clue to all hearts and all mysteries, can surely know to what extent a man, especially a man brought down as this man had been, can impose upon himself" (275). In order to maintain a balance, the narrator employs the externalist perspective that stresses those aspects of the mind that are outer, active, public, social, behavioral, evident, embodied, and engaged, when commenting of Mr Chivery that, "As to any key to his inner knowledge being to be found in his face, the Marshalsea key was as legible as an index to the individual characters and histories upon which it was turned" (346).

CHAPTER 5

Persuasion *and Other Novels*

*T*HIS CHAPTER is rather different in structure from the previous two. Those were in-depth analyses of single novels; this one is more wide-ranging. It focuses first on Anne Elliot in *Persuasion* and considers how she functions within the intermental network of the novel's storyworld. This analysis of a single character differs from the treatment of Lydgate in chapter 3 because there I analyzed the construction of his character at a very basic level (by examining, for example, its "gappiness"). Here, I take the analysis a stage further and look at how the intermental nature of Anne's social mind is central to our understanding of the whole novel. The second section of this chapter looks at the topic of characters' emotions in *Persuasion*. The subject of emotions is a huge one that would require another book to do it justice. I will therefore limit myself to a few brief words in order to give an indication of what such a full study might look like. The third section will make a few general points about a wide range of nineteenth-century novels. The intention here is to demonstrate that the intense interest in social minds shown by my three main example texts is entirely typical of the century as a whole. I use the fourth and final section to summarize some of the similarities and differences to be found in the novels under discussion.

SOCIAL MINDS IN *PERSUASION*

Persuasion, like *Middlemarch* and *Little Dorrit*, is preoccupied with the balance between public and private thought, intermental and intramental functioning, social and individual minds. Like the other two, it contains frequent references to attributions of mental states, theory of mind, and intermental thought. These include general statements about the functioning of minds such as the narrator perceptively commenting that "Husbands and wives generally understand when opposition [to the wishes of their spouse] will be vain" (81). There are also many more specific instances. The Musgrove daughters are able to see their mother's thought: "mamma is thinking of poor Richard" (91). Anne Elliot, who is generally, as we shall see, a good mind reader, "is ready to do good by entering into [Henrietta's] feelings" (124).

The character of Anne Elliot cannot be seen in isolation. Her mind is public, social, and engaged. In Bakhtinian terms, it is dialogic, frequently anticipating the views of others, successfully or not, and often judged by others, again favorably or not. This inescapability of the social has a profound effect on the value judgments that are made about her mind by others and also about others by her. When she is deciding whether she likes Mr Elliot or not, she arrives at this damning judgment: "Mr Elliot was rational, discreet, polished,—but he was not open" (173). This word "open" is an important one within the debate on social minds and requires further analysis. On the one hand, for people such as Anne and Clennam, whose default assumption about others is that their minds should work together to share the benefits of their mental functioning, honesty, goodwill, and openness are of great significance. She likes people whose minds are responsive, spontaneous, and generous. This coincides with the prevailing cultural preference in Austen's novels, in which secrecy is disliked and characters such as Darcy in *Pride and Prejudice* and Jane Fairfax in *Emma* are criticized for being "cold" or "reserved."

On the other hand, when it comes to the most important elements of Anne's mind, her feelings for Wentworth, she does not share them with anybody else until the indirect indication in chapter 23 that she gives in her speech to Harville that finally gives Wentworth the spur he needs to propose to her. And she never tells Lady Russell her conclusions about taking her advice. Nor is she open with Mary about her thoughts on Mary's behavior. So it is certainly not a simple matter of being open at all times. The fact that Anne is closed on these points is a result of moral choices, and they are moral choices that the implied author appears to approve of. It is legitimate to be closed in certain circumstances: for example, for reasons of politeness and courtesy, or when openness would cause unnecessary hurt to others or to oneself. The open/closed binary is an important one, in my view, but, like so many others, it does not work in a simplistic right/wrong way. Difficult moral choices are required on the right level of openness to be adopted in specific circumstances.

The emphasis in the text of *Persuasion* on the social nature of cognitive functioning is relentless. In a discussion between Anne and Mr Elliot on what constitutes "good company," this phrase is used seven times in ten lines (162). There are also references on the following page to "society," "the connexion," "your family," "related," "acquaintance," "the relationship," "acquaintance" (again), and "society" (again). All of these terms convey a sense of the context of the large-scale group frame of society within which Anne as an individual and also her smaller-scale relationships function. Anne's behavior is inexplicable without an awareness of the pressures brought to bear by the group norms that are imposed on her. The following two passages explicitly acknowledge the importance of the role played by social minds in the novel. Furthermore, they show that Anne is self-consciously aware of this fact:

> Anne had not wanted this visit to Uppercross, to learn that a removal from one set of people to another, though at a distance of only three miles, will often include a total change of conversation, opinion, and idea. . . . Yet, with all this experience, she believed she must now submit to feel that another lesson, in the art of knowing our own nothingness beyond our own circle, was become necessary for her. (69)

> She acknowledged it to be very fitting, that every little social commonwealth should dictate its own matters of discourse; and hoped, ere long, to become a not unworthy member of the one she was now transplanted into.—With the prospect of spending at least two more months at Uppercross, it was highly incumbent on her to clothe her imagination, her memory, and all her ideas in as much of Uppercross as possible. (70)

These quotes, in demonstrating beyond doubt the narrator's awareness of the externalist perspective, may surprise you (as they surprised me) in spelling out so clearly the practical implications of the theoretical framework described in chapter 2. To me, they sound like George Eliot. Reading them, it is easy to see how *Middlemarch* will come to be written. The language is not as obviously cognitive as that of the later novel, but the sensibility, the sensitivity to the workings of social minds, is the same.

The Party

Anne is sometimes alone. At the end of chapter 3, she "left the room, to seek the comfort of cool air for her cheeks," thinking to herself, "a few months more and *he,* perhaps, may be walking here" (54). The passage in chapter 4 that gives the backstory specifies that Anne is alone while reviewing that story herself: "With all these circumstances, recollections, and feelings, she could not hear that Captain Wentworth's sister was likely to live at Kellynch, without a revival of former pain; and many a stroll and many a sigh were necessary to dispel the agitation of the idea" (58). Also, she must be alone for lengthy periods in order to do all that reading that she talks with Benwick about. However, despite her frequent longing for solitude, few of the scenes presented in the novel show her to be alone. When she is not with her father and Elizabeth, she is usually part of a shifting, ever-changing group of people that I am calling *the party.* The composition of the party changes from day to day but its core consists of Charles and Mary, Mr and Mrs Musgrove, Henrietta and Louisa, Admiral and Mrs Croft, Captain Wentworth, Captain and Mrs Harville, Captain Benwick, and Charles Hayter. As with all groups, the dynamics of the party raises interesting questions related to individuality, the self, and situated identity. Some of the members of the party such as Mrs Musgrove are difficult to imagine alone, as being an individual or a self apart from it. Others, though, remain distinct characters despite having part of their identity defined in terms of it. Wentworth is one such. He becomes the centre of its attention. There is "but one opinion of Captain Wentworth, among the Musgroves and their dependencies" (97). Unsurprisingly, when he is thinking of leaving the party to visit his brother, "the attractions of Uppercross induced him to put this off. There was so much of friendliness, and of flattery, and of everything most bewitching in his reception there; the old were so hospitable, the young so agreeable" (97).

Intermental units sometimes engage in joint decision making. For example, joint decisions have to be taken by the party during the period after Louisa's accident. In the moments immediately following her fall, under the impact of the trauma, the party fractures into individuals. Then, an initial decision, what to do with the injured Louisa, is required. It is an easy one for the group to make: "That Louisa must remain where she was, however distressing to her friends to be involving the Harvilles in such trouble, did not admit a doubt" (132). Later, more long-term plans are required. This time, the precise membership of the core decision-making subgroup of the party is specified. "Charles, Henrietta and Captain Wentworth were the three in consultation, and for a little while it was only an interchange of perplexity and terror . . . At first, they were capable of nothing more to the purpose than such exclamations . . . The plan had reached this point . . . The other two warmly agreed . . . One thing more and all seemed arranged" (133–34). Notice that, at first, they are capable only of sharing their emotions. However, they gradually find themselves able to take on the more cognitively oriented functions of short- and medium-term planning. The group then has second thoughts: "A much better scheme followed and was acted upon" (137). "It was soon determined that they would go" (138). This decision-making intermental unit is functioning well. It is decisive but, when flexibility is required, it is able to change its mind and adopt a better plan. It is noticeable that Anne is not a part of the decision-making process but is indispensible to it, as she is the chief means by which its decisions can be implemented.

Anne thinks constantly about her relationship with the party. She "admired again the sort of necessity which the family-habits seemed to produce, of every thing being to be communicated, and every thing being to be done together, however undesired and inconvenient" (106). "The two families were so continually meeting, so much in the habit of running in and out of each other's house at all hours, that it was rather a surprise to her to find Mary alone" (64). The word "Uppercross" is frequently used as a metonymy for the party (in the same way as the names of large houses in *Middlemarch* are used). "Scenes had passed in Uppercross, which made it precious" (139); "Anne could not but feel that Uppercross was already quite alive again" (148); and Anne "looked back, with fond regret, to the bustles of Uppercross" (149). Her warm feelings about the group are clearly apparent.

However, Anne is also ambivalent about what she calls the "domestic hurricane" (149). Sometimes she enjoys it as a welcome contrast to the sterility and coldness of her own family; Anne envies the Musgrove sisters "nothing but that seemingly perfect good understanding and agreement together, that good-humored mutual affection, of which she had known so little herself with either of her sisters" (67–68). But at other times, she wishes to be alone. During the crisis in Bath, when what she really wants is some space, "she gave herself up to the demands of the party, to the needful civilities of the moment" (194), but with some reluctance. At the end of novel, the value to Anne of being part of this intermental unit is heavily underscored. Although she is delightfully happy to be engaged again to Wentworth, she has "the consciousness of having no relations to bestow on him which a man of sense could value . . . nothing of respectability, of harmony, of good-will to offer in return for all the worth and all the prompt welcome which met her in his brothers and sisters" (252–53). Anne is uncomfortably aware that her own immediate family is of little value compared with the shared humanity and warmth of the party. As I said in chapter 2, our real-world knowledge tends to entail the default assumption that our theory of mind works better with spouses, friends, and immediate family than it does with total strangers. Sometimes, these default slots are filled; sometimes, when our assumptions are wrong, they are not. In the case of Anne's relationship with her father and older sister, where her word has "no weight," major reconstruction is required. By the end of the novel, Anne almost abandons her family in her eagerness to embrace a new one.

Anne and Smaller Intermental Units

Anne is constantly engaged with other minds, and her knowledge of them is generally pretty good. "With a great deal of quiet observation, and a knowledge, which she often wished less, of her father's character" (62), Anne generally knows how Sir Walter's mind is going to work. When he and Elizabeth talk to Anne in exaggerated terms about their renewed acquaintance with Mr Elliot, "allowances, large allowances, she knew, must be made for the ideas of those who spoke" (153). Anne's perceptive "quiet observation" is often of the body language of others, in particular of their looks and glances. That Elizabeth and Mrs Clay agree on the merits of Mr Elliot "seemed apparent [to Anne] by a glance or two between them" (154). When Mr Elliot talks to Anne about his supposed suspicions of Mrs Clay, but without mentioning her name, "he looked, as he spoke, to the seat which Mrs Clay had been late occupying, a sufficient explanation of what he particularly meant" (163). And Anne does know immediately what he means.

Nevertheless, the novel frequently demonstrates that care should be taken with the interpretation of evidence of the apparent mental functioning of others. When Anne confronts Mrs Clay with the fact that she, Anne, saw her talking to Mr Elliot, "It seemed to her [Anne] that there was guilt in Mrs Clay's face as she listened" (232). Anne is right about Mrs Clay's feelings of guilt, but wrong about their cause. Anne thinks that Mrs Clay feels guilty because she has been confronted by Mr Elliot about her designs on Sir Walter, whereas, in reality, it is because she thinks that her affair with Mr Elliot has been discovered. In another example of half-successful, half-mistaken theory of mind, Mrs Smith says to Anne, "Your countenance perfectly informs me that you were in company last night with the person, whom you think the most agreeable in the world" (210). She is right, but wrong about the identity of the "most agreeable" person. It is not Mr Elliot, as Mrs Smith thinks, but Captain Wentworth. This confusion throws Mrs Smith so completely that she later says, "Now, how I do wish I understood you! How I do wish I knew what you were at!" (203).

One of the major reasons for theory of mind breakdown is the solipsistic tendency that we all have to forget that other people have minds too and that they work differently from ours. Anne is conscious of this possibility in herself. She has to remind herself that not everyone knows or even cares about her feelings. Most of the time, her reminders to herself work. She is usually acutely conscious of other minds and knows that it is sometimes not possible to predict the reactions of others: "She had spoken it; but she trembled when it was done, conscious that her words were listened to, and daring not even to try to observe their effect" (229). But at other times, as Anne herself knows, her tendency to solipsism can get the better of her. On one occasion, Anne thinks that Mrs Croft is talking about Captain Frederick Wentworth when she is actually referring to her other brother, Edward Wentworth. Anne "immediately felt how reasonable it was, that Mrs Croft should be thinking and speaking of Edward, and not of Frederick; and with shame at her own forgetfulness, applied herself to the knowledge of [Edward's] present state, with proper interest" (75). Anne has noticed that her "forgetfulness" is of the fact that Mrs Croft has a mind that will necessarily work differently from hers. The important point is that she realizes that her misreading of Mrs Croft's mind is caused by her understandable absorption in Wentworth's arrival. Another example of Anne's (admittedly fairly mild) solipsistic tendency is an elaborate set piece that takes up a whole page of text. When Anne is walking with Lady Russell in Bath she sees Captain Wentworth approaching on the other side of the road. During the course of a long paragraph Anne attributes a variety of states of mind to Lady Russell on the assumption that she has seen him and still disapproves of him. She anticipates a meeting between the two with growing dread. Finally, however, Lady Russell bathetically reveals that all she has been thinking about are curtains! On hearing this, "Anne sighed and blushed and smiled, in pity and disdain, either at her friend or herself" (189).

The last-mentioned misunderstanding is indicative of the complexity of the friendship between Anne and Lady Russell. Although Lady Russell is referred to as Anne's "one very intimate friend" (36), it is also mentioned that, after her refusal of Wentworth, Anne and Lady Russell "knew not each other's opinion, either its constancy or its change" (57). The point is made again: "It was now some years since Anne had begun to learn that she and her excellent friend could sometimes think differently" (160). And repeated: "They did not always think alike" (160). The relationship then strengthens again. When Anne discovers Mr Elliot's true nature, one of her first thoughts is that "She must talk to Lady Russell, tell her, consult with her" (218). And, when matters are resolved, "Anne knew that Lady Russell must be suffering some pain in understanding and relinquishing Mr Elliot, and be making some struggles to become truly acquainted with, and do justice to Captain Wentworth" (251). But, although the *friendship* is restored, they are never really a strong intermental unit. Anne has turned out to be a much better judge of character with regard to both Wentworth and Mr. Elliot, and, as a result, she is not open with her about the differences in their views on other people generally. It is hardly a friendship of equals.

The Croft marriage is an interesting attributional case study. On the one hand, the strongly intermental nature of the relationship between the Admiral and Mrs Croft is frequently emphasized. In Uppercross, "The Admiral and Mrs Croft were generally out of doors together . . . dawdling about in a way not endurable to a third person" (97). In Bath, they "brought with them their country habit of being almost always together . . . [Anne] delighted to fancy she understood what they might be talking of" (179). Anne responds to them as a couple, not as individuals: The Crofts "were people whom her heart turned to very naturally" (174). While thinking about her earlier engagement to Wentworth, she pays them this heartfelt tribute: "With the exception, perhaps, of Admiral and Mrs Croft, who seemed particularly attached and happy, (Anne could allow no other exception even among the married couples) there could have been no two hearts so open, no tastes so similar, no feelings so in unison, no countenances so beloved" (88). In addition to her emotional response to them, Anne is also aware that they function as a cognitive unit. She watches the Crofts "with some amusement at their style of driving," which involves their taking joint decisions on the steering, and "which she imagined no bad representation of the general guidance of their affairs" (114). There is only one occasion on which they are of different minds. When the Admiral warmly praises the Musgrove girls as possible objects of Wentworth's affection, Mrs Croft refers to them "in a tone of calmer praise, such as made Anne suspect that her keener powers might not consider either of them as quite worthy of her brother" (114).

On the other hand, much is also made of the Crofts' regular attributional breakdowns involving others. At one point, Admiral Croft talks to Wentworth "without taking any observation of what he might be interrupting, thinking only of his own thoughts" (92–93). When Anne wishes to be reassured by the Admiral that Wentworth is not grieving over losing Louisa to Captain Benwick, he is not sensitive enough to pick up on her emotional needs and "Anne did not receive the perfect conviction which the Admiral meant to convey" (183). To do him credit, he is sensitive enough to wish to convey the reassurance, but not sufficiently attuned to the workings of other minds to do so successfully. In addition, there is an enjoyably comic example of Mrs Croft's solipsism. When she is insistent to Mrs Musgrove about not referring to Bermuda or the Bahamas as "the West Indies," "Mrs Musgrove had not a word to say in dissent; she could not accuse herself of having ever called them any thing in the whole course of her life" (94). It is an interesting question whether it is a coincidence that the two individuals in the tightest intermental unit in the novel are also the ones who are among the most solipsistic in their relations with others. It is also worth comparing the centripetal nature of this unit with Anne's and Wentworth's centrifugal relationship as described at the end of the novel in the long quote (see page 156 below) with which this discussion of social minds in *Persuasion* concludes. The older couple are, in their cognitive relations with others, rather sealed off from them by their absorption with each other, while the love between the younger pair includes a heightened awareness of other minds.

Anne and Wentworth

The key to the novel is the construction of Wentworth's mind by Anne and by the reader. The central question posed by the text is: What does he now think of her? He appears at first to have no feelings for her and it then slowly becomes apparent that he does still love her. Anne experiences intense feelings of anguish toward the end of the novel when she is not sure what Wentworth is thinking. Her record in this respect is patchy. Sometimes she does know: "When he talked, she heard the same voice, and discerned the same mind" (88–89). And when he talks lightly of being ready to make a foolish match: "He said it, she knew, to be contradicted" (86). At other times she does not know. It is odd that this is a unit that does not function particularly well. As I said, though, when discussing *Little Dorrit,* this is consistent with the default assumptions contained in the cognitive frame for lovers, by which we assume that the course of true love never runs smooth and misunderstandings can often arise.

Anne's knowledge of Wentworth's views on others is generally accurate, but it is much less so when he is thinking about her. When he is listening to Mrs Musgrave becoming sentimental about her useless son, "there was a momentary expression in Captain Wentworth's face at this speech, a certain glance of his bright eye, and curl of his handsome mouth, which convinced Anne" that she knew what he was thinking, "but it was too transient an indulgence of self-amusement to be detected by any who understood him less than herself" (92). Anne can always discern his views on her family. When Mary makes an excessively snobbish remark to him about the Hayters, she "received no other answer, than an artificial, assenting smile, followed by a contemptuous glance, as he turned away, which Anne perfectly knew the meaning of" (19). When Sir Walter and Elizabeth ostentatiously offer him a visiting card because they know that he will "look well" in their drawing room, Anne "knew him; she saw disdain in his eye" (231). And when Anne sees Elizabeth snub Wentworth in the shop in Bath: "It did not surprise, but it grieved Anne to observe that Elizabeth would not know him. She saw that he saw Elizabeth, that Elizabeth saw him, that there was complete internal recognition on each side; she was convinced that he was ready to be acknowledged as an acquaintance, expecting it, and she had the pain of seeing her sister turn away with unalterable coldness" (186). (For a treatment of this scene as an example of "deep intersubjectivity," see Butte 2004, 3.)

In contrast, Anne's knowledge of his feelings about her is much more intermittent. It is fascinating to follow the fluctuations in their relationship in terms of the successes and the failures in their theory of mind. At the beginning, Anne lacks any knowledge of his state of mind. Before they meet again, "She would have liked to know how he felt as to such a meeting. Perhaps indifferent, if indifference could exist under such circumstances. He must be either indifferent or unwilling" (83). When it appears that the latter possibility is the correct one, "Anne understood it. He wished to avoid seeing her" (84); "Anne felt the utter impossibility, from her knowledge of his mind, that he could be unvisited by remembrance any more than herself" (88); and "She understood him. He could not forgive her,—but he could not be unfeeling" (113). Anne is wrong, though; she does not understand him because she is unaware of his growing renewed love for her. Nevertheless, she slowly begins to understand him better and to interpret his behavioral clues correctly. As is so often the case, there is a gap between characters' interpretations of others' minds and readers' interpretations of those minds. The reader will be ahead of Anne here in picking up on those clues about Wentworth's renewed love. Anne, who is such a good reader of others, does not understand him yet because she is afraid to let herself believe in his love. It makes her too vulnerable to the kind of pain that she experienced eight years before and that she is living with still.

In the scene in Lyme in which Anne, Wentworth, and Mr Elliot meet briefly, it seems to Anne that Wentworth sees that Mr Elliot is attracted to her: "It was evident that the gentleman . . . admired her exceedingly. Captain Wentworth looked round at her instantly in a way which shewed his noticing of it. He gave her a momentary glance,—a glance of brightness, which seemed to say, 'That man is struck with you,—and even I, at this moment, see something like Anne Elliot again'" (125). But, even in Bath, her success rate is mixed: "He was more obviously struck and confused by the sight of her, than she had ever observed before; he looked quite red . . . The character of his manner was embarrassment. She could not have called it either cold or friendly, or any thing so certainly as embarrassed" (185). This is another instance of partially successful theory of mind. She knows his mind well enough to know that he is embarrassed, but not well enough to know why. However, typically, she *knows* that she does not know what is troubling him: "She could not understand his present feelings, whether he was really suffering much from disappointment or not; and till that point was settled, she could not be quite herself" (187). Similarly, "Either from the consciousness, however, that his friend had recovered, or from other consciousness, he went no farther" (192). Anne does not know which.

Finally, Anne realizes that Wentworth *does* love her. The point at which she finally realizes this reads like an attribution manual in its analysis of the behavioral clues on which theory of mind rests. For this reason, the passage is worth quoting in full:

> His choice of subjects, his expressions, and still more his manner and look, had been such as she could see in only one light. His opinion of Louisa Musgrave's inferiority, an opinion which he seemed solicitous to give, his wonder at Captain Benwick, his feelings as to a first, strong attachment,—sentences begun which he could not finish—his half averted eyes, and more than half expressive glance,—all, all declared that he had a heart returning to her at least; that anger, resentment, avoidance, were no more; and that they were succeeded, not merely by friendship and regard, but by the tenderness of the past. She could not contemplate the change as implying less.—He must love her. (195)

But a problem remains—his jealousy of Mr Elliot. Anne does not realize this at first: "Anne knew not how to understand him" (239). As previously, she knows that something is the matter but does not know for sure what it is: "She saw him not far off. He saw her too; yet he looked grave, and seemed irresolute, and only by very slow degrees came at last near enough to speak to her. She felt that something must be the matter. The change was indubitable" (198). She correctly guesses the reason why: "Jealousy of Mr Elliot! It was the only intelligible motive" (199). Later, her guess is confirmed: "She had not mistaken him. Jealousy of Mr Elliot had been the retarding weight, the doubt, the torment" (243). In the meantime, the reader is given the only direct access in the novel to Wentworth's side of the relationship and, significantly, it is put in theory of mind terms. In his letter to her, he cries out in evident exasperation and suffering, "For you alone I think and plan.—Have you not seen this? Can you fail to have understood my wishes?" (240).

As I began this discussion with some large-scale group cognitive frames before going on to talk about medium- and then small-scale frames, I would like to conclude with a passage that brings us full circle by combining all three. The novel ends with Anne and Wentworth together. She is adjusting to her new life, and getting used to how her mind will be working together with other minds, and particularly Wentworth's, in the future. This passage beautifully encapsulates the functioning of Anne's social mind in action by showing her at the center of an intermental network:

> Mr Elliot was there; she avoided, but she could pity him . . . Lady Dalrymple and Miss Carteret; they would soon be innoxious cousins to her. She cared not for Mrs Clay, and had nothing to blush for in the public manners of her father and sister. With the Musgroves, there was the happy chat of perfect ease; with Captain Harville the kind-hearted intercourse of brother and sister; with Lady Russell, attempts at conversation, which a delicious consciousness cut short; with Admiral and Mrs Croft, every thing of peculiar cordiality and fervent interest, which the same consciousness sought to conceal;—and with Captain Wentworth, some moments of communication continually occurring, and always the hope of more, and always the knowledge of his being there. (247–48)

EMOTIONS IN *PERSUASION*

Much of the mental functioning that we attribute to fictional characters consists of strong emotions and feelings. Emotions drive narratives. They are the teleological motors of narratives. A novel with all of the emotions and feelings taken out would not make much sense. This crucially important element in the whole fictional mind was neglected by traditional, structuralist-derived, Genettian narratology for three reasons, I think. One is that it is difficult to find room for the messiness and complexity of emotions within a character paradigm limited to actants with carefully defined roles within the text. The second is that structuralist narratologists historically thought of the representation of consciousness in the novel in terms of linguistic categories such as stream of consciousness, interior monologue, and free indirect discourse, and these categories do not lend themselves easily to analysis in terms of the concept of emotion. (See *Fictional Minds,* chapter 3, for the theoretical background to this problem.) The final, more general reason is that emotions are difficult—in particular, they are difficult to talk about systematically and analytically. Whenever I discuss with other narrative theorists my interest in fictional emotions, I often sense a blank in their minds, a moment of panic arising from an inability to see how such a theoretical study could be undertaken. This is so despite the fact that so much of their actual, practical criticism involves talking about specific emotions. I recognize this panic because I so often feel it myself. Of all of the various elements of fictional minds that I have tried to explore, I have found emotions to be much the most difficult. It is with a feeling of relief, if I am honest, that I can say that, within the confines of this study, it is only possible to hint at the complexity of the subject.

However, it should be said that the current position on theoretical interest in emotions and fiction is now much healthier than before. Quite a bit of attention has been paid to this topic recently within other, nonstructuralist traditions. Of particular importance is the rhetorical criticism of the Chicago School, exemplified by the work done by James Phelan (1989) and Peter Rabinowitz (1987), who take account of characters' emotions while investigating readers' emotions. Much of their work is concerned with reasoning back from the emotional effects of a work on the reader to the causes of those effects in the interaction of authorial choices and readerly knowledge of narrative conventions. Philosophers such as Martha Nussbaum link emotions with ethics, and, in particular, turn to the novel to investigate ethics in ways that supplement analytic philosophy, because the novel recognizes the cognitive value of the emotions (for example, Nussbaum's *Love's Knowledge* [1992]). In *Having a Good Cry* (2002), Robyn Warhol foregrounds the emotional dimensions and cultural consequences of readers' engagement with popular-culture narratives. Finally, postclassical narrative theorists such as David Herman (2007a) and Patrick Colm Hogan (2003) have also made important advances in the theorizing of characters' emotion. As a small contribution to this process, I will briefly discuss the presentation of emotions in chapter 23 of *Persuasion*.

In order to reinforce the point made just now about the centrality of emotion to narrative, I want to present here a set of short quotes from *Persuasion*. Taken together, they compose a kind of condensed abstract of some of the emotions to be found in this novel. It is only a selection. A list of all of the references to emotions in the novel would be far longer than this one. I have focused on the most extreme and deeply felt emotions only for maximum impact.

"The pride, the folly, the madness of resentment" (244). "Her heart revelled in angry pleasure, in pleased contempt" (140). "You must allow for an injured, angry woman" (206). "The inevitable sufferings of her situation had been such as could not be related without anguish of spirit" (215). "She had used him ill; deserted and disappointed him" (86). "He is totally beyond the reach of any sentiment of justice or compassion. Oh! He is black at heart, hollow and black" (206). "Anger, resentment, avoidance were no more" (195). "[It] made her shudder at the idea of the misery which must have followed" (216). "[She] fully submitted, in silent, deep mortification" (85).

"Treading back with feelings unutterable" (131), "He exclaimed in the bitterest agony" (130). "[Her] shudderings were to her herself alone" (90). "As if overpowered by the various feelings of the soul" (132), "they were sick with horror" (132). "The horror of that moment to all who stood around . . . in an agony of silence" (129). "The horror and distress you were involved in—the stretch of mind, the wear of spirits" (193), "How could I look on without agony?" (246). "What wild imaginations one forms, where dear self is concerned." (199).

"All the overpowering, blinding, bewildering, first effects of strong surprise were over with her. Still, however, she had enough to feel! It was agitation, pain, pleasure, a something between delight and misery" (185). "She was deep in the happiness of such misery, or the misery of such happiness, instantly" (233). "As if wholly overcome" (135), he said: "You pierce my soul. I am half agony, half hope" (240).

"She could not command herself enough to receive that look" (242). "Her sensations on the discovery made her perfectly speechless . . . She could only hang over [him] with most disordered feelings . . . Such a confusion of varying, but very painful agitation, as she could not recover from" (103). "Her own emotions still kept her fixed. She had much to recover from, before she could move" (111). "For a few minutes she saw nothing before her. It was all confusion. She was lost" (185). "She gave herself up to the demands of the party . . . with exquisite, though agitated senses" (194). "She heard nothing distinctly; it was only a buzz of words in her ear, her mind was in confusion" (235). "She could not immediately have uttered another sentence; her heart was too full, her breath too much oppressed" (238). "Full of astonishment and emotion, she quitted [the place]" (135).

"She had some feelings that she was ashamed to investigate. They were too much like joy, senseless joy!" (178). "Every moment rather brought fresh agitation. It was an overpowering happiness" (240). "[Her] spirits were dancing in private rapture" (242).

Chapter 23 of *Persuasion* is the one in which Wentworth overhears Anne's discussion with Harville about love and gender differences. Wentworth writes his letter to Anne, who then has great difficulty in finding an opportunity to be alone with him once she has read it. However, they do eventually manage to meet and are finally reunited. This chapter contains a passage of three and a half pages in which, in effect, the plot of the novel is retold from Wentworth's point of view. What follows is a list of the emotions and feelings that are explicitly referred to in this passage.

Jealousy, torment, pouring out his feelings, love, indifference, anger, suffering, fortitude and gentleness, angry pride, pride (again), the "madness of resentment," horror, remorse, being "startled and shocked," not caring, feelings, happiness, pleasure, warm attachment, pride (yet again), astonishment, happiness (again), feelings (again), love (again), "exquisite moments," hope, despondence, feelings (yet again), reluctance, indifference (again), agony, indifference (yet again), feelings of being "overwhelmed, buried, lost" that he had "smarted under," and a "year of misery."

And all this in less than four pages.

You may need to remind yourself at this point that the novel in question is by Jane Austen, and not, say, a Gothic novelist of the period, or even an overwrought Russian novelist such as Dostoevsky. There has long been a tradition of unthinkingly assuming that what emotions there are to be found in Jane Austen are of a rather thin, attenuated, and bland variety. For example, in Charlotte Brontë's view, "the Passions are perfectly unknown" to Jane Austen (Letter to W. S. Williams, 12 April 1850). This view persists to the present day. In her introduction to the Penguin edition of Anne Brontë's *The Tenant of Wildfell Hall* (1848), Stevie Davies states of the Brontë novel that "Social comedy after the manner of Jane Austen characterizes Markham's letters but they also incorporate glimpses of *another, emotionally* and intellectually *ampler world*" (1996, xiv; my emphasis). The assumption behind her unfavorable comparison is that the world of Jane Austen novels is emotionally impoverished. Anyone who has shared this view will probably join with me in the sense of surprise that I felt when I completed the two lists and discovered the sheer amount, density, and extremity of the emotions to be found in a Jane Austen novel.

A potential drawback to cognitive approaches to literature is the possibility that they will focus only or mainly on the more obviously cognitive aspects of the mind such as what philosophers call *practical reasoning*: decisions on alternative courses of action. In studying the whole mind, we need to consider other, less obviously cognitive areas such as emotions and feelings. The need to recognize the importance of emotion is especially pressing because cognitions cause emotions; emotions cause cognitions. Emotions are therefore woven so deeply into the fabric of fictional discourse that it is difficult to separate them out from the other elements of a narrative. In the words of the psychologists Jerome Singer and John Kolligian, "Our ways of knowing the world are intrinsically bound up with our ways of feeling" (1987, 548), and, in the view of Antonio Damasio, "consciousness and emotion are not separable" (2000, 16). Psychologists and philosophers stress repeatedly that cognition and emotion are inextricably linked (Damasio 2000, Elster 1999, Le Doux 1999). In addition, the psychologist Keith Oatley maintains that "emotions are not on the periphery but at the center of human cognition" (1992, 3) and that, as a result, "most philosophical work on emotions has been cognitive" (1999, 274). In the context of fictional minds, Lubomír Doležel feels that emotions have "regained their status as powerful motivational factors but continue to elude theoretical grasp" (1998, 65). While discussing real minds, Damasio refers to "the scientific neglect of emotion" (2000, 39) but reassures us that, in recent years, "both neuroscience and cognitive neuroscience have finally endorsed emotion" (2000, 40). It is good that narrative theory is now following suit.

It seems to me that there are two broad and general tendencies in theoretical approaches to emotions. One is to emphasize their irrational, uncontrollable quality. This is the view of the emotions as *passions*. The other broad tendency is the stress, as in the previous paragraph, on the *cognitive* role of the emotions, especially in relation to the achievement of goals and plans. Oatley (1992) argues that emotions consist of four elements. Two of them— (a) private, subjective experiences such as conscious preoccupation and phenomenological tone; and (b) public bodily disturbances, facial expressions, and gestures—belong to the former tendency. The other two—(c) judgments, reactions relating to goals and plans, appraisal significance, and evaluation; and (d) action readiness—belong to the latter. With regard to the second, more cognitive tendency, I said just now that emotions function as the teleological motors of narrative. I want to pursue this point a little further. Fictional emotion has to be evaluated in the context of the interrelated issues of attribution, motivation, and teleology. Readers comprehend narratives primarily by means of their *attributions* of characters' states of minds as stated or implied in the text. Much of this attribution process concerns *motivation*—attributing motives, intentions, plans, goals, reasons for, or causes of, actions. And a good deal of the motivation for characters' actions arises from their *emotional* reactions to what happens to them. Once characters' motivations, and especially those related to their emotions, are apparent to the reader, the plot will unfold. It is in this way that attributions of motivation arising from emotions are the basis of teleology.

As I say, Oatley works within a teleological perspective on the emotions that focuses on their role in relation to the achievement of goals and plans. His central argument is that "Emotions are a human solution to problems of our simultaneous multiple goals, of our limitations and uncertain knowledge, and of our interactions with others" (1992, 411). Specifically, "emotions can communicate the need for cognitive change" (1992, 412) and the "normal function of an emotion is to change goal priorities and to load into readiness a small suite of plans for action" (1992, 89). (Notice how far we have come from uncontrollable passions.) Emotions communicate both to ourselves and to others that goals are being met or that they are not, and what action is appropriate. Obviously, positive emotions relate to the fulfillment of plans and goals, and negative emotions to the various disjunctions that occur between our expectations or hopes and the actual situation. With regard to fictional minds, readers and characters are sometimes fairly sure about the teleological implications of a particular emotion. "She had not mistaken him. Jealousy of Mr Elliot had been the retarding weight, the doubt, the torment" (243). This is a free indirect representation of what may be called *historical* motivation. It is Anne's third-person attribution of the emotion of jealousy to Wentworth in order to explain his past conduct. She knows now that she was right to think that the motivation behind his behavior was the emotion of jealousy. In addition, though, the use of the word "retarding" has a teleological implication. His jealousy has, in effect, retarded for a short while the story of their reignited romance. Now that she is sure of this, she can try to bring about their eventual reconciliation. She can, to adopt Oatley's language, load into readiness a small suite of plans for action. Her long-term goal is this reconciliation but shorter-term ones include, ideally, being alone with him or, at the least, if they are in public, trying to adopt the best course of dramaturgical action that will reassure him that he has no reason to feel any jealousy.

Anne's third-person attribution of an emotional state to Wentworth is then supplemented by Wentworth's own first-person attribution of emotional states to himself to explain his conduct: "He had imagined himself indifferent, when he had only been angry" (244). So Wentworth was for some time mistaken about his own emotional states. This is yet another example of the unreliability of first-person attribution that, although I said in chapter 2 would not be systematically pursued in this study, has cropped up with some regularity during my discussions of the reliability of third-person attribution.

The two broad tendencies in the approaches to emotions are reflected in Oatley's important distinction between the *semantic messages* and the *control messages* that are sent by emotions. Semantic messages are those that have a specific cognitive content. They are *intentional*. (I am again using this word in the sense that I referred to in chapter 2, not with the normal, everyday meaning relating to motivation but in its technical, philosophical sense of a mental state that is about something, that is directed out into the world.) Emotions and feelings often contain cognitive judgments on states of affairs in the world. Decisions to act in certain ways are made up, on the one hand, of desires, emotions, and feelings, and, on the other hand, of beliefs and cognitions. And these two elements are difficult to disentangle. I desire something because I believe that it is good; I believe that it is good because I find that I desire it. Many of the cognitive judgments of characters in *Persuasion* are presented in terms of their feelings. Characters are happy or sad that something, in their view, is the case. Presenting characters' cognitive judgments in terms of their feelings allows the narrator to register their approval or disapproval of these states of affairs. In many of these cases, the causation may be said to be *forward*. A character feels an emotion that is based on a cognitive judgment about an aspect of the storyworld and so takes action in order to change the current situation. The emotion causes a future action. Anne's feelings of relief and happiness that she now knows what was causing Wentworth's behavior and also her belief that she is able to do something about it will, together, result in future action—specifically, her attempts to be alone with him.

By contrast, the control messages that are sent by emotions are nonsemantic. They function as a kind of alarm system. They arise out of the emotions as uncontrollable passions. These are the occasions when Anne is overcome by emotion to the point where she does not know what is happening around her. "Anne heard nothing distinctly; it was only a buzz of words in her ear, her mind was in confusion" (235). "She could not immediately have uttered another sentence; her heart was too full, her breath too much oppressed" (238). There is often a correlation between control messages and the physical manifestations of emotions: starting, blushing, stammering, crying, and so on. In these cases, the causation is typically *backward*. Anne feels an emotion because of what has just happened: the event causes the emotion; the emotion is a reaction to the event. In practice, of course, emotions will often form part of a causal chain, and specific examples of emotions will have both backward and forward elements. In any event, though, as is so often the case, the distinction between the semantic messages and the control messages that are sent by emotions is more of a spectrum than a dichotomy. Take this example: "She was deep in the happiness of such misery, or the misery of such happiness" (233). Although this is a reaction to past events that is similar in some respects to the examples of Anne being overwhelmed by emotions cited earlier in this paragraph, it has a more cognitive element than they have, I think. This sentence involves a judgment that Anne is a long way from fulfilling her objective. However, it does not contain any semantic messages and does not involve any element of planning for future action. So I would put this example roughly in the middle of the semantic/control spectrum.

Moving back to the semantic end of the spectrum, attributions of emotions can contain *local* (or short-term) motivation or *extended* (or teleological) motivation, and often both. Take these two examples: "In desperation, she said that she would go home" (241). "Anxious to omit no possible precaution, Anne struggled and said . . ." (241). In these cases, the motivation is both local (or short-term)—the examples explain Anne's specific actions at that point in the story—and also teleological (or long-term)—they are geared to Anne's long-range plan of being reunited with Wentworth. To take another illustration, Anne overhears a conversation between Mrs Musgrove and Mrs Croft on the desirability of short engagements. "Anne found an unexpected interest here. She felt its application to herself, felt it in a nervous thrill all over her, and at the same moment . . . her eyes instinctively glanced towards [Wentworth]" (235). Anne's nervous thrill results from her cognitive judgment on the applicability of the conversation to her situation. She appraises it in terms of her long-term goal of a rekindled relationship with Wentworth. It is also the motivation for her short-term response—the glance toward Wentworth.

Oatley's use of the term *control* is significant. Much of the teleological value of the emotions is related to the *expression* of emotions. Sometimes emotions are involuntarily expressed, for example by blushing, crying, and facial expressions. At other times, it is possible to control the expression of emotions in order to conceal them. In those cases, decisions can be made about how much emotion to express. One consequence of the concealment of strong emotion is that misunderstandings will arise. Initially, Wentworth and Anne do not express their emotions either to each other or to other people. This makes it more difficult for them to know what the other is feeling and thinking. Later, they do see signs of emotions in each other—one sees that the other is moved or disturbed—but they do not know what is causing the emotion. Doubt can arise because much of the action resulting from the feeling of an emotion is related to the concealment of that emotion. There is a need for her to control her "overpowering happiness" (240). "Anne could command herself enough to receive that look" (242); and "Smiles reined in and spirits dancing in private rapture" (242).

The reasons for the need for concealment are complex. One is the general issue of social constraint. Anne has great concern for feelings of others: when her brother-in-law insists for the kindest of reasons in interfering with her desire to see Wentworth at the climax of the novel, thereby infuriating her almost beyond endurance, "She set off with him, with no feeling but gratitude apparent" (242). As she has been conditioned by the duty to be polite, her dramaturgical action is faultless. A second reason for concealment is the unreliability of first-person attribution. Characters are often not sure themselves precisely what their feelings mean or what their causes are, and so are apprehensive about expressing them. Wentworth thought he was feeling indifference when, as he eventually discovers about himself, he was experiencing anger. A third, related reason for concealment is the knowledge that emotions may cause actions that can be misinterpreted. Wentworth's rekindled love for Anne causes him to undertake kind actions toward her. He takes the boisterous nephew off her back when she is obviously bothered by him, and he lifts her into the carriage at the end of a long walk when she is noticeably exhausted. Anne, however, mistakenly attributes these acts to his general thoughtfulness, rather than to any remaining feelings of love for her.

SOME OTHER NOVELS

I thought it would be a good idea at this point in the book to supplement detailed consideration of the three main texts with some remarks on other nineteenth-century novels. In this way, I can demonstrate some breadth as well as depth. In particular, I want to show that the explicit and self-conscious debate on the balance between public and private thought, intermental and intramental functioning, social and individual minds that is such a striking feature of my main example texts is also characteristic of the fiction of the period as a whole. Within this balance, authors will use differing emphases to display the balance. Jane Austen, Wilkie Collins, Charles Dickens, Maria Edgeworth, George Eliot, Elizabeth Gaskell, and Anthony Trollope tend toward the social end of the spectrum. Their novels are characterized by an assumption that characters' thought processes are frequently transparent and public. It is for this reason that secrets (the device around which so many of their plots revolve) are so difficult to keep. In fact, several of the novels discussed below, and especially Maria Edgeworth's *Helen,* Elizabeth Gaskell's *Wives and Daughters,* Charlotte Brontë's *Shirley,* and Wilkie Collins's *No Name* (1862), would certainly benefit from the kind of in-depth analysis given earlier to *Middlemarch* and *Little Dorrit.* In contrast, other writers such as Walter Scott and Henry James are rather more ambivalent about social minds and are often more comfortable with the assumption that minds are usually inaccessible and private.

The Warden is one of the many novels of the nineteenth century in which characters read the minds of others: "Mr Harding knew that the attorney-general regarded him as little better than a fool, but that he did not mind; he and the attorney-general had not much in common between them; he knew also that others, whom he did care about, would think so too; but Eleanor, he was sure, would exult in what he had done, and the bishop, he trusted, would sympathize with him" (155). This passage vividly indicates the necessity for seeing the character of Mr Harding as situated within a distributed cognitive network. As part of this network, he and the bishop form a small intermental unit of long standing. "The bishop and Mr Harding loved each other warmly" (24), and, for this reason, "Mr Harding determined to open his mind and confess his doubts" (25). He feels able, in this telling phrase, to "open his mind" to the mind of another, and, as in the passage from *Helen* that was quoted at the beginning of this book, there is often no need for words. As with the characters of Dickens, gestures can be enough: when the bishop puts his hand on his knee as a gesture of comfort, "Mr Harding well knew what that pressure meant" (26).

Shirley is another text that debates the epistemological and ethical implications of mind reading: "Men rarely like such of their fellows as read their inward nature too clearly and truly" (215). This novel is extraordinary in combining a large amount of staginess, awkwardness, and clunkiness in the presentation of the internalist perspective on characters' minds (by such means as elaborate spoken soliloquies, highly unlikely diary entries, and the like) with great sensitivity, fluidity, and insight in the externalist perspective. One of the many examples of the latter is a beautiful and moving passage in which, following a period of estrangement, the minds of Shirley and Louis Moore start to work together again in perfect unison. They renew themselves as an intermental unit by slipping into their previous, familiar roles of tutor and pupil (378–89).

The externalist perspective is, as I have said, an opportunity to widen and deepen our conception of such apparently internalist notions as character, interiority, subjectivity, and identity. Individuals do not exist in a vacuum. As the passage quoted above shows, Mr Harding can only be fully understood in terms of his functioning within intermental units. Similarly, other characters such as Lydgate in *Middlemarch* can be seen in relation to the units that they are *not* part of (for example, when they are identified as outsiders, scapegoats, and so on). There are many other ways in which a social-minds approach can be used to identify patterns in relationships that may not be apparent from the use of more orthodox tools. In *The Tenant of Wildfell Hall*, there are few examples of characters knowing what other characters are thinking. The one exception is the relationship between Helen, the eponymous heroine, and Hargrave, the sexual predator who tries unsuccessfully to seduce her. During their brief passages of dialogue, there are at least seven explicit references to one of them being able to read the mind of the other. To put this in context, I have discovered only six other examples in the rest of the book. On the face of it, this finding seems surprising. Helen says that she finds Hargrave's attentions abhorrent. However, the evidence of the closeness of their joint mental functioning suggests that her feelings for him may be deeper and more complex than her own narration, as contained in her diary, is willing to admit.

Wilkie Collins is similar to Charles Dickens in his emphasis on the surface: the looks, facial expressions, bodily movements, and sign language by which characters communicate with others. This is unsurprising, given the close working relationship between the two men. "Surface" is a word that recurs throughout *No Name*. There is hardly any direct report of internal thought in this novel, but there is a good deal of highly visible thinking. "When [Magdalen] withdrew [her hands from her face], all the four persons in the room noticed a change in her. Something in her expression had altered, subtly and silently; something which made the familiar features suddenly look strange, even to her sister and Miss Garth; something, through all after years, never to be forgotten in connection with that day—and never to be described" (124). Magdalen's sister, governess, solicitor, and family friend can see the change in her mental functioning. It is so marked that they find it unforgettable. But there is an internalist side too. Although others can see the alteration in Magdalen's face, it is strange to them. They do not know its precise nature. The change in her appearance arises from a decision that she had just made: her intention to avenge the wrong done to her and her sister. The others do not know this because she has also made another decision: to keep her desire for revenge a secret.

Magdalen now has a secret. Edgeworth's Helen also has a secret. Its beginnings are apparent in the passage with which this book began. The general comes to believe that the dead man was Helen's lover, not Cecilia's. Out of loyalty to Cecilia, Helen cannot tell him that he is wrong. The plot of *Helen* hinges on this secret. *Shirley* and *Wives and Daughters* are similarly preoccupied with secrets: How much can be concealed from others? For how long? And for what purpose? In *Wives and Daughters,* Mrs Gibson has a secretive disposition; Osborne is secretly married; Roger and then Molly discover the marriage and are forced to keep Osborne's secret too; Cynthia conceals her relationship with Preston; Molly, again, finds it out and has another secret to keep. There are several passages in this novel, often involving Cynthia, in which characters either think about or discuss the difficulty of hiding aspects of their minds. And it is this *difficulty* of concealment that is precisely the point. On the face of it, the combination of secrets with social minds might seem paradoxical. But the juxtaposition of these apparently disparate elements highlights the epistemological and ethical dilemmas that characters face while trying to keep secrets from other minds within a community in which people tend to be open and cognitively available to each other. The characters who are attempting to hide something are forever fearful that their actions, facial expressions, looks, blushes, and silences will give them away, especially to other characters who know them well. (For an analysis of secrets in Wilkie Collins, see Bachman 2010.)

The strong sense of social entanglement (especially through the medium of gossip) that is characteristic of the nineteenth-century novel is reinforced by the visibility of thought. People will gossip when they notice that someone blushes when a particular person comes into the room. Once the object of the gossip becomes aware that they are talked about, they will blush all the more. In Jane Austen's *Sense and Sensibility,* Marianne in particular suffers from the extremely public ways in which what she regards as her innermost feelings are openly discussed by such prying gossips as Mrs Jennings. Marianne in turn can cause suffering to others by her own behavior, specifically her displays of emotion. Brandon, on entering the room on one occasion, sees Marianne rush past him because she cannot contain her intense disappointment that he is not Willoughby. This pains him deeply. It is against this background of intensely public thought that I will now discuss some of the different types of intermental units to be found in my selection of nineteenth-century novels. After starting with a few large and medium-sized units, I will focus on small ones that comprise parents and daughters, and then sisters or near-sisters.

I mentioned in chapter 1 that Mr Harding quotes an old proverb in *The Warden:* "Every one knows where his own shoe pinches!" (114). I said that this is an internalist motto that vividly expresses the apparent truth that only we know what we are experiencing and no one else can. Oddly, this contribution to the internalist/externalist debate in the nineteenth-century novel is totally at odds with the whole tenor of this profoundly externalist novel. Mr Harding feels that "all the world knew" (23) about his circumstances. "All Barchester was by the ears about it" (59). Susan Sniader Lanser (1992) has shown that the town of Cranford in Elizabeth Gaskell's novel of that name works in much the same sort of way as Barchester does. The village of Raveloe in George Eliot's *Silas Marner* is another example. The role of the local community, in the form of "gossip," "rumour," and "scandal" (all words used in *The Warden*), is as important in these places as it is in Middlemarch, and so the sense of oppression that, for example, Mr Harding feels is similar to that felt by Dorothea, Lydgate, and Ladislaw. In *Wives and Daughters,* the collective mind of the town of Hollingford exerts perceptible pressure on Mr Gibson to marry again (he asks himself, "Why did people think" that he had to remarry? [104]), and its speculations about Mr Gibson's past are similar to those about Lydgate's. (In fact, there are curious parallels between the characters of Gibson and Lydgate: though at different stages in their lives, both are cultivated country-town doctors who are interested in scientific research, but who blunder into unfortunate marriages to similarly shallow women.)

It could be argued that the main character of Joseph Conrad's *The Nigger of the 'Narcissus'* (1897) is the medium-sized intermental unit formed by the crew of the ship. At one point, the men of the crew attempt to rescue the black man of the title, James Wait:

A rage to fling things overboard possessed us. We worked fiercely, cutting our hands and speaking brutally to one another . . . The agony of his fear wrung our hearts so terribly that we longed to abandon him, to get out of that place . . . to get out of his hearing, back on the poop where we could wait passively for death in incomparable repose. (54)

This is extremely complex intermental thought. It starts with an emotion (rage) that is presented *causally,* that is, as an intention to perform an action (flinging things overboard) and therefore as a cause of that action. The intention is presumably unfulfilled and so the action remains hypothetical. The passage then presents realized joint action: intense labor and the unintended consequence of hands being cut, then speech. Both actions are expressed in ways that vividly convey shared states of mind: working fiercely and speaking brutally. Next a complex of strong emotions (hearts being wrung) are described as a response to an individual's emotion (Wait's agony of fear). This is followed by another causal emotion (longing), presented as an unfulfilled intention that relates to two decisions that are not made (wanting to abandon him and to get out of his hearing). This short passage concludes with a hypothetical desire (to wait passively for death). In addition, some emotions are implied, but not openly stated: compassion, fear, desperation, and so on. The thought processes are initially focused on an individual, Wait, but then become almost mystical or metaphysical ("waiting passively for death in incomparable repose") in a way that is characteristic of this narrative, but is completely alien to all of the other novels under discussion in this section.

This passage is an example of a "we" narrative (as explained in chapter 2, these are written predominantly in the first-person plural). As such, it is an indication of the presence of what might be called, in parallel, "*we*" *cognition:* that is, intermental thought. As this book's focus on heterodiegetic narratives will have demonstrated, "we" narration is only one such indicator. "*Narcissus*" oscillates weirdly between this sort of narration and what might be called "*they*" *narration,* and both indicate the presence of intermental thought. Analysts of "we" narration often express concern about what they regard as "illicit" access to individual mental functioning in texts of this sort. "How can the homodiegetic narrator know what is going on in the minds of his shipmates?" It seems to me that an important consequence of situating "we" narration within the much wider context of "we" cognition is that concerns of this sort can, to a certain extent, be allayed. Within the externalist perspective, at least some knowledge of the mental states of others is the expected norm, not a mysterious aberration. This is a good example of a narrative that can be illuminated by a discussion of its social minds. Within the tradition of the action novel, this is a novel of collective action; within the tradition of the novel of consciousness, this is a novel of collective consciousness.

Close cognitive relationships between parents and daughters are a notable feature of several novels of the nineteenth century. In *Shirley*, while Caroline is being nursed by her mother, Mrs Pryor, the two "coalesced in wondrous union" (331). "Mrs Pryor could not complete her broken sentences . . . but Caroline comprehended" (296). Shirley does not need to be told that Caroline and Mrs Pryor are mother and daughter—she sees it by watching them together. However, she conceals from them the fact that she knows it: "I may be communicative, yet know where to stop" (354). When the mother and daughter discuss love and marriage, they contribute to the social-minds debate by disagreeing over the degree of intermentality to be expected within a marriage. Caroline suggests that, "Where affection is reciprocal and sincere, and minds are harmonious, marriage *must* be happy." Her mother disagrees, arguing that "It is never wholly happy. Two people can never literally be as one" (300). There is an equally close relationship between Mr Gibson and his daughter Molly in *Wives and Daughters*, and there are frequent references to their ability to know what the other is thinking. "We understand each other" (76). Molly feels great pain at her father's decision to suspend the openly acknowledged working of the unit following his marriage. He does this because he quickly realizes that his mind and that of the new Mrs Gibson will never be "harmonious." By continuing to be as obviously close to his daughter in the future as he was in the past, he would, he thinks, appear to be disloyal to his new wife. Molly is sad that they now no longer share their minds. They enter into an unspoken pact that the intermental quality of their relationship should from now on be implicit. Of course, by doing so, the father and daughter reinforce the intermental element in their relationship, albeit by different means.

Mr Harding is another father who forms a close unit with his daughter. He notices quickly that Eleanor loves John Bold. She knows that he is upset by the affair of the hospital. However, even this relationship contains misunderstandings and concealments. He wrongly thinks at one point that she is more worried about herself than she is about him. Initially, Mr Harding suffers in silence, and for a long time he cannot tell anyone, even Eleanor, what he is thinking and feeling. On the other hand, he cannot "prevent her from seeing that he was disturbed" (83). "Eleanor saw well how it was" (83). His isolation hurts her: her desire is "to be allowed to share his sorrows" (84). Tellingly, she exclaims, "Oh! papa, your face tells so much; though you won't speak to me with your voice, I know how it is with you every time I look at you" (88). She knows some of what he is thinking, but not all. She knows that he is suffering, but not that it is bad enough to make him want to resign as warden. When he eventually tells her everything, "he laid bare the inmost corners of his heart to her" (89). Their mind reading also works well when they undertake joint actions. Mr Harding gives Eleanor a letter to his son-in-law that explains that he is going to London to speak to the attorney general "with the perfect, though not expressed, understanding that its delivery was to be delayed" (138). Eleanor knows that Mr Harding wants the letter to arrive only after it is too late for his son-in-law to stop him going.

Another interesting pattern to emerge from novels of this period is the high degree of intermentality between sisters or near-sisters. Examples include Elinor and Marianne in *Sense and Sensibility* (real sisters), Molly and Cynthia in *Wives and Daughters* (stepsisters), Shirley and Caroline in *Shirley* (close friends who become sisters-in-law), and Helen and Cecilia in *Helen* (almost-foster sisters). Shirley and Caroline have a fascinating conversation in which they debate the visibility of thought, and emotion in particular. Caroline: "I saw you disturbed." Shirley: "You saw nothing, Caroline. I can cover my feelings." But then, Shirley: "You can never tell how your look, mien, carriage, shook me . . . I soon saw you were diffident" (340). Shirley then "took Caroline in her arms, gave her one look, one kiss, then said—'You are better'" (353). However, the familiar theme of the patchiness and unreliability of intermental thought recurs. Caroline remarks to Shirley: "I thought I knew you quite well: I begin to find myself mistaken" (357). In another similarly complex scene, Caroline tells Robert Moore about an intimate conversation between her and Shirley that probes the mechanics of intermentalism (474–75). In summary, Caroline explains to Robert that Shirley tells her some things but not others; Caroline can guess and infer some aspects of Shirley's mind but not all of them. What neither finds out about the other is the identity of the person they love. In *Wives and Daughters*, there are frequent occasions on which Molly and Cynthia know what the other is thinking and they are able to communicate this knowledge by means of looks and gestures (for example, their shared disapproval of Mrs Gibson's behavior). The picture is mixed again, though; Cynthia does not know about the most important aspect of Molly's mind, because she does not suspect Molly's feelings for Roger.

Any survey of internalist and externalist perspectives in the nineteenth-century novel would be incomplete without a brief discussion of Henry James. I will, therefore, comment at this point on a curious feature of one of his unjustly neglected books, *The Tragic Muse* (1890). Misunderstandings between characters can occur when, during a conversation, one will not quite follow what the other has said and will ask them to explain what they meant to say. In *The Tragic Muse* there are, extraordinarily, at least 175 examples of this phenomenon. (That is not a typing error—it does indeed happen at least one hundred seventy-five times.) You may be thinking that this is Henry James, after all, and his characters are prone to employ masterly indirection in order to avoid being understood or to pretend misunderstanding. However, this novel is different from other James novels in that it has few Machiavellian schemers and plotters. Characters here are trying to be straightforward with each other, and so the vast majority of their non-understandings are genuine. It is just that the minds in this novel are private, solitary, and mysterious. As a result, characters' conversations are too gnomic for easy communication. The tone is typically cagy—people circle each other watchfully, never saying precisely what they mean, not through deceit, but through self-absorption. Only rarely does a reader get a clear sense of a character knowing another's mind. Specifically, they do not put themselves in somebody else's place and ask themselves: What does that person already know, and what do I need to tell them in order to make myself intelligible? In almost every conversation in the novel, statements have to be made more explicit because the original formulation is unclear to the interlocutor. As a result, communication is a laborious effort. The predominant feeling is one of apartness. There is never any sense of a meeting of minds, of two characters being on the same wavelength. Revealingly, the narrator describes two participants in one conversation as "speaking a different language" (346).

Consider the contrast between the storyworld of this novel and those of the novels of Austen, Edgeworth, Gaskell, and Eliot. In cognitive terms, it is a huge distance to travel from *The Tragic Muse*—where characters do not know what others are thinking, despite their endlessly trying to explain—to the many earlier novels in which characters often know perfectly well what others are thinking without the need for speech. Within the externalist paradigm, the emphasis is on *ease* of communication; within the internalist one, it is on its *difficulty*. However, it is important not to exaggerate the differences between Henry James and these other novelists. It is certainly not black and white—we are talking about shades of grey. In the James novel, characters do occasionally know what others are thinking. Equally, as I have shown, there are many secrets and frequent misunderstandings and mind-misreadings in the other novels. There are more secrets, in fact, in the externalist novels than in *The Tragic Muse*. Nevertheless, the general tendency is unmistakably different. The few examples of intermentality in the James novel have to be set against the 175-odd occasions when it is conspicuously absent.

COMPARISONS BETWEEN THE NOVELS

At this point in the book I will return to the three main example texts in order to comment on some of the similarities and differences between them. I will also refer occasionally to some of the novels discussed in the previous section.

•

The default setting for the sharing of thought is speech. When we want to let someone know what we are thinking, the obvious way to do so is to tell them in words. This is why communication by such nonverbal means as the look, the face, and body language presupposes more intermentality than speech. These communicative mechanisms are particularly salient in both *Little Dorrit* and *No Name*. Because there is a good deal of emphasis in both these novels on the visibility of thought, much is often deliberately left unsaid. Dickens in particular had an extraordinarily visual sense of cognitive functioning that accounts, I think, for much of the distinctively vivid and dramatic quality of his writing. In other novelists there is a little more stress on characters unconsciously betraying themselves, rather than consciously communicating by signs. In addition, George Eliot had a characteristic interest in the complex, intricate development of large, medium, and small units over time. It should be stressed, however, that these are all differences of emphasis only.

•

Most nineteenth-century novels contain intermental minds (that is, high-functioning units). The town of Middlemarch is well defined enough to be thought of as a group mind. Indeed, it is a major character in that novel. The village of Santa Dulcina delle Rocce is another good example. Other towns such as Barchester, Cranford, and Hollingford function in similar ways. The candidates for group-mind status in *Persuasion* and *Little Dorrit* tend to be small units. I am thinking here of such pairings as the Crofts, the clever ones (Flintwinch and Mrs Clennam), and the Meagles. The parent-daughter and sister pairings that were referred to in the previous section, together with the crew of the "Narcissus," also qualify, in my view.

•

All intermental units contain a balance between long-term dispositions to behave in certain ways and short-term, immediate, individual mental events. In some cases a knowledge of the former does not assist very much with the latter. Clennam knows that his mother has a secretive disposition, but he does not know the precise nature of her biggest secret, the one that forms the plot of the novel. In other cases, knowledge of dispositions does help with day-to-day awareness of the mind of the other.

•

Characters try to read other minds from a variety of motives—selfishness, altruism, curiosity, ambition, and so on. Like intramental thought, intermental thought is morally neutral in itself. It is not necessarily good or bad, although, of course, specific examples will be. All of the novels interpreted in this study show evidence of beneficial, ethical, and rewarding and also of stupid, selfish, and destructive intermental thought. The range in terms of quality and ethics is similar to that for intramental thought.

•

Arthur Clennam, Anne Elliot, Dorothea Brooke, Mr Harding, Helen, and others are open characters who believe in social minds, favor openness in others, and are disposed to form intermental relationships. This does not preclude the possibility of secrecy for good reasons. Other characters are devious, secretive, and self-absorbed by nature. They are inclined to use mind reading for selfish and exploitative reasons and they manipulate the theory of mind of others. They do not take part in intermental units at all or else they form dysfunctional and unbalanced ones. Examples of closed characters are Mr Elliot, Mrs Clennam, Gowan, Miss Wade, Mr Casby, and Casaubon. Some of these like mindfucking for the pleasure of it; other minds are closed out of weakness.

•

Open or closed minds can often be linked to the issue of *control*. In *Wives and Daughters,* Mrs Gibson vents her ill humor on Molly, "from whom she feared neither complaint nor repartee" (439). In other words, she selfishly makes use of her awareness of Molly's mind, safe in the knowledge that she is able to manipulate and control her. Characters with closed minds tend to try to control others: Sir Walter and Elizabeth try to control Anne; the clever ones control Affery and try to control Clennam; Casaubon tries to control Dorothea; Rosamond tries to control Lydgate.

•

All of the novels contain examples of small intermental units that function well. Middle-aged and elderly couples such as the Crofts, the Meagles, and the Vincys seem to be the template in this respect. In these cases, the degree of intermentality, cognitive or emotional, is balanced or symmetrical; other units function differently. All of the novels that I have studied for this book portray small intermental units such as friendships, lovers, and marriages that are both balanced and unbalanced. In their different ways, the destructive relationship between Flintwinch and Mrs Clennam and the beneficial one between Little Dorrit and Pet are well balanced and symmetrical. The relationships between the clever ones and Affery, and between Clennam and Gowan, are not. There are also imbalances between Casaubon and Dorothea, and between Lydgate and Rosamond.

•

Imbalances are frequently related to the link between emotions and cognition. Little Dorrit and Pet often know what the other is *thinking* on an obviously cognitive level because they instantly developed a strong and immediate emotional bond and therefore know what the other is *feeling* too. But there are relationships in which this is not the case. The clever ones are a good example. Casaubon and Rosamond do not acknowledge Dorothea's or Lydgate's feelings.

•

It is interesting to note that dysfunctionality arises in the context of small units and, also, to an extent, with medium-sized units, but not in the case of large units. It is difficult to imagine what it would mean to say that a whole town such as Middlemarch is dysfunctional. It might be too sweeping to say that it would be impossible, rather that it would be much less likely than, say, a dysfunctional marriage.

•

Anne and Clennam are major characters whose theory of mind is fairly good. This would also tend to be true of the major characters featured in the novels briefly referred to in the previous section (for example, Molly and Helen). Dorothea and Lydgate, however, are rather too self-absorbed and focused on their high ambitions to be keen observers of other people. As a result, they make big mistakes and end up in unhappy marriages with manipulative spouses. Both Anne and Clennam self-consciously confront the dangers of solipsism, while Dorothea and Lydgate do not.

•

There is a good deal of emphasis in *Little Dorrit*, *Persuasion*, and the other novels on the workings of families; perhaps surprisingly, there is much less in *Middlemarch*. The nearest that this novel comes to the sustained presentation of the workings of a family unit is the Vincy family, but they do not have the central place in the novel that the Dorrits or the Elliots have. The three main characters, Lydgate, Dorothea, and Ladislaw, are not shown as having relationships with parents. (The roles that Mr Brooke and Casaubon play as the guardians of Dorothea and Ladislaw, respectively, hardly count in this context.)

•

I mentioned in chapter 4 that some families have a strong self-image. The Dorrits (minus Little Dorrit and Frederick) are one example, and the Elliots (minus Anne) are another. The common factor is social insecurity. The Dorrits would like to be regarded as members of the middle class despite being in the debtors prison. Sir Walter and Elizabeth would like to be regarded as members of the upper class despite having to leave their family home. Pride and vanity have important roles to play in this social insecurity. Little Dorrit and Anne have a similar position (skepticism) on the question of the family honor. Oddly, as I say, there is no comparable family in *Middlemarch*. The question of class insecurity is much less of an issue in this novel than one might expect. The Chettams have a concern about Dorothea aligning the family with a man such as Ladislaw, who is "not quite out of the top drawer" (an obnoxious British phrase that used to be employed in these circumstances), but this concern is hardly of the same scale as the paranoia that grips both the Elliots and the Dorrits.

•

Dickens was acutely aware of the phenomenon of physically distributed cognition and, in keeping with his absorption in the surface, and therefore physical, nature of thought, showed a greater interest in it than other nineteenth-century novelists (with the possible exception of Wilkie Collins).

•

There are several examples of collective action and joint decision making in *The Nigger of the "Narcissus"* in particular, but also in *Persuasion*, *The Warden*, and others. It is perhaps a little surprising that there is little combined joint decision making in *Middlemarch*. I mentioned that Lydgate and Rosamond do not engage in any joint actions. Obviously, an engagement is a joint decision, but Lydgate and Rosamond's is noticeably accidental and contingent. There is at no point a real meeting of minds. Similarly, Clennam rather drifts into his joint decision with Pancks to invest in Merdle.

•

Several novels contain characters who function as mouthpieces for the local intermental minds. In their different ways, Sir James Chettam and Mrs Cadwallader have this role in *Middlemarch*, as do Lady Russell in *Persuasion* and Mrs Merdle in *Little Dorrit*.

•

On a related point, many of the novels feature large and medium-sized units that are relentlessly judgmental of individuals such as Dorothea and Lydgate. *Wives and Daughters* and *The Warden* are good examples also. Group focalization is a particular feature of *Middlemarch*. There is also group focalization of Anne (by her family) and Clennam (by the clever ones and the public in the passage from *Little Dorrit* that I used as an example of action theory). A linked issue is the transgression of group norms. Some major characters such as Dorothea, Lydgate, and Ladislaw, in their different ways, are all norm-transgressors, while others such as Anne and Clennam are much less so.

•

Fuzzy sets (intermental units with imprecise memberships) are a noticeable feature of *Middlemarch*, where there are several discussions on the subject. There is little specific reference to this issue in the other novels.

•

Scapegoating occurs with depressing frequency in most novels: for example, Bulstrode and Lydgate; Clennam in relation to the Dorrits; Mrs Smith in relation to the Elliots; Anne briefly for refusing Mr Elliot; Mr Harding for taking a principled stand.

•

Unsurprisingly perhaps, the intermental units that are made up of lovers do not function particularly well. As I said when discussing *Little Dorrit*, this is consistent with the default assumptions contained in the cognitive frame for lovers. Difficulties may also be necessary in order to ensure that storylines can be sustained over the course of a novel.

•

In most cases, readers have to be aware of what may be called the sociogeography of the storyworld. This is most obviously true of the novels that are set in market towns such as *Middlemarch, Wives and Daughters,* and *The Warden*. Sociogeography can ensure that the class structure of a storyworld is precisely and vividly delineated. It is necessary to an understanding of *Little Dorrit* to know that the Marshalsea prison, Bleeding Heart Yard, and the home of the Barnacles have different sociogeographical locations. Similarly, it is important to be aware of the significance of the different country houses in *Persuasion*. The names of such houses are often used as metonymies for the upper middle class. One also needs to know about the geopolitical significance of Bath in Austen. However, sociogeography is taken to the highest level of sophistication in *Middlemarch*.

•

I referred in chapter 3 to what I called the intermental rhythm in *Middlemarch*. The only other novel considered by this study that shares this feature is *"Narcissus."* For example: "Some thought . . . others disagreed . . . the boatswain said . . . many did not understand, others did not care; the majority further aft did not believe . . ." et cetera (66).

•

The ephemeral quality of many of the intermental units in *Middlemarch* is unique; none of the other books have anything like it. The same is true of intermental free indirect thought.

•

By contrast, all of the novels feature intramental functioning that has a strong intermental component (in particular in anticipating the thought of others). For example: "Even much stronger mortals than Fred Vincy hold half their rectitude in the mind of the being they love best." (*Middlemarch,* 167).

•

The use of the passive voice for the purpose of constructing large-scale intermental thought is quite common. (See the beginning of chapter 3 for detailed examples from *Middlemarch*.)

•

To summarize this summary: for depth, complexity, and subtlety, and despite being in a high-quality field made up of truly wonderful novels, *Middlemarch* is in a class of its own.

CHAPTER 6

Conclusion
(Including Enduring Love*)*

Shared minds create all we know.
    —*Colwyn Trevarthen*

THIS FINAL CHAPTER is divided into four parts. In the first, I comment briefly on some of the issues that would arise from a rigorously diachronic approach to the study of social minds in the novel. The second part consists of an analysis of the intermental thought to be found in Ian McEwan's novel *Enduring Love*. In the third section I discuss possible future developments in the study of social minds in narratives in other media. The fourth and final section is, as promised in the first chapter, a rhetorical flourish.

A HISTORY OF SOCIAL MINDS

It is an obvious truth that historical periods are necessarily arbitrary. The novel form does not, of necessity, change utterly at the beginning of each century to suit the classificatory needs of future literary historians. Indeed, it is always necessary to complicate and question such easy and neat categories as "the nineteenth-century novel." On the other hand, though, it is possible to paint a picture of the history of the English novel that does, as it happens, fit quite neatly into divisions into centuries. There *was* a change at the beginning of the nineteenth century, due in the main to the genius of Jane Austen, and it is possible to trace a satisfying line of descent from Austen through Edgeworth and the Brontës to Dickens and Collins, Gaskell and Eliot, and then on to Conrad and James. There was then a very different change at the beginning of the twentieth century with the beginnings of the modernist movement. Many features of the English novel will not fit comfortably into this satisfyingly schematic picture. However, from the externalist perspective on social minds with which this book is concerned, the picture is a genuinely illuminating one. The novel of this period explores the tensions between the internalist and externalist perspectives, between social and private minds, in ways that are noticeably different from both the eighteenth-century novel and the twentieth- and early-twenty-first-century novel. This is not to say that the novels of other periods are not interested in social minds. The differences lie in the degree of interest, and the ways in which this aspect of the novel is presented and examined.

The standard story for the historical development of the representation of consciousness follows what might be termed the *speech category trajectory* (see chapter 1 for a definition of the term *speech category approach*). Roughly, this begins with the reliance of narratives before Jane Austen on authorial thought report. Then, from Austen onwards until, say, Henry James, novels are marked by a growing preponderance of free indirect discourse. With the modernist novels of the early twentieth century, stream of consciousness and interior monologue become the dominant speech category modes. Leaving aside any quibbles regarding the accuracy of this history (its possible overestimation, perhaps, of the amount and importance of free indirect discourse at the expense of thought report), it is an indispensible aid to an understanding of the history of the novel. However, if we want a *complete* picture of the historical development of the representation of *whole* fictional minds, then the speech category trajectory has to be supplemented by others such as the history of social minds. This narrative might well intersect at a number of points with the speech category account. It could be, perhaps, that Jane Austen was the first great English novelist of social minds, just as she was the first of free indirect discourse. That sounds quite likely to me.

Given that the history of social minds that I envisage would study all of the novelists discussed in this book, as well as many others, as historically embedded figures, several questions would arise. These might include the following: Are the workings of social minds more salient in the novels of the authors examined here than in the other authors of the same period who are not here for reasons of space? And are they more salient than in the novels of earlier and later periods? If the answer to the second question is yes, then further questions arise: Was the nineteenth century a privileged moment in which these great writers caught the *universal* condition that we all share and that has since been obscured by assumptions that have limited the power of narrative to expose the full extent of this condition? Or, alternatively, were social minds a unique characteristic of the nineteenth-century British society that was the subject matter of those authors?

Kate Summerscale, the author of *The Suspicions of Mr Whicher or the Murder at Road Hill House,* a work of popular history that was a bestseller in the UK, suggests that the mid-Victorians were fascinated

> by the idea that faces and bodies could be "read", that the inner life was imprinted on the shapes of the features and the flutter of the fingers. Perhaps the fascination stemmed from the premium placed on privacy; it was terrifying and thrilling that thoughts were visible, that the inner life, so jealously guarded, could be instantly exposed. (2008, 84–85)

Her theory is that these concerns arose out of the intense public interest during this period in the ability of detectives, both real and fictional, to read suspects' faces and body language for clues. I am sure that equally plausible alternative explanations could be found. Clearly, any attempt to address the questions asked in the previous paragraph will have to be a major cultural studies research project.

I think that it may eventually be possible to construct historical arguments along these lines in terms of the relationship between narrative technique and cultural conceptions of the self. Such scholarship might involve a revaluation of Dickens as the novelist who captures perhaps more vividly than any other the universal, *trans-historical* fact that, in cognitive terms, we spend almost all of our lives on the surface, on the outside, and who is therefore undeserving of the condescension accorded him by advocates of the more internalist Henry James. On the other hand, it will also have in mind that Jane Austen, George Eliot, Anthony Trollope, and other novelists of the period were also acutely attuned to the workings of social minds. I say that it may *eventually* be possible to construct these sorts of arguments because, while I think that this sort of perspective will be of great value in aiding our understanding of the historical development of the novel, it should only be employed once the necessary detailed textual work has been done on the operation of social minds in a wide chronological range of novels. Once the evidence has been assembled, then such historical patterns will probably become apparent. But it would be unwise, in my view, to theorize too widely and too soon in advance of the textual evidence.

The sort of theorizing that I have in mind could be taken in a number of different directions, social, historical, and cultural. In this context, *The Tragic Muse* makes an interesting comparison with the other, earlier nineteenth-century novels. Like them (in the main and apart from Dickens), it portrays a homogenous social group—the leisured upper-middle classes. I mention this because being of the same social class seems to be one of the enabling factors for the formation of social minds. Others include being of the same age; characters liking or loving each other; knowing each other for a long time; the absence of solipsistic characteristics, and so on. This is not to say that these factors guarantee social minds, only that they make them a little more likely. But how then can we explain the reasons for the stark differences in perspective between the James novel and the others? The two obvious reasons are that they are written by different people and at different periods of time. But how can we know which factor is the more important? Is it the difference between two aspects of British upper-middle-class society, or simply the difference between Dickens, Eliot, and the others and Henry James? That is assuming, of course, that the novels discussed in this book are typical of their authors, and they may not be; other Henry James novels may be less internalist than *The Tragic Muse*.

Fictional social minds have many other ideological, gendered, historical, and cultural implications that I hope will be explored in the future but cannot be addressed here for reasons of space. One single book cannot go in all the directions that will, I am sure, have occurred to readers of this book. There are many studies of nonverbal communication from a variety of perspectives (anthropological, sociological, sociolinguistic, and so on) that I have not referred to. As an illustration of one important future direction, at the end of the discussion of *Enduring Love* in the next section I refer to the need for a rhetorical and ethical perspective on analyses of social minds. Also, attribution theory can be used to differentiate between the techniques of characterization formation and consciousness representation that are characteristic, not just of different historical periods, but also of genres, authors, and types of characters. Finally, I will discuss later in this chapter my belief that the externalist perspective can fruitfully be applied to narratives in other media such as films and graphic novels. However, any comparative study of the fictional minds realized by contrasting narrative styles, periods, genres, and media should, I propose, pay as much attention to the large number of underlying and persistent similarities as to the marked and undeniable differences.

A history of social minds in the novel will, I am sure, show that an interest in them did not end with the beginning of the twentieth century. This is James Joyce's characteristically playful take on the subject:

> What, reduced to their simplest reciprocal form, were Bloom's thoughts about Stephen's thoughts about Bloom and about Stephen's thoughts about

Bloom's thoughts about Stephen?

He knew that he thought that he was a jew whereas he knew that he knew that he knew that he was not. (*Ulysses*, 558)

Social minds play an important role in another, very different modernist novel: Ford Madox Ford's *The Good Soldier*. The unreliable narrator of that novel appears at first to be describing an intermental unit formed by two couples: he and his wife, Florence, and Edward and Leonora Ashburnham. He refers in the second sentence of the novel to their "extreme intimacy" (1) and later to "the swiftness with which intimacy had grown up between us" (40–41). However, he reveals later that, in reality, he knew nothing at all of the true nature of the relationships within this foursome (in particular, that his wife was having an affair with Ashburnham) until after his wife's suicide. The actual intermental unit comprised the other three, who all shared their knowledge of the real state of affairs. When the focus of attention then moves onto the relationship between the Ashburnhams and their ward, Nancy, the narrator remarks that "that wretched fellow [Ashburnham] knew—by a curious instinct that runs between human beings living together—exactly what was going on" (217). In the final scene of the novel, the narrator is aware that Ashburnham is going to commit suicide but decides not to stop him. "When he *saw* that I did not intend to interfere with him, his eyes became soft and almost affectionate" (229; my emphasis). There *are* social minds of a sort in this novel, but, as you would expect of a modernist classic, they are partial, fractured, and deeply dysfunctional.

The twenty-first-century novel has so far been characterized by an explicit interest in the workings and, in particular, the malfunctionings of characters' minds. The first half of Ian McEwan's *Atonement* is about the development of the thirteen-year-old Briony's theory of mind and her growing ability to attribute mental states to others. She frequently muses self-consciously on the subject: "Was everyone else really as alive as she was? . . . If the answer was yes, then the world, the social world, was unbearably complicated, with two billion voices, and everyone's thoughts striving in equal importance and everyone's claim on life as intense, and everyone thinking they were unique, when no one was" (36). Within two paragraphs, the text refers to "three points of view" (40), "separate minds" (40), "other minds" (40), "different minds" (40), and again to "other minds" (40). Unfortunately, though, catastrophe results from a misattribution by Briony to Robbie. She thinks that Robbie wants to attack Cecilia when in fact he loves her. In contrast to this part of *Atonement,* which shows how Briony's mind is opening up and acquiring some knowledge of the existence of other minds (although what knowledge she has does not prevent her from fatally misreading Cecilia's and Robbie's minds), in the epilogue, many years later, she realizes that, because of her progressive dementia, "my brain, my mind, is closing down" (354).

The modernist novel is characterized by a move away from the heterodiegetic narration that is typical of the realist novel and toward an experimental and impressionistic emphasis on subjectivity, inner states of consciousness, and fragmentary and discontinuous character construction. These sound like deeply internalist preoccupations. And my guess is that, when the companion volume to this one comes to be written on the twentieth- and twenty-first-century novel, the presence of social minds will be found to be much patchier than in the nineteenth century. However, David Herman's chapter on the modernist novel in his edited collection *The Emergence of Mind* illuminatingly examines the modernist novel in terms of situated or distributed cognition. In any event, it should be stressed that the absence of social minds is as significant as their presence. If social minds in twentieth- and twenty-first-century fiction are fractured, attenuated, or even absent, then that, in itself, is an important fact.

I have maintained throughout this study that both perspectives, the internalist and the externalist, are necessary for a full picture of the workings of fictional minds in novels. In my view, this is as true of the twentieth- and twenty-first-century novel as it is of the nineteenth. The purpose of the discussion in the following section is to enrich, deepen, and complicate the picture of social minds that was presented in the earlier chapters on nineteenth-century canonical novels. I will now jump to the contemporary period in order to show that the concerns of the previous chapters are still relevant. I do this by giving a single example of a social-minds analysis of a modern novel. I have chosen Ian McEwan's *Enduring Love* for this purpose. McEwan is a good choice because his work reflects an interest in the whole history of the novel, even as he works in both modernist and postmodernist ways to represent fictional consciousness. As shown above, he is a novelist who has a self-conscious interest in fictional minds. The energy of *Enduring Love* is keyed to the subject of intermentality and, in particular, to the attribution breakdown within the intermental unit formed by the couple at the heart of the novel (Joe and Clarissa). We readers, as interpreters, are drawn into this breakdown if we assume, from the beginning, that the relationship between Joe and Clarissa will be robust enough to withstand the shock caused by the eruption of a mad person into their lives. It may well be that pressures and shocks of this sort will be found by a history of fictional social minds to be characteristic of the modern novel.

ENDURING LOVE

The character-narrator of this novel, Joe, is a popular science writer who, following a hot-air balloon accident in which a man dies, is stalked by a young man, Jed Parry. Jed is in love with Joe and believes that Joe is in love with him. Joe comes to understand that Jed is suffering from *de Clerambault's syndrome* or *erotomania* (a real complaint), which causes the sufferer to fall in love with someone who is usually older and of a higher social status, and who, sufferers often think, sends them signals of their love, for example by drawing their curtains. Sufferers typically stalk their victims and often attack them when they are rejected. However, Joe's partner, Clarissa, does not take Jed seriously, is skeptical of Joe's concerns, and thinks that Joe should have handled Jed better. The police are also unhelpful. After an unsuccessful attempt on Joe's life, Jed threatens Clarissa with a knife and Joe shoots and wounds him. Jed is then detained in a psychiatric hospital. At the end of Joe's narrative he and Clarissa are separated. The novel ends with an academic paper on the case (apparently thought to be genuine by some reviewers) which mentions briefly and in passing that Joe and Clarissa are later reconciled.

My purpose in discussing this novel is to examine the nature of the attributions of madness to Jed by Joe and Clarissa, and to show how these attributional differences cause the breakdown of that couple's intermental unit. I conclude the discussion with an analysis of Clarissa's character—and, in particular, the question of whether her behavior is sufficiently motivated or not—from a number of different aspects: characterization theory, empathy, rhetorical and ethical criticism, and gender studies. It is in this way that I will be looking at the process by which *attributions* (a cognitive term) become *judgments* (an ethical term). Put bluntly, I think McEwan's treatment of the character of Clarissa does not work. This section is, therefore, intended in part to show that a social-minds approach can form the basis of aesthetic appraisals of texts that bear a greater resemblance to mainstream literary criticism than the earlier, rather formalist and descriptive treatments of the nineteenth-century novels. (For a persuasive and highly productive disagreement with my position on Clarissa from a rhetorical perspective, see James Phelan's "Cognitive Narratology, Rhetorical Narratology, and Interpretive Disagreement: A Response to Alan Palmer's Analysis of *Enduring Love*" [2009].)

I referred in chapter 1 to the debate about whether people regard their lives as narratives and whether this is a good thing. *Enduring Love* contributes to this debate by repeatedly and explicitly drawing attention to its characters' attempts to make sense of and control their experiences by turning them into narratives. Four different perspectives on the storyworld of the novel are directly presented in the text:

- Joe (the bulk of the text consists of his first-person narrative);
- Clarissa (one chapter is written by Joe but focalized through her; and her letter to Joe is also reproduced within Joe's narrative);
- Jed (two of his letters to Joe are also reproduced); and
- the authors of the academic article that follows Joe's narrative.

These perspectives comprise narratives that, in different ways, account for, and try to make sense of, the events that occur in the storyworld. Unsurprisingly, it emerges that life is aspectual. The words *narrative* and *story* recur continually, and even rather heavy-handedly, as ever-present reminders of aspectuality throughout the text. A minor character, Mrs Logan, has a "story" (122), "a narrative that only grief, the dementia of pain, could devise" (123). Joe asks whether Jed believes "in his private narrative" that he was sparing Clarissa's feelings (144). "It was only when they reached us that our story could continue" (173). "I had my story" (196). "I want to hear this story at first hand" (224). There are references to the "narrative compression of storytelling" (213) and "Lacy's story" (220). And this is just a selection. Given this plethora of stories and narratives, an objective view of the aspectual events of the storyworld will not be possible. To reinforce the point, the impossibility of such objectivity is referred to twice: "There could be no private redemption in objectivity" (181); and, "Besides, there isn't only ever one system of logic" (214). This point becomes particularly significant when Joe's reliability as a narrator of the events in the storyworld is called into question.

Both Joe and Clarissa obsessively retell the story of the accident. They turn it into a narrative. They are shown to be "circling it, stalking it, until we had cornered and began to tame it with words" (29). Reinforcing the need to "tame" events by means of narrative, Joe says later that, "Over the days and weeks, Clarissa and I told our story many times to friends, colleagues and relatives" (36). During this period, "our story was gaining in coherence; it had shape, and now it was spoken from a place of safety" (36). (Incidentally, this process is rather reminiscent of Briony's narrativizings, her continual and self-conscious retellings and reshapings, of the events in *Atonement*.) When describing Jed's request that they pray together, he tells "the prayer story as comedy" (30). The need to narrativize the accident lessens once the event has been tamed: "Talking the events over with friends no longer seems to help because, she thinks, she has reached a core of senselessness" (80).

Joe also likes to narrativize other events. Just before the murder attempt in the restaurant, Joe confesses that "I would have liked to tell the story of my encounter with Inspector Linley, spice it up a little and squeeze some amusement from it" (164). His need to narrativize is also apparent after the restaurant shooting: "A day or so later it became a temptation to invent or elaborate details about the table next to ours, to force memory to deliver what was never captured . . . It also became difficult to disentangle what I discovered later from what I sensed at the time" (166). So much so that some of the details that he gives to the police are later contradicted by others.

As Joe is a popular science writer, his job consists of narrativizing science: "I can spin a decent narrative out of the stumblings, back-trackings and random successes that lie behind most scientific breakthroughs" (75). But he is ambivalent about his work because he wants to be a "real" scientist and occasionally makes unsuccessful attempts to get back into serious science. In particular, he feels revulsion at the professional necessity to narrativize his subject: "Narrative—my gut tightened at the word. What balls I had written the night before" (56). He feels guilty about his dishonest methodology: the use made of a small number of convenient examples together with a total disregard for the many other counterexamples. In his science writing, as with his urge to spice up and tell as comedy his narratives of the events in his life, he is imposing an arbitrary and aspectual framework on the inchoate flux of facts and events.

Because of his occupation, Joe has a tendency to come up with scientific explanations for things. Some of these relate to the question of attribution. When Joe is waiting at the airport for Clarissa and looking at the other people in the crowd, he decides that the expressions on their faces confirm "Darwin's contention that the many expressions of emotion in humans are universal, genetically inscribed" (4). Later, there is a long and general scientific discussion on the age-old question of whether we can ascribe behavior to nature or nurture (70–77). These discussions form a context for the specific attributional problems that are caused by madness. The notion of madness arises from the difficulty in reliably projecting mental states onto others. To say that behavior is obsessive, mad, or insane is to admit that it is not possible to ascribe reliable motives, reasons, and intentions for actions, and so other explanations must be found. When the standard process does not work, the default explanation is "he must be mad." Mad people have unreadable minds; they do not have social minds. There is a significant emphasis in the text on madness as a complete, self-contained, solipsistic world that sane people cannot enter: Jed's "world was emotion, invention and yearning" (147); "His was a world determined from the inside, driven by private necessity, and this way it could remain intact . . . He illuminated the world with his feelings, and the world confirmed him at every turn his feelings took" (143). "He was inviolable in his solipsism" (144). The scientific paper explains that, as a "well-encapsulated delusional system" (238), "erotomania may act as a defence against depression and loneliness by creating a full intrapsychic world" (239).

As Joe is initially unable to narrativize Jed's behavior according to the usual rules, he characteristically seeks a scientific explanation. At the first mention by Jed of Joe drawing his curtain, it is apparent to Joe that the curtains have an *attributional* significance for him. "A curtain used as a signal. Now I was closer than before. I almost had it" (92). Joe has a faint memory of the importance of the signal from the "lover" for de Clerambault sufferers, but cannot quite place it at first. Finally he remembers the existence of de Clerambault's syndrome: "The name was like a fanfare, a clear trumpet sound recalling me to my own obsessions. There was research to follow through now and I knew exactly where to start. A syndrome was a framework of prediction and it offered a kind of *comfort*. I was almost *happy*... It was as if I had at last been offered that research post with my old professor" (124; my emphasis). He is deeply relieved when he is able to attach a scientific label to this disruptive and inexplicable event in his life. He sees Jed's behavior as "a love whose morbidity I was now *anxious* to research" (127; my emphasis). The point is reinforced even more strongly a little later: "Studying Parry with reference to a syndrome I could tolerate, even *relish*, but meeting him yet again, in the street, especially now that I had read his first letter, had frightened me" (130; my emphasis). Although "comfort," "happy," and "relish" are odd words to use in this context, the reader knows why he uses them. He feels reassured by his knowledge: "I had read the literature and knew the possibilities" (153). He now has some control over the situation. Also, he makes it explicit that part of the reason for his frantic scientific study of Jed's madness is to bring him closer to Clarissa again: "What could I learn about Parry that would restore me to Clarissa?" (128). And he feels better even though the conclusions are not necessarily reassuring in themselves, and do not appear to suggest that any such control is going to be possible: "Well over a half of all male de Clerambaults in one survey had attempted violence on the subjects of their obsessions" (142).

Having found a coherent narrative that can serve as an explanation for Jed's behavior, it is also important for Joe that, in addition, it be narrativized as criminal. Joe stresses that "Parry's behaviour had to be generalised into a crime" (73). However, it is noticeable that this move is always resisted by everyone else associated with the case. Clarissa certainly does not see Jed as a criminal, and she never takes seriously the possibility that he might become violent. Joe's narrative also differs from the official one. After Joe describes Jed's behavior to a policeman, he is told that it is not possible to establish that what Jed is doing is against the law. The response is that "There's nothing here that's threatening, abusive or insulting as defined by Section Five of the Public Order Act" (157). The aspectual nature of the narrative that Joe has constructed for Jed is thereby given additional emphasis.

Joe's theoretical or scientific interest in Jed's mental illness may in part explain his dilemma over how to deal with the madman. Joe frequently engages with Jed and then immediately experiences a marked desire to disengage. Their encounters are characterized by a continual seesawing of movement toward him, then withdrawal. "'What do you want?' Even as I said the words, I wanted them back. I did not want to know what he wanted, or rather, I did not want to be told" (59). Sometimes Joe gives in to his undeniable feelings of curiosity and also pity. At other times he withdraws and refuses to humor him in any way. He agonizes a good deal over this recurring pattern. "I was quite interested to know, although I also wanted to get away" (64); "I should have walked on, but his intensity held me for the moment and I had just sufficient curiosity to echo him" (65); and "I had decided to say nothing more to him, but I couldn't help myself" (68). Joe's ambivalence has serious consequences for his relationship with Clarissa when she accuses him of leading Jed on. Joe links the two issues of scientific curiosity and attributional failure when he says that "When this story was closed it would be important to know something about Parry. Otherwise he would remain as much a projection of mine as I was of his" (60). There is a laudable awareness here of one of the chief pitfalls in the attribution process—the temptation to project one's self into others. This is the concern that Clennam has about turning Little Dorrit into a "domesticated fairy." It could even be argued that Joe goes too far in this direction because, when encounters with Jed go badly wrong, he seems to imagine himself "accused" of "a failed extension into mental space" (128). He appears to feel guilty that he does not realize immediately that Jed is mad. But why? This seems to me to be an overreaction. It is surely praiseworthy to be reluctant to attribute madness too quickly.

Meetings between the two men tend to revolve around the issues of control and intimacy. Jed remarks, "It's all about control, isn't it?" (62). Joe is understandably disturbed at the apparent closeness of their relationship. He finds himself "talking to a stranger in terms more appropriate to an affair, or a marriage on the rocks" (67). To his horror, he thinks, "I'm in a *relationship*" (73). In an oddly intimate form of words, Joe refers to Jed as "my de Clerambault" (207). The use of the possessive when referring to Jed strikes a jarring note. The issues of power, control, and intimacy become an important element in the conflicts between Joe and Clarissa when she begins to have doubts about Joe's handling of the situation: "Was I giving her the impression that I was secretly flattered by Parry's attention, or that I was unconsciously leading him on, or that without recognising the fact, I was enjoying my power over him, or—perhaps she thought this—my power over her?" (102).

It is hardly surprising that the group of people including Joe and Jed who are suddenly thrown together in the hot-air balloon accident at the beginning of the novel do not form an intermental unit. What is more surprising, though, is the fact that the narrative explicitly draws attention to the absence of intermentality. Joe states, "I should make something clear. There may have been a vague communality of purpose, but we were never a team" (10). The point is an important one, because he repeats it a few pages later: "But as I've said, there was no team, there was no plan, no agreement to be broken" (14). Nevertheless, the academic article that follows Joe's narrative speculates that Jed's participation in this loose social unit, however fleeting and ephemeral it may have been, has a profound psychological effect on him. The authors suggest that "Such a transformation, from a 'socially empty' life to intense *team-work* may have been the dominating factor in precipitating the [de Clerambault's] syndrome" (239; my emphasis). The article is proposing that Jed's participation in what he thinks is an intermental unit (although Joe does not agree and it is doubtful whether any of the other participants would either) is the proximate cause of his descent into madness. Whether or not this is a plausible theory in this specific case, it is a telling acknowledgment of the power and importance of intermental units.

At the start of the novel, Joe and Clarissa form a fairly well-functioning unit. Initially, their attributions of states of mind to the other appear to be accurate and successful. There was nothing, Joe says, until the Jed affair, that "threatened our free and intimate existence" (8). However, as with most relationships, there are some fine, potential fault lines. One is Joe's desire to become a real scientist again. Clarissa finds Joe's occasional unsuccessful attempts to do so rather upsetting because they are doomed to failure and they disturb the equilibrium of their relationship. Another is Clarissa's inability to have children. Both of them would like to have a family. When these fault lines crack wide open on the impact of the invasion into their lives of a madman, then their relationship ceases to be intermental. The reason for the split is that they attribute different states of mind to Jed. They narrativize him intramentally. They never achieve a stable consensus on this issue. Joe's attributions, as we have seen, construct a double cognitive narrative for Jed as a threatening, dangerous, potentially violent madman. Clarissa initially denies that Jed is mad at all. She narrativizes him as a joke, implies that Joe is unreliable in his accounts of Jed's behavior, and trivializes the matter as a nuisance. Then, once she does accept the reality, she sees him as capable of being, in effect, tamed and domesticated. She also alleges that, in any event, it is all Joe's fault (56–58).

Clarissa's views on Jed, are, on the whole, focalized through Joe. To put the point another way, Joe is exercising his theory of mind on what Clarissa thinks of Jed. Clarissa is only able to speak for herself directly when she writes her letter to Joe, but this letter is placed near the end of Joe's narrative. Joe refers frequently to what he thinks (reliably, in my view) is Clarissa's view of Jed, and tries hard to be convinced by it: "Clarissa was right, he was a harmless fellow with a strange notion, a nuisance at most, hardly the threat I had made him out to be" (61). While in general Joe sees Jed as dangerous, he is constantly aware that Clarissa regards him as harmless and he pays careful attention to her views. "Then he [Jed] represented the unknown, into which I projected all kinds of inarticulate terrors. Now I considered him to be a confused and eccentric young man who couldn't look me in the eye, whose inadequacies and emotional cravings rendered him harmless. He was a pathetic figure, not a threat after all, but an annoyance, one that might frame itself, just as Clarissa had said, into an amusing *story*" (69; my emphasis). Later, Jed's first letter to Joe appears to Clarissa to be "such an unfaked *narrative* of emotion" (101; my emphasis) that she is convinced that it is Joe who is at fault. However, despite Joe's attempt to reconcile the two narratives, they soon diverge. Trying on Clarissa's attributions does not work for Joe for long. In the next passage, written by Joe but focalized through Clarissa, the note of skepticism is unmistakable: "She thinks she understands Parry well enough. A lonely inadequate man, a Jesus freak who is probably living off his parents, and dying to connect with someone, anyone, even Joe" (81). She has constructed a detailed life story for Jed that is fairly accurate, but what she leaves out is his potential for violence.

Joe's awareness of Clarissa's ambivalence about Jed's madness is well caught in this passage: "She seemed to agree with me that he was mad and that I was right to feel harassed. 'Seemed' because she was not quite wholehearted, and if she said I was right—and I thought she did—she never really acknowledged that she had been wrong. I sensed she was keeping her options open, though she denied it when I asked her" (100). The reliable mind reading on which any successful intermental unit is based is under threat here. It has become dangerously intermittent. Joe knows that something is not quite right, but he is simply not sure of the extent to which Clarissa's views on Jed diverge from his own. In particular, he is not sure what Clarissa's "options" might be. Perhaps the divergence with the greatest impact on their relationship is Clarissa's insistence on holding Joe responsible, at least in part, for Jed's obsession. Joe thinks that Clarissa is fooled by Jed's "artful technique of suggesting a past, a pact, a collusion, a secret life of glances and gestures" (100). In other words, Jed has constructed a (nonexistent) narrative that Clarissa finds plausible. Multiple levels of theory of mind result: Joe thinks that Clarissa believes that Jed knows that Joe loves him too. In a key statement in her letter near the end of the novel, Clarissa writes to Joe, "I accept that Parry is mad in ways I could never have guessed at. All the same, I can understand how he might have formed the impression that you were leading him on" (218). This is in part because "You went your own way, you denied him everything, and that allowed his fantasies, and ultimately his hatred, to flourish" (218). These first-person views show that Joe was right all along to think that Clarissa had strong reservations about his handling of the affair. Both these statements put a good deal of the blame for the harm caused by Jed's actions on Joe. What is noticeable about them is how intolerant they are of Joe's perceived shortcomings. Clarissa certainly cuts Joe no slack whatsoever. I will come back to this point later.

As a result of these intramental divergences, the unit is put under great pressure. The two individuals start to separate. They both acknowledge that it is Jed who has caused the divide. Joe says of the period before he invaded their lives, "Now I could not quite imagine a route back into that innocence" (127). Understandably, he is reluctant to talk to Clarissa about Jed: "Another reason for not talking now of our problem was that we would be bound to let Parry into our bedroom" (145). Clarissa also knows that they are drifting apart: "She remembers too that they love each other and happen to be in very different mental universes now, with very different needs" (82). However, intermentality is still a factor in their relationship. During their row, she realizes that, despite her best efforts, "She has let herself be drawn into Joe's mental state, his problems, his dilemmas, his needs" (85). Nevertheless, Joe refers to "the fine crack of estrangement that had appeared between Clarissa and me" (99). Their attributions of states of mind to each other become judgmental and confrontational. In Joe's words, "We were hardly at war, but everything between us was stalled . . . To her I was manic, perversely obsessed, and, worst of all, the thieving invader of her private space. As far as I was concerned she was disloyal, unsupportive in this time of crisis, and irrationally suspicious" (139).

Any attempts at communication are inconclusive because they have less knowledge of the other's mind than they used to: Joe "felt that we had been denied a conclusion . . . I thought that there remained between us an unarticulated dispute, though I wasn't certain what it was" (101). Joe's illicit and totally unjustified reading of Clarissa's letters seems to her to be "a statement, a message, from you to me, it's a signal. The trouble is, I don't know what it means" (132). Clarissa tells Joe that a "stranger invaded our lives, and the first thing that happened was that you became a stranger to me" (218). However, it is noticeable from these statements that some vestigial traces of intermental thought remain, even though the gaps between them widen. They know what they do not know. In Donald Rumsfeld's phrase, these are known unknowns. What would be even worse, I suppose, would be unknown unknowns: not knowing that they do not know what the other is thinking, and assuming that everything is still fine when it is not. Given these pressures, it is inevitable that, toward the end, they drift apart. Joe refers to the "speed with which this mate, this familiar, was transforming herself into a separate person" (221). He talks slightingly of her letter: "I disliked its wounded, self-righteous tone, its clammy emotional logic, its knowingness that hid behind a highly selective memory" (222). As far as both of them are concerned, "The matter of our differences was unbroachable" (223). (However, as stated in a brief aside in the academic paper, they are eventually reconciled and adopt children.)

A powerful irony operating in the novel is the fact that, when the perfectly sane Joe is faced by the mad Jed, both Clarissa and even Joe himself develop doubts about *Joe's* own sanity. At one point Joe feels like a "mental patient at the end of visiting hours. *Don't leave me here with my mind*, I thought" (58). Clarissa feeds these fears. In the chapter in which Joe speculates about what Clarissa thinks about how his mind is working, he writes (from her point of view): "The trouble with Joe's precise and careful mind is that it takes no account of its own emotional field. He seems unaware that his arguments are no more than *ravings*, they are an *aberration* and they have a cause" (83; my emphasis). Clarissa is wondering hard about Joe's mental health: "Perhaps Parry, or the Parry as described by Joe, does not exist." During their row, she says, "You were so intense about him as soon as you met him. It's like you invented him" (86). "You ought to be asking yourself which way this fixation runs" (86). During another exchange, she exclaims, "I'm talking about your mind." When Joe replies, "There's nothing wrong with my mind," she responds, "Don't you realise you've got a problem" (148). Joe decides that "Now it was settled in her mind I was unhinged" (150). "Clarissa thought that her emotions were the appropriate guide, that she could feel her way to the truth, when what was needed was information, foresight and careful calculation. It was therefore natural, though disastrous for us both, that she should think I was mad" (150). That "therefore" is surely a stretch. Why should Clarissa relying on her emotions and feeling her way to the truth *necessarily* cause her to think that he is mad?

His alleged mania is linked to his growing sense of loneliness. Because the intermental unit has been broken and Clarissa has doubts about Joe's sanity, he is alone: "We continued to live side by side, but I knew that I was on my own" (149). "Clarissa thought I was mad, the police thought I was a fool, and one thing was clear: the task of getting us back to where we were was going to be mine alone" (161). "I was on my own" (175). "I felt my isolation and vulnerability" (177). This isolation is self-reinforcing. The more alone he feels, the more Clarissa feels it too: "Your being right is not a simple matter . . . Shoulder to shoulder? You went it alone, Joe" (216). "You were manic, and driven, and very lonely" (217). These discussions about Joe's sanity and the emphasis on his aloneness will reinforce any doubts about the reliability of Joe's narration.

Enduring Love is an instructive lesson in the aspectuality of narrative and of life generally. It turns out that Joe was right all along to think that Jed was a dangerous madman and that Clarissa was wrong not to take Joe's views seriously. He *was* a reliable narrator. Clarissa does not know *at the time* that Joe is right. Fair enough—we all make mistakes. But for me, the issue is not Clarissa being wrong. It is whether she should believe in Joe more at the time and trust in him more than she does. From her aspectual view of the storyworld, what she undeniably *does* know is that they have a loving, trusting relationship and that he is intelligent and reliable. So why does she not believe him? Why does she not accept his narrative and, instead, create one of her own? Why does she not accept his attributions to Jed and replace them with hers? What evidence (what T. S. Eliot called the "objective correlative") is there that this character, Clarissa, would behave in this way? What would justify such a breach of faith by such an intelligent person within such a trusting relationship? How likely is it that this character, Clarissa, would think that this character, Joe, would wish to lead Jed on or even make it all up? How likely is it that she would be so unyieldingly critical of him? Why did she not make allowances for the fact that he is being stalked by a madman? Putting the question even more tendentiously: Is Clarissa's why-didn't-you-just-invite-this-homicidal-maniac-in-for-a-cup-of-tea? strategy *meant* to sound as utterly stupid, inadequate, and pathetic as it does to me?

This discussion of Clarissa's behavior, and in particular the talk of evidence for the workings of characters' minds, raises interesting questions about characterization. The evidence that I have been discussing comprises the data that readers slot into the cognitive characterization frame that they create for the Clarissa character. My frame is as follows: a highly intelligent, sensitive, self-aware, and conscientious person who loves her partner, tries hard to behave well, and has a considerable degree of insight into herself, other people, and the mechanics of relationships generally. So, can I account, within this frame, for a person who would *immediately* be so utterly distrustful of the man that she loves that she instantly jumps to the conclusion that he is making things up? Would not the character that I have created give him some considerable benefit of the doubt? So, what happens next? Should another frame be created? But I am not sure what that other frame would be, given that it would contain data that, to me, seems inconsistent with what is already there. So perhaps we simply say that this is a characteristic of the text of this novel that we should simply accept. OK, people *are* inconsistent, they *are* complex. We're not robots. But even though I know this to be true, why do I find it unsatisfying as an answer in this case?

In order to explore this question further, I will summarize Clarissa's criticisms of Joe as follows:

(1) Joe may be making it all up.
(2) Joe is guilty of leading Jed on.
(3) Joe does not show sufficient empathy for Jed: if Joe had invited him into the house he may not have become violent.
(4) Joe cuts himself off emotionally from Clarissa and goes his own way.
(5) Joe reads her letters.

The last point is easily dealt with. He is wrong to read her letters. This is something that Joe should not have done. It was a morally indefensible act. However, her lack of trust in him had begun before then. The other criticisms deserve closer examination. (1), (2), and (3) appear to be contradictory. If he is making it up, then the possibilities of leading Jed on and not dealing with him properly do not arise. (2) and (3) are equally at odds. Surely, showing more empathy and inviting him into the house would be the clearest possible case of leading him on. As for the substance of (2), Joe is certainly ambivalent about how best to deal with Jed, but whether he can then be said to be "leading him on" seems to me to be debatable. With regard to Joe going off on his own (4), this looks like a chicken-and-egg situation in which, if Clarissa had been more supportive, Joe would not have felt the need to go it alone.

It is sometimes said that the relations between men and women are made difficult by the fact that they are governed by two completely different impulses: men by shame and women by fear. The typical dynamics of arguments between men and women can, it is argued, be explained in these terms. This view might be applied to this case by suggesting that Joe feels shame at the growing closeness and intimacy of his relationship with Jed, and Clarissa feels fearful that Joe is drifting away from her and she is losing the person she loves. "It's always been a fear that she'll live with someone who goes crazy. That's why she chose rational Joe" (83). In addition, there are the underlying tensions in the relationship that I referred to earlier: Joe wanting to go back into real science while Clarissa knows that he has left it too late; and Clarissa's inability to have children. Perhaps these latent conflicts can explain Clarissa's behavior, especially if she perceives Joe as irresponsibly attempting to avoid the problems in their relationship by throwing himself into the research into Jed's condition?

It may help at this point to focus on one particular event: Jed's first phone call. Joe errs in not telling Clarissa about it at the time and waiting for a day or two before he mentions it. "It may have been exhaustion, or perhaps my concealment was protective of her, but I know I made my first serious mistake" (37). He also explains the delay by saying that it was because he could not cope with it at that time so soon after the balloon accident and he did not want to disrupt the intermental equilibrium that they had only just managed to recover following this accident. ("Would it have been right then . . . to intrude upon our happiness with an account of Parry's phone call?" [53].) Let us look at this issue first in terms of empathy. (See Suzanne Keen's *Empathy and the Novel* [2007] for an extended treatment of this topic.) If I were to put myself into Clarissa's position, I would find Joe's explanation satisfactory. I suppose this is because I do that sort of thing myself. I sometimes wait before I tell someone something because I need time to process it myself first. But it seems to me that this is not what empathy is: it is not me trying to imagine being *myself* in that position; it is me trying to imagine being *Clarissa* in that position. And to do that, we have to ask: What caused her to behave in the way that she did? In other words, the reader must attribute reasons, causes, motives, and intentions to her actions, bringing us back, once again, to the question of evidence. So we need to return once more to attribution theory.

Our well-researched tendency to overvalue the reasons for actions that focus on the individual ("he did that because he's that kind of person") and undervalue those that focus on the context ("he did that because that's what everybody tends to do in that kind of situation") is referred to by psychologists as the *fundamental attribution error*. Within this attributional framework, it is possible to see Joe's decision not to report the call in situational or contextual terms. That is, "Well, anyone in his situation—tired, stressed, wanting a little respite—would have done the same." It is equally plausible, though, to see the decision as an example of a dispositional fallibility: his need to control the narrative. The combination of Joe's personality flaw and Clarissa's understandable fear of loss of intimacy might form the beginnings of an ethical justification of her behavior. But is it enough to set against the contrary case? Is not her distrust a distinct overreaction both to her fear of Joe drifting away and to Joe's apparent faults? After all, there are worse things in life than being rather controlling. In any event, how much of a control freak is Joe? Agreed, his disposition is to use narrative as a controlling device, but don't we all? He may have an ambivalent attitude toward Jed because he is curious about the syndrome, but this hardly seems to me to amount to an illegitimate exercise in power and control. And the careful and respectful attention that he pays to Clarissa's initial views on Jed is anything but controlling.

At this point I have to confess that, when I read this novel for the first time, and again when I was studying it for the purpose of writing this chapter, I found myself getting angry with Clarissa. This is shaming to admit, but true nevertheless. I thought to myself, How dare she distrust and undermine Joe and leave him, a man alone, to face this homicidal maniac! Why was she not by his side? (My reaction, as you can see, had a rather "High Noon" flavor.) On the other hand, I have been equally conscious of a parallel, contradictory response: this is to doubt that Clarissa's behavior is sufficiently motivated by McEwan the novelist. I have discussed some of the possible reasons for her behavior—her fear of losing the man she loves, her concern over Joe's desire to be a serious scientist, her pain at not being able to have children with Joe. Nevertheless, I personally am not convinced by them. For me, they do not fully explain her behavior cognitively (as well as not justifying it ethically). These instabilities do not seem to me to constitute sufficient causes for the dramatic widening of the hairline cracks in their relationship under the impact of Jed's madness. And, in particular, I simply do not see what evidence Clarissa has for thinking that it may be Joe who is the madman. So, if I cannot find the evidence to explain or justify Clarissa's behavior, then it seems to me that the choices are these:

- I am an incompetent reader;
- McEwan is an incompetent author; or
- Clarissa is an unethical character.

In other words, the evidence is in the text but I cannot see it, so I am incompetent. Or the evidence is not there and this lack is unintended. This is therefore an aesthetic fault in McEwan the novelist and so he is incompetent. Or the evidence is not there, this is intended, and it therefore shows that Clarissa behaves in an unethical way. She is unjustified in behaving as she does. The question to ask can be simply put: Does Joe do enough wrong? On balance, I would say: no. A more nuanced question is this one: Does McEwan miscalculate in trying to set up a context within which Clarissa's mistrust of Joe can be understood and even forgiven? I would say: yes.

I wish to end this discussion with a tentative speculation that will take what is already a wide-ranging discussion into the area of gender studies. It is that I suspect that there may be a gender divide in readers over Clarissa's behavior. That is, I suspect that women readers may tend to sympathize with Clarissa's concern over what she perceives to be Joe's erratic behavior and her fear of losing him, while men may be more likely to identify with Joe and his anger at what he perceives to be Clarissa's disloyalty. The aspectual view of the novel's storyworld adopted by most women readers may have more in common with Clarissa's perspective than Joe's, and vice versa for male readers. This hypothesis might benefit from some empirical investigation.

SOCIAL MINDS IN OTHER MEDIA

Narratology studies the nature, form, and functioning of all narratives irrespective of their mode or medium of representation. Indeed, many narratological concepts are particularly suited to multimodal analysis (Ryan 2004). As is well known, the story of Cinderella can be told in any number of different discourses or media (a short story, a film, a play, a ballet, a cartoon) and still remain the same story. In considering whether the study of social minds is applicable to narratives in other media, I conclude that it is surprisingly adaptable and is just as revealing about fictional minds across a range of media as it is about written texts. I say that the approach is *surprisingly* adaptable because it was built specifically for written narratives and, before I undertook this exercise, I expected it to be geared far more specifically to novels than in fact it is. In particular, I think that the sort of approach to narrative outlined in this book is well suited to graphic novels and related narrative forms. In his article "Presenting Minds in Graphic Narratives" (2008), Kai Mikkonen argues that the medium of graphic novels "stimulates the viewer's engagement with the minds of characters by recourse to a wide range of verbal modes of narration in a dynamic relation with images that show minds in action" (2008, 302). Mikkonen is extremely successful in exploring the nature of that relation. In addition, it strikes me that a social-minds perspective would work really well in film studies. I will now briefly indicate what such a study might look like by commenting on two scenes in *The Godfather Part I* and a scene from *The Usual Suspects.*

In *The Godfather Part I,* Sollozzo, "the Turk," while putting a business proposition to Don Corleone and his associates, mentions that the rival Tattaglia family will be able to guarantee security. The Don's son, Sonny, starts to object to the implicit slight to the Corleone family, but the Don stops him with a motion of his hand. (After the meeting, the Don tells him, don't ever again tell anyone outside the family what you're thinking.) Following the gesture, there are three split-second close-ups showing the reactions of Sollozzo and two others, Tom Hagen and Clemenza. These lightning-quick shots show in an instant that all three understand perfectly what has just happened: the insiders Hagen and Clemenza know that the outsider Sollozzo knows that Sonny has been humiliated and shown to be an unreliable hothead who is unsuitable to become the eventual head of the family, and that the Don has been forced to acknowledge this weakness publicly; Hagen and Clemenza are embarrassed by their knowledge; Sollozzo is wondering what use he can make of such knowledge, and so on. And the viewer learns about this substantial amount of mental functioning from a section of the film that lasts about a second.

Later in the same film, another son, Michael, is standing at the entrance to the deserted hospital where his seriously ill father is recovering from an assassination attempt. Michael is with a young baker who happened to be visiting at the same time. Although both are unarmed, they successfully pretend to be gunmen and so the car containing the men who have come to kill the Don drives past. Once the crisis is over, the baker is unable to light his cigarette because his hand is shaking so violently. Michael lights the cigarette with a perfectly steady hand and then pauses for a second, looking with surprise and interest at the steadiness of his hand. The self-attributional process in this case involves the sort of external physical evidence relating to body language that is usually thought to be characteristic of third-person attribution. Michael is taking the advice offered by the psychologist Timothy Wilson in chapter 2 and is deducing the nature of his hidden mind by looking outward at his behavior. He has just discovered something about himself from observing his own body, and this discovery is of great teleological importance to the narrative (he knows now that he has the courage to become the leader of the family). And again, the shot lasts little more than a second.

My other film example is included here in order to illustrate how postmodern and unnatural narratives can complicate, disrupt, and subvert the creation and maintenance of social minds in a fictional storyworld. In the famous climax to *The Usual Suspects* it is revealed that the confession being given in a police station by Verbal Kint, an apparent loser, was untrue in many respects and that he is, in fact, the master criminal Keyser Söze. His interrogator discovers this by seeing that many of the details of Verbal's story were taken from the office notice board. As much of the film consists of flashbacks illustrating Verbal's story, viewers find themselves in a similar position to readers of *Atonement*. As an apparently authoritative world-creating narrative has been revealed to be unreliable, how then do we know what *really* happened?

Let us approach the question systematically. Some of the film is authoritative because it is independent of Verbal's narrative, in particular the investigation into the shootout on the ship. Of the content of his story, some of the detail is unimportant—his singing in a barbershop quartet and going to Guatemala. Of the rest, two of the characters in the story are revealed to have made-up names inspired by objects in the police station: Kobayashi and Redfoot. Interestingly, though, we see "Kobayashi" drive Verbal/Söze away from the police station, so, even though his name cannot be "Kobayashi," we do at least know that he exists within the whole film storyworld. But what about Redfoot? Does this character exist at all in the film storyworld? Are the scenes that feature him pure fantasy? Or does he exist under another name? We do not know. Also, the gang, the usual suspects of the title, must exist in the storyworld because the police investigators refer to them. But we do not know about the conversations between them that Verbal describes, or about the power relations between them. Most importantly, was Keaton really the leader of the gang, as Verbal portrays him? So, the fictional minds presented in the film have been radically destabilized. We do not know whether some of these minds existed at all (Redfoot), and we do not know whether others operated in the way that the film shows (Keaton). Oddly, these ontological and epistemological uncertainties tend to be forgotten when, for example, Keaton's characterization is being discussed by film critics. Can we say with any certainty where Keaton's identity is situated, when nearly all of what we know about him is told to us by a proven liar? For the same reason, we cannot know the extent to which the gang of usual suspects ever became a social mind.

Another area in which I believe this sort of cognitive analysis would have rewarding results is in the study of narratives about real minds: history, biography, and autobiography. Once you are alerted to the internalist/externalist divide, surprisingly explicit references to it crop up in the most unexpected places. The British politician Leo Amery said of the prime ministers David Lloyd George and Winston Churchill: "LG was purely external and receptive, the result of intercourse with his fellow men, and non-existent in their absence, while Winston is literary and expressive of himself with hardly any contact with other minds" (*Times Literary Supplement,* page 14, 25 September 2009). It is significant that the so-called group biography is currently becoming fashionable. These books are based on the premise that it can be at least as informative to write biographies of groups as of individuals. The author Richard Holmes made his name by writing conventional biographies of Shelley and Coleridge, but his book *The Age of Wonder* (2008), which won the 2009 Samuel Johnson Prize, is a group biography that examines the life and work both of the scientists of the Romantic age who laid the foundations of modern science and of the Romantic poets who responded to the new science.

My final example of internalist and externalist perspectives in media or genres other than fiction is pure self-indulgence. It is simply an excuse to refer to my first love: American popular music such as blues, jazz, country and western, soul, and gospel music. Consider the highly contrasting worldviews of two famous country gospel songs. First, the opening verse of a beautiful song made famous by the Carter Family called "Lonesome Valley":

> You've got to walk that lonesome valley
> You've got to walk it by yourself
> Ain't nobody here can walk it for you
> You've got to walk it by yourself

This is internalism taken to a chillingly Beckettian conclusion. By contrast, enjoy the thrillingly externalist chorus of an equally wonderful, and rather more typical, gospel song called "Farther Along":

> Farther along we'll know all about it
> Farther along we'll understand why
> Cheer up my brother and walk in the sunshine
> We'll understand it all by and by

CONCLUSION

In his foreword to a book titled *The Shared Mind: Perspectives on Intersubjectivity* (2008), from which the motto for this chapter was taken, Colwyn Trevarthen asserts that "human life and culture is incomprehensible without intersubjective processes" (2008, vii). His conclusion is that "We need a science of the imaginative fictions persons so easily share" (2008, vii). Trevarthen is actually talking about the real-mind sciences. To take his reference to "fictions" more literally, it could be argued that we already have a "science of imaginative fiction": it is called narratology. The purpose of this book has been to attempt to add the last four words of his statement to the existing science.

When a phenomenon is identified that does not fit within a well-established paradigm, an anomaly is created. And, as Thomas Kuhn explained in *The Structure of Scientific Revolutions*:

> Discovery commences with the awareness of anomaly, that is, with the recognition that nature has somehow violated the paradigm-induced expectations that govern normal science. It then continues with a more or less extended exploration of the area of anomaly. And it closes only when the paradigm theory has been adjusted so that the anomalous has become the expected. (1996, 52–53)

The widespread and pervasive existence of fictional social minds and intermental thought constitutes an anomaly within the traditional narratological paradigm for the presentation of consciousness in the novel. The proof is the invisibility of intermental thought within the current theory. However, following a more or less extended exploration of this area and of all of the other aspects of the whole of the social mind in action, the paradigm theory can be adjusted to take full account of their importance. Social minds in the novel will then be anomalous no longer; they will be expected.

WORKS CITED

Abbott, H. Porter. *The Cambridge Introduction to Narrative*. 2nd ed. Cambridge: Cambridge University Press, 2008.
———. "Unreadable Minds and the Captive Reader." *Style* 43.4 (2009): 448–67.
Alber, Jan. "Impossible Storyworlds—And What to Do With Them." *Storyworlds* 1.1 (2009): 79–96.
Austen, Jane. *Emma*. Edited by Ronald Blythe. Harmondsworth, UK: Penguin, 1966 (1816).
———. *Persuasion*. Edited by D. W. Harding. Harmondsworth, UK: Penguin, 1965 (1818).
———. *Pride and Prejudice*. Edited by Vivien Jones. Harmondsworth, UK: Penguin, 2003 (1813).
Bachman, Maria. "Concealing Minds and the Case of *The Woman in White*." In *Victorian Secrecy: Economies of Knowledge and Concealment*. Edited by Albert Pionke. Farnham: Ashgate, 2010.
Bakhtin, Mikhail. *Problems of Dostoevsky's Poetics*. Translated by Caryl Emerson. Manchester, UK: Manchester University Press, 1984.
Bal, Mieke. *Narratology: Introduction to the Theory of Narrative*. 2nd ed. Toronto: University of Toronto Press, 1997.
Bamberg, Michael. "Positioning." In *The Routledge Encyclopedia of Narrative Theory*, edited by David Herman, Manfred Jahn, and Marie-Laure Ryan. London: Routledge, 2005. 445–46.
Bateson, Gregory. *Steps to an Ecology of Mind: A Revolutionary Approach to Man's Understanding of Himself*. New York: Ballantine, 1972.

Berlin, Isaiah. *The Hedgehog and the Fox.* London: Weidenfeld and Nicolson, 1953.
Blackmore, Susan. *Consciousness: A Very Short Introduction.* Oxford: Oxford University Press, 2005.
Brontë, Anne. *The Tenant of Wildfell Hall.* Edited by Stevie Davies. Harmondsworth, UK: Penguin, 1996 (1848).
Brontë, Charlotte. *Shirley.* London: Everyman, 1975 (1849).
Bruner, Jerome. *Actual Minds, Possible Worlds.* Cambridge, MA: Harvard University Press, 1986.
Butte, George. *I Know That You Know That I Know: Narrating Subjects from* Moll Flanders *to* Marnie. Columbus: The Ohio State University Press, 2004.
Carruthers, Peter. "The Evolution of Consciousness." In *Evolution and the Human Mind: Modularity, Language and Meta-cognition,* edited by Peter Carruthers and Andrew Chamberlain. Cambridge: Cambridge University Press, 2000. 254–75.
Case, Alison and Harry E. Shaw. *Reading the Nineteenth-Century Novel: Austen to Eliot.* Oxford: Blackwell, 2008.
Chatman, Seymour. *Story and Discourse: Narrative Structure in Fiction and Film.* Ithaca, NY: Cornell University Press, 1978.
Clark, Andy. *Supersizing the Mind: Embodiment, Action, and Cognitive Extension.* Oxford: Oxford University Press, 2009.
Clark, Andy and David Chalmers. "The Extended Mind." *Analysis* 58 (1998): 7–19.
Cohn, Dorrit. *Transparent Minds: Narrative Modes for Presenting Consciousness in Fiction.* Princeton, NJ: Princeton University Press, 1978.
Collins, Wilkie. *No Name.* Edited by Mark Ford. Harmondsworth, UK: Penguin, 1994 (1862).
Conrad, Joseph. *The Nigger of the 'Narcissus' and Other Stories.* Edited by J. H. Stape and Allan H. Simmons. Harmondsworth, UK: Penguin, 2007 (1897).
Culler, Jonathan. *Structuralist Poetics: Structuralism, Linguistics, and the Study of Literature.* London: Routledge, 1975.
Culpeper, Jonathan. *Language and Characterisation: People in Plays and Other Texts.* London: Longman, 2001.
Damasio, Antonio. *The Feeling of What Happens: Body, Emotion and the Making of Consciousness.* London: Heinemann, 2000.
Davidson, Donald. *Essays on Actions and Events.* Oxford: Oxford University Press, 1980.
Dennett, Daniel C. *Consciousness Explained.* Harmondsworth, UK: Penguin, 1991.
———. *Kinds of Minds: Towards an Understanding of Consciousness.* London: Weidenfeld and Nicholson, 1996.
Dickens, Charles. *Hard Times.* Edited by Kate Flint. Harmondsworth, UK: Penguin, 2003 (1854).
———. *Little Dorrit.* Edited by John Holloway. Harmondsworth, UK: Penguin, 1967 (1857).

Doležel, Lubomír. *Heterocosmica—Fiction and Possible Worlds*. Baltimore: Johns Hopkins University Press, 1998.
Donald, Merlin. *A Mind So Rare: The Evolution of Human Consciousness*. New York: Norton, 2001.
Eco, Umberto. *The Role of the Reader: Explorations in the Semiotics of Texts*. London: Hutchinson, 1981.
Edelman, Gerald. *The Remembered Present: A Biological Theory of Consciousness*. New York: Basic Books, 1989.
Edgeworth, Maria. *Helen*. Northridge, CA: Aegypan Press, 2007 (1837).
Edwards, Derek. *Discourse and Cognition*. London: Sage, 1997.
Edwards, Derek and Jonathan Potter. *Discursive Psychology*. London: Sage, 1992.
Eliot, George. *Middlemarch*. Edited by Bert G. Hornback. New York: Norton, 1977 (1872).
Elster, Jon. *Alchemies of the Mind: Rationality and the Emotions*. Cambridge: Cambridge University Press, 1999.
Emmott, Catherine. *Narrative Comprehension: A Discourse Perspective*. Oxford: Clarendon, 1997.
Ermarth, Elizabeth Deeds. *Realism and Consensus in the English Novel: Time, Space and Narrative*. Edinburgh: Edinburgh University Press, 1998.
Fludernik, Monika. *The Fictions of Language and the Languages of Fiction: The Linguistic Representation of Speech and Consciousness*. London: Routledge, 1993.
———. *An Introduction to Narratology*. London: Routledge, 2009.
———. *Towards a "Natural" Narratology*. London: Routledge, 1996.
Ford, Ford Madox. *The Good Soldier*. Harmondsworth, UK: Penguin, 1972 (1915).
Frith, Chris and Daniel Wolpert. *The Neuroscience of Social Interaction: Decoding, Influencing and Imitating the Actions of Others*. Oxford: Oxford University Press, 2004.
Gaskell, Elizabeth. *Wives and Daughters*. Edited by Frank Glover Smith. Harmondsworth, UK: Penguin, 1969 (1865).
Geertz, Clifford. *The Interpretation of Cultures: Selected Essays*. London: Fontana, 1993.
Gould, Stephen Jay. *The Hedgehog, the Fox, and the Magister's Pox: Mending the Gap Between Science and the Humanities*. New York: Harmony Books, 2003.
Habermas, Jürgen. *The Theory of Communicative Action*. Translated by T. McCarthy. Boston: Beacon, 1984.
Harré, Rom and Grant Gillett. *The Discursive Mind*. London: Sage, 1994.
Heider, Fritz. *The Psychology of Interpersonal Relations*. New York: Wiley, 1958.
Herman, Luc and Bart Vervaeck. *Handbook of Narrative Analysis*. Lincoln: University of Nebraska Press, 2005.
Herman, David. "Cognition, Emotion and Consciousness." In *The Cambridge Companion to Narrative,* edited by David Herman. Cambridge: Cambridge

University Press, 2007a. 245–59.

———. "1880–1945: Re-minding Modernism." In *The Emergence of Mind: Representations of Consciousness in Narrative Discourse in English,* edited by David Herman. Lincoln: University of Nebraska Press, 2011.

———, ed. *The Emergence of Mind: Representations of Consciousness in Narrative Discourse in English.* Lincoln: University of Nebraska Press, 2011.

———. "Hypothetical Focalization." *Narrative* 2.3 (1994): 230–53.

———. "Narrative Theory and the Intentional Stance." *Partial Answers* 6.2 (2008): 233–60.

———. "Regrounding Narratology: The Study of Narratively Organized Systems for Thinking." In *What is Narratology: Questions and Answers Regarding the Status of a Theory,* edited by Tom Kindt and Hans-Harald Muller. Berlin: de Gruyter, 2003a. 303–32.

———. "Scripts, Sequences, and Stories: Elements of a Postclassical Narratology." *PMLA* 112.5 (1997): 1046–59.

———. "Stories as a Tool for Thinking." In *Narrative Theory and the Cognitive Sciences,* edited by David Herman. Stanford, CA: CSLI Press, 2003b. 163–92.

———. *Story Logic: Problems and Possibilities of Narrative.* Lincoln: University of Nebraska Press, 2002.

———. "Storytelling and the Sciences of Mind: Cognitive Narratology, Discursive Psychology, and Narratives in Face-to-Face Interaction." *Narrative* 15.3 (2007b): 306–34.

Hogan, Patrick Colm. *The Mind and Its Stories: Narrative Universals and Human Emotion.* Cambridge: Cambridge University Press, 2003.

Holmes, Richard. *The Age of Wonder: How the Romantic Generation Discovered the Beauty and Terror of Science.* New York: HarperCollins, 2008.

Hutchins, Edwin. *Cognition in the Wild.* Cambridge, MA: MIT Press, 1995.

Hutto, Daniel D. *Folk Psychological Narratives: The Sociocultural Basis of Understanding Reasons.* Cambridge, MA: MIT Press, 2008.

Jahn, Manfred. "Frames, Preferences, and the Reading of Third Person Narratives: Towards a Cognitive Narratology." *Poetics Today* 18.4 (1997): 441–68.

James, Henry. *The Portrait of a Lady.* Edited by Geoffrey Moore. Harmondsworth, UK: Penguin, 1984 (1882).

———. *The Tragic Muse.* Edited by Philip Horne. Harmondsworth, UK: Penguin, 1995 (1890).

James, William. *The Principles of Psychology.* Cambridge, MA: Harvard University Press, 1983 (1890).

Joyce, James. *Ulysses.* Edited by Hans Walter Gabler. Harmondsworth, UK: Penguin, 1986 (1922).

Kafalenos, Emma. *Narrative Causalities.* Columbus: The Ohio State University Press, 2006.

Keen, Suzanne. *Empathy and the Novel.* Oxford: Oxford University Press, 2007.

———. *Narrative Form.* Basingstoke, UK: Palgrave, 2003.

Kelley, Harold. "The Processes of Causal Attribution." *American Psychologist* 28 (1973): 107–28.

Knapp, John V. *Striking at the Joints: Contemporary Psychology and Literary Criticism.* Lanham, MD: University Press of America, 1996.

Kuhn, Thomas. *The Structure of Scientific Revolutions.* Chicago: University of Chicago Press, 1996 (1962).

Lanser, Susan Sniader. *Fictions of Authority: Women Writers and Narrative Voice.* Ithaca, NY: Cornell University Press, 1992.

Le Doux, Joseph. *The Emotional Brain.* London: Orion, 1999.

Lodge, David. *Consciousness and the Novel: Connected Essays.* London: Secker and Warburg, 2002.

Lothe, Jakob. *Narrative in Fiction and Film: An Introduction.* Oxford: Oxford University Press, 2000.

MacIntyre, Alasdair. *After Virtue: A Study in Moral Theory.* Notre Dame, IN: University of Notre Dame Press, 1981.

Marcus, Amit. "A Contextual View of Narrative Fiction in the First Person Plural." *Narrative* 16.1 (2008): 46–64.

Margolin, Uri. "Characters in Literary Narrative: Representation and Signification." *Semiotica* 106.3–4 (1995): 373–92.

———. "Characters and Their Versions." In *Fiction Updated: Theories of Fictionality, Narratology, and Poetics,* edited by Calin-Andrei Mihailescu and Walid Hamarneh. Toronto: Toronto University Press, 1996a. 113–32.

———. "Telling Our Story: On 'We' Literary Narratives." *Language and Literature* 5.2 (1996b): 115–33.

———. "Telling in the Plural: From Grammar to Ideology." *Poetics Today* 21.3 (2000): 591–618.

McEwan, Ian. *Atonement.* London: Vintage, 2002 (2001).

———. *Enduring Love.* London: Vintage, 2006 (1997).

McGahern, John. *Amongst Women.* London: Faber and Faber, 2008 (1991).

McGinn, Colin. *Mindfucking.* Durham, NC: Acumen, 2008.

McHale, Brian. "Islands in the Stream of Consciousness: Dorrit Cohn's *Transparent Minds.*" *Poetics Today* 2.2 (1981): 183–91.

Mikkonen, Kai. "Presenting Minds in Graphic Narratives." *Partial Answers* 6.2 (2008): 301–21.

Mildorf, Jarmila. "Review of Alan Palmer's *Fictional Minds.*" *Anglia* 123.4 (2006): 775–79.

Moretti, Franco. *Atlas of the European Novel 1800–1900.* New York: Verso, 1998.

Nietzsche, Friedrich. *Beyond Good and Evil.* Translated by R. J. Hollingdale. Harmondsworth, UK: Penguin, 1990 (1886).

Nűnning, Ansgar. "On the Perspective Structure of Narrative Texts: Steps Towards a Constructivist Narratology." In *New Perspectives on Narrative Perspective*, edited by Willi van Peer and Seymour Chatman. Albany: State University of New York Press, 2000. 207–23.

Nussbaum, Martha: *Love's Knowledge: Essays on Philosophy and Literature*. Oxford: Oxford University Press, 1992.

Oatley, Keith. *Best Laid Schemes: The Psychology of Emotions*. Cambridge: Cambridge University Press, 1992.

———. "Emotions." In *The MIT Encyclopedia of the Cognitive Sciences*, edited by Robert A. Wilson and Frank C. Keil. Cambridge, MA: MIT Press, 1999. 273–75.

Palmer, Alan. *Fictional Minds*. Lincoln: University of Nebraska Press, 2004.

Perry, Menakem. "Literary Dynamics: How the Order of a Text Creates Its Meanings." *Poetics Today* 1.1–2 (1979): 35–64, 311–61.

Phelan, James. "Cognitive Narratology, Rhetorical Narratology, and Interpretive Disagreement: A Response to Alan Palmer's Analysis of *Enduring Love*." *Style* 43.3 (2009): 309–21.

———. "Editor's Column." *Narrative* 13.5 (2005): 205–10.

———. *Reading People, Reading Plots: Character, Progression, and the Interpretation of Narrative*. Columbus: The Ohio State University Press, 1989.

Pinker, Steven. *How the Mind Works*. Harmondsworth, UK: Penguin, 1997.

———*The Language Instinct: The New Science of Language and Mind*. Harmondsworth, UK: Penguin, 1994.

Priest, Stephen. *Theories of the Mind*. Harmondsworth, UK: Penguin, 1991.

Pynchon, Thomas. *The Crying of Lot 49*. London: Vintage, 1996 (1966).

Rabinowitz, Peter J. *Before Reading: Narrative Conventions and the Politics of Interpretation*. Columbus: The Ohio State University Press, 1987.

Richardson, Brian. *Unlikely Stories: Causality and the Nature of Modern Narrative*. Newark: University of Delaware Press, 1997.

———. *Unnatural Voices: Extreme Narration in Modern and Contemporary Fiction*. Columbus: The Ohio State University Press, 2006.

Rimmon-Kenan, Shlomith. *Narrative Fiction: Contemporary Poetics*. London: Routledge, 1983.

Ryan, Marie-Laure. "Diagramming Narrative." *Semiotica* 165.1/4 (2007): 11–40.

———, ed. *Narrative Across Media: The Languages of Storytelling*. Lincoln: University of Nebraska Press, 2004.

———. *Possible Worlds, Artificial Intelligence, and Narrative Theory*. Bloomington: Indiana University Press, 1991.

Ryle, Gilbert. *The Concept of Mind*. Harmondsworth, UK: Peregrine, 1963.

Scarry, Elaine. *Dreaming by the Book*. Princeton, NJ: Princeton University Press, 1999.

Schank, Roger C. and Robert P. Abelson. *Scripts, Plans, Goals, and Understanding: An Inquiry into Human Knowledge Structures*. Hillsdale, NJ: Erlbaum, 1977.

Scott, Walter. *Waverley*. Edited by Andrew Hook. Harmondsworth, UK: Penguin, 1972 (1814).
Searle, John R. "Minds, Brains, and Programs." *Behavioural and Brain Sciences* 3.3 (1980): 417–57.
———. *The Rediscovery of the Mind*. Cambridge, MA: MIT Press, 1992.
Semino, Elena. "Blending and Characters' Mental Functioning in Virginia Woolf's 'Lappin and Lapinova.'" *Language and Literature* 15.1 (2006): 55–72.
———. *Metaphor in Discourse*. Cambridge: Cambridge University Press, 2008.
Singer, Jerome and John Kolligian. "Personality: Developments in the Study of Private Experience." *Annual Review of Psychology* 38 (1987): 533–74.
Smith, Brian Cantwell. "Situatedness/Embeddedness." In *The MIT Encyclopedia of the Cognitive Sciences*, edited by Robert A. Wilson and Frank C. Keil. Cambridge, MA: MIT Press, 1999. 769–71.
Sperber, Dan and Lawrence Hirschfeld. "Culture, Cognition, and Evolution." In *The MIT Encyclopedia of the Cognitive Sciences*, edited by Robert A. Wilson and Frank C. Keil. Cambridge, MA: MIT Press, 1999. cxi–cxxxii.
Stockwell, Peter. *Cognitive Poetics*. London: Routledge, 2002.
Strawson, Galen. "Against Narrativity." *Ratio* 16 (2004): 428–52.
———. "The Self." *Journal of Consciousness Studies* 4.5–6 (1997): 405–28.
Summerscale, Kate. *The Suspicions of Mr Whicher or the Murder at Road Hill House*. London: Bloomsbury, 2008.
Thomas, Bronwen. "Multiparty Talk in the Novel: The Distribution of Tea and Talk in a Scene from Evelyn Waugh's *Black Mischief*." *Poetics Today* 23.4 (2002): 657–84.
Trollope, Anthony. *The Warden*. Edited by Robin Gilmour. Harmondsworth, UK: Penguin, 2004 (1855).
Turner, Mark. *Reading Minds: The Study of English in the Age of Cognitive Science*. Princeton, NJ: Princeton University Press, 1991.
van Dijk, Teun. "Philosophy of Action and Theory of Narrative." *Poetics* 5 (1976): 287–338.
Warhol, Robyn. *Having a Good Cry: Effeminate Feelings and Pop-Culture Forms*. Columbus: The Ohio State University Press, 2002.
Waugh, Evelyn. *Men at Arms*. Harmondsworth, UK: Penguin, 1964 (1952).
———. *Vile Bodies*. Harmondsworth, UK: Penguin, 1996 (1930).
Wertsch, James V. *Voices of the Mind: A Sociocultural Approach to Mediated Action*. Cambridge, MA: Harvard University Press, 1991.
Wilson, Timothy. *Strangers to Ourselves: Discovering the Adaptive Unconscious*. Cambridge, MA: Harvard University Press, 2002.
Wittgenstein, Ludwig. *Philosophical Investigations*. Oxford: Blackwell, 1958.
Woloch, Alex. *The One vs. the Many: Minor Characters and the Space of the Protagonist in the Novel*. Princeton, NJ: Princeton University Press, 2003.
Yates, Frances. *The Art of Memory*. Chicago: University of Chicago Press, 2001

(1966).

Zlatev, Jordan, Timothy Racine, Chris Sinha and Esa Itkonen, eds. *The Shared Mind: Perspectives on Intersubjectivity.* Amsterdam: John Benjamins, 2008.

Zunshine, Lisa, ed. *Introduction to Cognitive Cultural Studies.* Baltimore: Johns Hopkins University Press, 2010.

———. "Theory of Mind and Fictions of Embodied Transparency." *Narrative* 16.1 (2008): 65–92.

———. *Why We Read Fiction: Theory of Mind and the Novel.* Columbus: The Ohio State University Press, 2006.

INDEX

Abbott, H. Porter, 9, 28, 37, 45, 117
Abelson, Robert P., 24
actants, 8, 31, 68, 156. *See also* functions
action, 2, 9–11, 20–23, 43–44, 159–63, 202; communicative action, 140; discursive action, 135, 141–44; and dispositions, 29, 32–34; dramaturgical action, 96, 102, 110, 112, 139, 161, 163; intermental action, 135, 140–41, 168, 175–76; in *Little Dorrit*, 27, 36, 38, 108–10, 112, 121–22, 134–44; mediated action, 140; in *Middlemarch*, 65, 72–73, 76, 86, 93, 95–97, 99–100, 104; normatively regulated, 139; philosophy of action, 135–38; sociocultural action, 135, 139–40; teleological action, 139; theory of, 135–44; in various novels, 55–58, 155, 166, 168, 170, 175–76, 187, 192, 196, 198. *See also* behavior
Alber, Jan, 19
Ambassadors, The (James), 113–14
Amery, Leo, 200
Amongst Women (McGahern), 38
Anna Karenina (Tolstoy), 41
anthropology, 8, 182
Arabian Nights, The, 12

Archilochus, 19
artificial intelligence (AI), 6, 50
Ashbery, John, 44
aspectuality, 11–12, 40–41, 56; in relation to *Enduring Love*, 186–87, 189, 194, 197; in relation to *Little Dorrit*, 125, 129; in relation to *Middlemarch*, 94–95
Asperger syndrome, 21
Atonement (McEwan), 36, 183–84, 186, 199
attributions, 35–36, 49, 137–38, 184–85; attribution theory, 5, 10, 20–24, 142–43, 182, 196; of emotions, 156–64; in *Enduring Love*, 185–96; first-person and third-person, 15, 40, 59, 125, 130, 132, 161, 199; intermental, 88–89, 99, 101; in *Little Dorrit*, 125; in *Middlemarch*, 103; in *Persuasion*, 146, 151–52, 155
Austen, Jane, 146, 159, 164, 171, 177, 180–81. See also *Emma*; *Persuasion*; *Pride and Prejudice*; *Sense and Sensibility*
autism, 21

Bachman, Maria, 166

211

Bakhtin, Mikhail, 16, 86, 106. *See also* word with a sideways glance
Bal, Mieke, 8, 11, 27
Bamberg, Michael, 143
Bateson, Gregory, 43, 130
behavior, 22, 39, 136–44, 170, 199; and attribution, 20, 24–25; and behaviorism, 51–52; and dispositions, 29–30, 32, 34; in *Enduring Love*, 185–90, 194–97; in *Little Dorrit*, 36, 107–8, 121–22, 126, 129, 134; in *Men at Arms*, 58–61; in *Middlemarch*, 72–73, 87, 98, 102; in *Persuasion*, 146–47, 154–55, 161–62, 167. *See also* action
behaviorism, 18, 30, 51–52
Behn, Aphra. *See Orinokoo*
beliefs, 19, 11, 22, 29–31, 56, 84, 97, 161–62
Berlin, Isaiah, 19
Blackmore, Susan, 13
blues, the, 200
brain, the, 50–52, 184
Brontë, Anne, 180. *See also Tenant of Wildfell Hall, The*
Brontë, Charlotte, 159, 180. *See also Jane Eyre; Shirley*
Brontë, Emily, 180. *See also Wuthering Heights*
Brown, Dan. *See Da Vinci Code, The*
Bruner, Jerome, 13
bundles of habits, 30
Butte, George, 154

Carruthers, Peter, 21
Carter Family, The, 200
Case, Alison, 42–43
causality and causation, 9, 25, 28; forward causation, 162; backward causation, 162; and minds, 32, 56, 96, 98, 136, 142, 168
Cezanne, Paul, 75
Chalmers, David, 43
characterization theory, 9, 11–12, 200; and attribution theory, 20, 182; and cognitive frames, 24–26; and dispositions, 5, 27–29, 31; in relation to *Enduring Love*, 185, 194; in relation to *Middlemarch*, 67, 97, 101
Chatman, Seymour, 8
Chicago School, 157. *See also* rhetorical and ethical approaches to literature
Chinese Room experiment, 50
Churchill, Winston, 200
Cinderella, 198
Clark, Andy, 43, 51
classical view of the mind, 8. *See also* internalist perspective
cognitive approaches to literature, 5–8, 159
cognitive frames. *See* frames, cognitive
cognitive narratives, 12–14, 88, 90–92, 94, 97–98; double cognitive narratives, 12, 77, 88, 92, 95, 97, 99–103, 190
cognitive poetics, 6
cognitive stylistics. *See* cognitive poetics
cognitive turn in the humanities, 5
cognitivism, 7, 23, 52
Cohn, Dorrit, 8, 28, 49
Coleridge, Samuel Taylor, 200
colleagues, work, 2, 41, 47
collective thought. *See* intermental thought
Collins, Wilkie, 164–65, 175, 180. *See also No Name*
communal voice, 45
computers, 50
Conrad, Joseph, 180. *See also Nigger of the 'Narcissus,' The*
consciousness presentation in fiction. *See* thought and consciousness presentation in fiction
consensus, 48, 82, 144, 190; in relation to *Middlemarch*, 69, 73, 75, 77, 82, 86, 90, 99; in relation to *Little Dorrit*, 123, 133
continuing consciousness frame, 10–12, 26, 40–41, 94

control messages, 161–63
control, 5, 64, 163, 173; in relation to
    Enduring Love, 186, 188–89, 196;
    in relation to *Little Dorrit,* 110, 115,
    123, 125, 130–31; in relation to
    Middlemarch, 71, 102
country and western music, 200
Cranford (Gaskell), 167
Crying of Lot 49, The (Pynchon), 126
cue-reason words, 137
Culler, Jonathan, 27
Culpeper, Jonathan, 26
cultural approaches to literature, 7, 14,
    157, 181
culture, 22–24, 67, 135, 139, 181–82,
    201
*Curious Incident of the Dog in the Night
    Time, The* (Haddon), 21

Da Vinci Code, The (Brown), 18
Damasio, Antonio, 6, 9, 16, 30, 40,
    159–60
Darwin, Charles, 187
Davidson, Donald, 142
Davies, Stevie, 159
day job, my, 50
de Clerambault's syndrome, 185,
    188–90
decisions, 59, 96, 112, 138–39, 159, 161,
    163, 196; intermental, 33, 43–44,
    48, 55, 72, 148–49, 152, 168, 175–76
Defoe, Daniel. See *Robinson Crusoe*
Dennett, Daniel C., 6, 9, 13, 16, 30, 43,
    51, 106, 116
desires, 9, 11, 22, 55, 139, 161
Deuteronomy, 63
dialogicality, 40, 58, 74, 95, 99, 106–7,
    130, 146. *See also* Bakhtin, Mikhail
Dickens, Charles, 105, 164–65, 172, 175,
    180–82. See also *Hard Times; Little
    Dorrit*
direct thought, 93
discourse. *See* story and discourse
discursive intermental rhythm, 80–85,
    177
dispositions, 15, 27–34, 60, 137, 172–73,
    196; and attribution theory, 20, 142;
    and behaviorism, 18; and characterization, 5; in *Little Dorrit,* 107–9,
    121, 128; in *Middlemarch,* 72–73, 97
Doležel, Lubomír, 64, 160
Donald, Merlin, 30
Dostoevsky, Fyodor, 159. See also *Idiot,
    The*
double-voiced discourse, 71
drama, 6, 26, 46
dual attitudes, 59–63
dyads, 43

Eco, Umberto, 27
Edelman, Gerald, 13
Edgeworth, Maria, 164, 171, 180. See
    also *Helen*
Edwards, Derek, 142
Edzard, Christine, 95
Eliot, George, 76, 83, 95, 147, 164, 171–
    72, 180–82. See also *Middlemarch;
    Silas Marner*
Eliot, T. S., 194
Elster, Jon, 159
embedded narratives. *See* cognitive narratives
Emma (Austen), 5, 146
Emmott, Catherine, 6, 25
emotions, 20, 27, 29, 31, 36, 142, 145,
    156–64, 168, 174
empathy, 101, 129, 185, 195–96
encyclopedias, 64
Enduring Love (McEwan), 27, 36–37,
    182, 184–98
epistemological debate on social minds,
    4, 64, 165–66
Ermarth, Elizabeth Deeds, 82
erotomania, 185. *See also* de Clerambault's syndrome
ethical debate on social minds, 4, 64,
    165–66
events, 9–10, 18, 25, 40, 55, 135, 142,

162, 186–88
evolution, 21
experiences, 9, 12–13, 24, 29, 40, 55–58, 62, 105, 139, 160
experientiality, 11
extended cognition. *See* intermental thought
externalist perspective, 2–4, 8, 26, 34, 38–42, 49, 52, 180–84, 200; on *Little Dorrit,* 35–36, 105–8, 144; on *Middlemarch,* 69; on *Persuasion,* 147; on various novels, 58, 60, 165, 167–68, 170–71

fabula. *See* story and discourse
families, 2, 25, 41, 47, 49, 175; Corleone family, 198–99; family systems therapy, 41; in *Little Dorrit,* 4, 35, 37, 111–12, 118, 120–23, 126; in *Middlemarch,* 73, 76, 82, 95; in *Persuasion,* 147, 149–50, 153, 176
"Farther Along," 201
Faulkner, William. *See* "A Rose for Emily"
feeling rules, 59–63
feelings, 10, 36, 139, 156, 159, 161–62, 165, 167, 170; in *Enduring Love,* 186–89; in *Little Dorrit,* 106–7, 110, 123, 125–28, 143; in *Men at Arms,* 58, 60–62; in *Middlemarch,* 73, 174; in *Persuasion,* 64, 101, 146, 149–55, 158–59, 163–64
feminist approaches to literature, 7
Ferguson, Sir Alex, 141
fictional minds, 7–12, 14, 31, 40, 44, 64, 97, 198–200; and the externalist perspective, 49, 156, 160–61; history of, 17, 180, 182, 184; in *Men at Arms,* 55; and real minds, 19, 26; and social minds, 49, 52, 144
Fielding, Henry. See *Tom Jones*
films, 6, 37, 63, 95, 182, 198–200
first-person narrators. *See* narrators
Fludernik, Monika, 6, 8, 11, 25, 28

focalization, 8, 12, 40–41, 57, 186, 190–91; intermental, 84–85, 176; in relation to *Little Dorrit,* 124, 127, 141; in relation to *Middlemarch,* 65, 68, 70, 76–78, 87–88, 92–94
folk psychological narratives, 22–23
Ford, Ford Madox. See *Good Soldier, The*
frame narratives, 12
frames, cognitive, 11, 24–26, 46, 49, 55, 57, 153, 177, 194; in relation to *Middlemarch,* 67, 73, 96–97; in relation to *Persuasion,* 147, 155. *See also* continuing consciousness frame
free indirect discourse, 8, 31, 39, 156, 161, 180; intermental free indirect thought, 67, 71, 77, 87, 177; in *Middlemarch,* 74, 87, 89, 93, 100
free indirect thought. *See* free indirect discourse
Freudian unconscious, 59
friendship, 2, 41, 47–49, 76, 149, 156, 170, 174; in *Little Dorrit,* 109, 132–33; in *Middlemarch,* 79, 101; in *Persuasion,* 148, 151–52, 154–55
Frith, Chris, 43
functionalist perspective, 50
functions, 8. *See also* actants
fundamental attribution error, 196

gappiness: in relation to consciousness, 13; in relation to narrative, 93–94, 145
gaps in storyworlds, 11, 25, 57, 61
Gaskell, Elizabeth, 164, 171, 180. See also *Wives and Daughters; Cranford*
Geertz, Clifford, 30, 43
gender, 158, 182, 185, 197
genre, 25–26, 182, 200
Gillett, Grant, 142
Godfather Part I, The, 198–99
Gone with the Wind (Mitchell), 94
Good Soldier, The (Ford), 12, 183
gospel music, 200
Gothic, 159

Gould, Stephen Jay, 19
graphic novels, 182, 198
group biography, 200
group thought. *See* intermental thought
groups, 16, 20, 25, 41–48, 52, 139–41, 176, 190, 200; in *Little Dorrit,* 4, 36, 107, 118, 120, 182; in *Men at Arms,* 54, 56, 58; in *Middlemarch,* 69–72, 75–78, 80–92, 98–100, 172; in *Persuasion,* 147–49, 155
groupthink, 44, 141

Habermas, Jürgen, 139–40
habits, 29–30, 34, 51, 60, 116
Haddon, Mark. See *Curious Incident of the Dog in the Night Time, The*
Hamilton, William, 60
hard cognitive sciences, 8
Hard Times (Dickens), 117
Harré, Rom, 142
Heider, Fritz, 20
Helen (Edgeworth), 1–2, 4, 14, 164–66, 170
Herman, David, 6, 8, 17, 25, 45, 78, 157, 184
Herman, Luc, 28
heterodiegetic narrators. *See* narrators
High Noon, 197
Hilton, Paris, 21, 138
Hirschfeld, Lawrence, 43
historical approaches to literature, 7, 17, 36, 179–82
Hogan, Patrick Colm, 157
Holmes, Richard, 200
homeostasis, 25
homodiegetic narrators. *See* narrators
Hutchins, Edwin, 9, 27, 43
Hutto, Daniel D., 22–24

ideology, 11, 48, 88, 118, 120, 123, 182
Idiot, The (Dostoevsky), 94
implied author, 14, 127, 146
indicative description, 137

individual thought. *See* intramental thought
inner speech, 8, 93, 106
inner thought. *See* intramental thought
intentionality (philosophical sense), 57, 161
intentions, 9, 11, 22, 24, 89, 136–43, 160, 168, 187, 196
interior monologue, 8, 31, 39–40, 67, 74, 156, 180
intermental attributional breakdowns, 49, 125, 127, 150, 152, 184–85
intermental encounters, 2, 46–49
intermental minds, 48, 50, 56, 58, 60, 172, 176; in *Little Dorrit,* 120, 131; in *Middlemarch,* 70, 75, 80, 88–89, 99
intermental thought, 4, 36, 38, 40–41, 44, 46–50, 136, 140, 201–2; in *Little Dorrit,* 106, 113, 118, 124; in *Middlemarch,* 67, 70, 75–76, 80–81, 84, 87, 92, 101; in *Persuasion,* 146; in various novels, 52–53, 168, 170, 173, 178–79, 192
intermental typology, 46–49
intermental units, 35–37, 41, 43, 45–49, 52, 64; in *Little Dorrit,* 111–12, 117–20, 122–25, 128, 130–31, 133–34, 141; in *Middlemarch,* 73, 75–76, 81–83, 85–87, 90, 97, 102–4; in *Persuasion,* 148–51, 153; in various novels, 164–65, 167, 172–77, 183–85, 190–93
internalist perspective, 3–4, 8, 23, 26, 34–43, 52, 58, 165–67, 170–71, 180–84, 200; on *Little Dorrit,* 106, 144; on *Middlemarch,* 67
intersubjectivity, 20, 22, 41, 201; deep intersubjectivity, 154
intramental thought, 4, 35, 40–44; in *Little Dorrit,* 106–7, 121, 131, 138; in *Middlemarch,* 67, 72, 74–75, 80, 82–91, 99; in *Persuasion,* 146; in various novels, 56, 58, 164, 173, 177, 190, 192

introspection, 29, 40, 125

Jahn, Manfred, 25
James, Henry, 105, 133, 164, 170–71, 180–82. See also *Ambassadors, The; Portrait of a Lady, The; Tragic Muse, The*
James, William, 30
Jane Eyre (Charlotte Brontë), 42
jazz, 200
joint thought. *See* intermental thought
Joyce, James. *See Ulysses*

Kafalenos, Emma, 9
Keane, Roy, 141
Keen, Suzanne, 28, 196
Kelley, Harold, 20
Knapp, John V., 8, 31, 41, 45, 47
Kolligian, John, 159
Kuhn, Thomas, 201

Laclos, Pierre Choderlos de. *See Liaisons Dangereuses, Les*
Lanser, Susan Sniader, 45, 167
Lawrence, D. H. *See Sons and Lovers*
Le Doux, Joseph, 159
Liaisons Dangereuses, Les (Laclos), 41
linguistic turn in the humanities, 5
linguistics, 6, 31, 156; psycholinguistics, 7, 9, 16; sociolinguistics, 8, 182
literary studies, 2, 5, 24, 31, 46, 82
Little Dorrit (Dickens), 3, 35–38, 42, 48, 64; action in, 10, 27, 134–44; comparisons with other novels, 76, 94, 145, 153, 164, 172, 174–77, 189; film of, 95; large intermental units in, 117–20; physically distributed cognition in, 116–17; small intermental units in, 120–34; social minds in, 14, 42, 44, 105–8; visible thought in (including the face, the look, and nonverbal communication), 108–16

Lloyd George, David, 200
Lodge, David, 8
"Lonesome Valley," 200–201
Lothe, Jakob, 28

MacIntyre, Alasdair, 13
Marcus, Amit, 45
Margolin, Uri, 27, 45
marriage, 35, 47–48, 126, 141, 166–67, 169, 174; in *Little Dorrit*, 107, 120, 133; in *Middlemarch*, 35, 72–73, 75–76, 79–80, 89, 92, 96, 102–4; in *Persuasion*, 152
Marxist approaches to literature, 7
mass hysteria, 141
McEwan, Ian, 184. *See also Atonement; Enduring Love*
McGahern, John. *See Amongst Women*
McGinn, Colin. *See Mindfucking*
McHale, Brian, 49
media, 37, 179, 182, 198–200
Men at Arms (Waugh), 35, 41, 44, 52–63, 65, 89
mental events, 9, 28–31, 33–34, 60, 97, 101, 108–9, 137, 172
mental functioning, 3–4, 7–9, 17–18, 23, 27, 36, 39, 55, 135–36, 199; intermental, 20, 41–42, 44, 46–47, 58–59, 65, 69, 72, 74; in *Little Dorrit*, 4, 106, 109, 119, 130–31, 133, 135; in *Middlemarch*, 65, 69, 72, 74, 76, 78–79, 82–85, 88, 93, 97; in *Persuasion*, 146, 150, 156; in various novels, 164–66, 168, 177
mental network, 9, 22, 56, 136
mental states, 20, 24, 30, 57, 142, 146, 168, 183, 187
metaphor, 6, 44, 65, 74, 141
metarepresentation, 15
Middlemarch (Eliot), 11–12, 16, 27, 35, 37–38, 42, 141; comparisons with other novels, 44, 107, 113–14, 117–18, 131, 145–49, 164–67, 172–78; the Middlemarch mind, 64–75;

Middlemarch minds, 48, 75–93; social minds in, 141
Mikkonen, Kai, 198
Mildorf, Jarmila, 16
mind beyond the skin, 42–43
mind blindness, 21
Mindfucking (McGinn), 133
mindfucking, 173
mind inside the skull, 42, 74
mind reading, 2, 21–24, 46–47, 165, 170, 173, 191; inadvertent, 47; in *Little Dorrit*, 124–25, 127, 133, 137; in *Middlemarch*, 72–73, 100–101; reciprocal, 47
mind-ruts, 30, 106
Mitchell, Margaret. See *Gone with the Wind*
mob rule, 141
Modernism, 34, 180, 183–84
moments of embodied transparency, 47
Moretti, Franco, 78
motives and motivation, 9, 11, 22, 24, 32–33, 64, 136–43, 173; and emotions, 160–63; in *Enduring Love*, 185, 187, 196–97; in *Middlemarch*, 65, 98–99, 101; in *Persuasion*, 155
multiparty talk, 78–79
multiperspectivalism, 84
multiple drafts of consciousness, 13

narrative comprehension, 6, 17–18, 25, 54
narrative imperialism, 14
narrative practice hypothesis, 23
narrative theory. See narratology
narrativity, 13; ethical narrativity thesis, 13; psychological narrativity thesis, 13
narratology, 19, 42, 160, 198, 201; classical or traditional, 4, 6, 8–12, 14, 17–19; cognitive, 5–6; fault line in, 27–29, 31; structuralist, 135, 156
narrators, 9, 14, 64; heterodiegetic or third-person, 20, 46; homodiegetic or first-person, 20, 168; in *Little Dorrit*, 3–4, 107–10, 117–18, 121, 126–27, 131–33, 138, 142–44; in *Middlemarch*, 65, 70–71, 77, 81–84, 87–88, 91–93, 101–3, 107; in *Persuasion*, 146–47, 162; unreliable, 23, 183; in various novels, 12, 57, 62, 171, 185–86, 194
neuroscience, 7–9, 160; social neuroscience, 43
new view of the mind, 8. See also externalist perspective
Nietzsche, Friedrich, 141
Nigger of the 'Narcissus,' The (Conrad), 167–68, 175, 177
nineteenth-century novel, 17, 36–37, 42, 70, 179, 185; social minds in, 4, 46, 64, 145, 164–67, 170, 172, 175
No Name (Collins), 164–66, 172
non-conscious thought, 59. See also unconscious thought
nonfiction, 6, 200
Nünning, Ansgar, 84
Nussbaum, Martha, 157

Oatley, Keith, 159–63
Occam's razor, 52
Orinokoo (Behn), 139

parallel discourses, 9
party, the (in *Persuasion*), 48, 147–49
passive voice, 71–72, 86, 123, 178
Perry, Menakem, 46, 73
personality, 10, 20, 28–33, 60, 196; in *Little Dorrit*, 108, 115, 128, 131; in *Middlemarch*, 97
Persuasion (Austen), 35–36, 38, 113–14; character of Anne Elliot, 27, 64, 88, 94; emotions in, 156–64; social minds in, 42, 44, 48, 76, 145–56, 172, 175–77
Phelan, James, 14, 28–29, 157, 185
phenomenology, 160

philosophy, 16, 30, 42, 157; of action, 21, 135–39, 142; of mind, 7, 9, 26, 57
physically distributed cognition, 35, 51–52, 116–17, 175
Pinker, Steven, 6, 9
plot, 9–11, 42, 45, 64, 140, 158, 160, 164, 166, 173; of *Middlemarch*, 35, 73, 89
poetry, 6, 200
point of view. *See* focalization
Portrait of a Lady, The (James), 27, 29, 32–34, 133, 137
positioning, 143–44
Postmodernism, 13, 19, 184, 199
Poststructuralism, 18
Potter, Jonathan, 142
practical reasoning, 159. *See also* problem solving
presentation of consciousness in fiction. *See* thought and consciousness presentation in fiction
presupposition, 71–72, 86
Pride and Prejudice (Austen), 15, 146
Priest, Stephen, 30
primacy effect, 73
principle of minimal departure, 55
private thought. *See* intramental thought
problem solving, 43–44, 48, 97. *See also* practical reasoning
psychology, 9, 16, 30–31, 42, 60; cognitive psychology, 7; discursive psychology, 7–8, 26, 141–43; folk psychology, 20, 22–23, 31; social psychology, 7–8, 26
Pynchon, Thomas. *See Crying of Lot 49, The*

Rabinowitz, Peter J., 157
readable minds, 44–45, 47
reader competence, 25, 98
real minds, 7–8, 11, 14, 19–20, 26, 29–31, 55, 160; real-mind discourses, 7, 9, 16, 42, 200–201
reasons, 9, 20, 22–23, 32, 64, 104, 136–42, 173, 187; in *Enduring Love*, 196–97; in *Little Dorrit*, 122–23, 133; in *Men at Arms*, 62; in *Middlemarch*, 83, 89, 90, 96, 99; in *Persuasion*, 155, 160–63
rhetorical and ethical approaches to literature, 7, 157, 182, 185. *See also* Chicago School
Richardson, Brian, 9, 19, 45
Rimmon-Kenan, Shlomith, 8, 27–28
Robinson Crusoe (Defoe), 41
"Rose for Emily, A" (Faulkner), 41, 46
Ross, Martin, 39, 44
Rowe, Keith, 44
Rumsfeld, Donald, 192
Ryan, Marie-Laure, 6, 11, 45, 55, 198
Ryle, Gilbert, 30, 96

scapegoating, 44, 122–23, 165, 176
Scarry, Elaine, 6
Schank, Roger C., 24
schemas, 24. *See also* frames, cognitive
Schuyler, James, 44
Scott, Walter, 43, 164. See also *Waverley*
Searle, John R., 9, 12, 16, 50
secrecy, 2, 63–64, 164, 166, 171, 173; in *Little Dorrit*, 106, 108, 123, 128, 134, 172; in *Middlemarch*, 95; in *Persuasion*, 146
Secret History, The (Tartt), 41
self, the, 13–14, 28–32, 40–42, 60, 139, 175; in *Little Dorrit*, 110, 120, 126, 129; in *Persuasion*, 148
semantic messages, 161–63
Semino, Elena, 6, 48
semiotics, 19, 31, 45, 54, 56
Sense and Sensibility (Austen), 167
Seurat, Georges, 75
shared thought. *See* intermental thought
Shaw, Harry E., 42–43
Shelley, Percy, 200
Shirley (Charlotte Brontë), 36, 164–66,

169–70
Silas Marner (Eliot), 167
simulation theory. *See* theory of mind
Singer, Jerome, 159
situated cognition. *See* intermental thought
situated identity, 10, 15, 30, 40–41, 64, 164, 200; in *Little Dorrit,* 129–30; in *Middlemarch,* 90, 93, 97; in *Persuasion,* 148
sjuzhet. *See* story and discourse
skills, 11, 22, 30
Skinner, B. F., 18
Smith, Brian Cantwell, 8
social class, 111, 175, 177, 182; in relation to *Middlemarch,* 70, 72–3, 75, 78–82, 85–87, 89, 97, 103
social minds, 4–5, 16–17, 34–46, 49, 201–2; and characterization, 27; history of, 179–84; in *Little Dorrit,* 104, 111, 129, 131; in *Middlemarch,* 76, 80; in *Persuasion,* 145–47, 153, 155; purposes of, 63–64; and real-mind discourses, 8–9; and the unconsciousness, 58; in various media, 198–201; in various novels, 14, 32, 164–66, 168–69, 173, 185, 187
socially distributed cognition. *See* intermental thought
society, 181–82; in *Little Dorrit,* 117–19; in *Middlemarch,* 71, 79, 88; in *Persuasion,* 48, 147
socio-geography, 78, 177
sociology, 182
soft cognitive sciences, 8, 26
solipsism, 47, 103, 108, 123, 150–53, 174, 182, 187–88
Somerville, Edith, 39, 44
Sons and Lovers (Lawrence), 41
soul music, 200
speech category: approach, 8, 180; trajectory, 180
Sperber, Dan, 43
stereotypes, 26, 31, 61, 67, 93

Stockwell, Peter, 6
story analysis, 8, 12, 68
story and discourse, 11–12, 17, 96, 135–36, 138, 198
storyworlds, 18, 25, 135, 162, 199–200; and fictional minds, 4, 8–12, 14, 20–21, 40–42, 63–64; in *Little Dorrit,* 108, 128, 140; Lydgate storyworld, 35, 91, 93–104; in *Middlemarch,* 67, 74–75, 78, 88; in *Persuasion,* 145; in various novels, 52–61, 171, 177, 186, 194, 197
Strawson, Galen, 13–14
stream of consciousness, 8, 13, 31, 34, 39–40, 67, 74, 156, 180
subjectivity, 11, 14, 40–41, 136, 139, 165, 184
Summerscale Kate. See *Suspicions of Mr Whicher or the Murder at Road Hill House, The*
Suspicions of Mr Whicher or the Murder at Road Hill House, The (Summerscale), 181

Tartt, Donna. See *Secret History, The*
teleology, 89, 139, 156, 160–63, 199
Tenant of Wildfell Hall, The (Anne Brontë), 159, 165
theory of mind, 20–24, 40–41, 46, 49, 173–74, 183, 191; in *Little Dorrit,* 124, 126, 132–33, 138; in *Men at Arms,* 52–53, 55, 62; in *Persuasion,* 88–89, 146, 149–50, 154–55; simulation theory, 22–23; theory-theory, 22–23
theory-theory. *See* theory of mind
third-person narrators. *See* narrators
Thomas, Bronwen, 79
thought and consciousness presentation in fiction, 8, 12, 28, 63, 182
thought report, 67, 74, 80, 93, 180; contextual, 96, 106–7
thought-action continuum, 10, 136
Tolstoy, Leo. See *Anna Karenina*

220 | Index

Tom Jones (Fielding), 10
Tragic Muse, The (James), 170–71, 181–82
Trainspotting, 63
Trevarthen, Colwyn, 179, 201
Trollope, Anthony, 164, 181. See also *The Warden*
Turner, J. M. W., 75
Turner, Mark, 6

Ulysses (Joyce), 10, 18, 34, 182–83
unconscious thought, 35, 52–54, 58–63; Freudian unconscious, 59
unnatural narratives, 19, 199
unreadable minds, 44–45, 187
unreliable narrator. *See* narrators
Usual Suspects, The, 199–200

van Dijk, Teun, 140–41
Venn diagrams, 45, 83
Vervaeck, Bart, 28
Victorian Literary Studies Archive, 113–14
Vile Bodies (Waugh), 43, 101, 104, 136

Warden, The (Trollope), 23, 36, 164–65, 167, 169–70

Warhol, Robyn, 157
Waugh, Evelyn. See *Men at Arms*; *Vile Bodies*
Waverley (Scott), 3
"we" narratives, 45, 168
Wertsch, James V., 9, 43
wetware, 50–51
Whitman, Walt, 15
whole mind, the, 9, 28–31, 39, 109, 159
Wilde, Oscar, 1, 4, 105
Wilson, Timothy, 20, 58–62, 199
Wittgenstein, Ludwig, 30, 120, 136
Wittgenstein's question, 136
Wives and Daughters (Gaskell), 36, 164, 166–67, 169–70, 173, 176–77
Woloch, Alex, 27
Wolpert, Daniel, 43
word with a sideways glance, 73, 76, 86, 90
Wuthering Heights (Emily Brontë), 12

Yates, Frances, 51

Zlatev, Jordan, 22
Zunshine, Lisa, 6–7, 15–16, 21, 47

THEORY AND INTERPRETATION OF NARRATIVE
James Phelan and Peter J. Rabinowitz, Series Editors

Because the series editors believe that the most significant work in narrative studies today contributes both to our knowledge of specific narratives and to our understanding of narrative in general, studies in the series typically offer interpretations of individual narratives and address significant theoretical issues underlying those interpretations. The series does not privilege one critical perspective but is open to work from any strong theoretical position.

Social Minds in the Novel
  Alan Palmer

Narrative Structures and the Language of the Self
  Matthew Clark

Imagining Minds: The Neuro-Aesthetics of Austen, Eliot, and Hardy
  Kay Young

Postclassical Narratology: Approaches and Analyses
  Edited by Jan Alber and Monika Fludernik

Techniques for Living: Fiction and Theory in the Work of Christine Brooke-Rose
  Karen R. Lawrence

Towards the Ethics of Form in Fiction: Narratives of Cultural Remission
  Leona Toker

Tabloid, Inc.: Crimes, Newspapers, Narratives
  V. Penelope Pelizzon and Nancy M. West

Narrative Means, Lyric Ends: Temporality in the Nineteenth-Century British Long Poem
  Monique R. Morgan

Understanding Nationalism: On Narrative, Cognitive Science, and Identity
  Patrick Colm Hogan

Joseph Conrad: Voice, Sequence, History, Genre
  Edited by Jakob Lothe, Jeremy Hawthorn, James Phelan

The Rhetoric of Fictionality: Narrative Theory and the Idea of Fiction
  Richard Walsh

Experiencing Fiction: Judgments, Progressions, and the Rhetorical Theory of Narrative
  James Phelan

Unnatural Voices: Extreme Narration in Modern and Contemporary Fiction
  Brian Richardson

Narrative Causalities
  Emma Kafalenos

Why We Read Fiction: Theory of Mind and the Novel
   Lisa Zunshine

I Know That You Know That I Know: Narrating Subjects from Moll Flanders *to* Marnie
   George Butte

Bloodscripts: Writing the Violent Subject
   Elana Gomel

Surprised by Shame: Dostoevsky's Liars and Narrative Exposure
   Deborah A. Martinsen

Having a Good Cry: Effeminate Feelings and Pop-Culture Forms
   Robyn R. Warhol

Politics, Persuasion, and Pragmatism: A Rhetoric of Feminist Utopian Fiction
   Ellen Peel

Telling Tales: Gender and Narrative Form in Victorian Literature and Culture
   Elizabeth Langland

Narrative Dynamics: Essays on Time, Plot, Closure, and Frames
   Edited by Brian Richardson

Breaking the Frame: Metalepsis and the Construction of the Subject
   Debra Malina

Invisible Author: Last Essays
   Christine Brooke-Rose

Ordinary Pleasures: Couples, Conversation, and Comedy
   Kay Young

Narratologies: New Perspectives on Narrative Analysis
   Edited by David Herman

Before Reading: Narrative Conventions and the Politics of Interpretation
   Peter J. Rabinowitz

Matters of Fact: Reading Nonfiction over the Edge
   Daniel W. Lehman

The Progress of Romance: Literary Historiography and the Gothic Novel
   David H. Richter

A Glance Beyond Doubt: Narration, Representation, Subjectivity
   Shlomith Rimmon-Kenan

Narrative as Rhetoric: Technique, Audiences, Ethics, Ideology
   James Phelan

Misreading Jane Eyre: *A Postformalist Paradigm*
   Jerome Beaty

Psychological Politics of the American Dream: The Commodification of Subjectivity in Twentieth-Century American Literature
Lois Tyson

Understanding Narrative
Edited by James Phelan and Peter J. Rabinowitz

Framing Anna Karenina: *Tolstoy, the Woman Question, and the Victorian Novel*
Amy Mandelker

Gendered Interventions: Narrative Discourse in the Victorian Novel
Robyn R. Warhol

Reading People, Reading Plots: Character, Progression, and the Interpretation of Narrative
James Phelan